LEEDS UNITED
The Official History of the Club

A team of household names—the League Cup Winners in 1968—left to right (back row)—Norman Hunter, Paul Madeley, Jack Charlton, Gary Sprake, Mick Jones, Jimmy Greenhoff, Eddie Gray, (Front row)—Paul Reaney, Terry Cooper, Billy Bremner, Johnny Giles, Peter Lorimer.

LEEDS UNITED

Don Warters

Published by
WENSUM BOOKS (NORWICH) LTD
33 ORFORD PLACE
NORWICH

First Published
OCTOBER 1979

ISBN 903619 32 6

Printed and Bound by
McCorquodale (Newton) Ltd
Newton-le-Willows

Contents

Introduction by Billy Bremner 7
Formation: United rise from ashes 8
First Division in four years 12
War, Decline, and the Major 19
The legendary John Charles 27
Disaster: Charles departs and fire destroys the West Stand 31
How Don Revie became Manager 37
Foundation for success 42
Glory, glory Leeds United 50
The Battlefields of Europe 67
Eyes on the future 79
Statistical Appendix 92

Introduction

Though my energies these days are concentrated very much on soccer management and what I hope will turn out to be a successful bid to bring a change of fortunes to Fourth Division Doncaster Rovers, one thing remains certain—I will never forget my days as a player with Leeds United.

The true glory days for me, and the greater majority of the fine players who were at Elland Road under Don Revie's expert management, are now over, but the memories linger on.

We enjoyed immense success—much of it beyond the wildest dreams of even the most optimistic among us—and we wrote a true rags to riches story.

When I first became associated with Leeds United as a keen but very raw schoolboy recruit from Stirling there was little at Elland Road to suggest to me that such an exciting future was in store.

Indeed there were some very unhappy days for me in the early part of my career. For one thing I could not settle down in Leeds. It was not that I disliked the place, far from it. But I was homesick for my native Scotland, so much so in fact that I was allowed leave of absence for a time because I felt so badly about being away from my family home.

In addition I had to struggle to get into the side. Then Don Revie arrived on the scene and after a short spell as a player the master stroke was made and he became Team Manager.

That appointment proved to be the key that turned the lock to open the door to success and glory for Leeds United not only in England but in Europe too. It was a dream come true for all of us and I regard myself as being privileged to have been able to play a part in it.

People of my age group tend to relate to the 1960s and the early 1970s and this is undoubtedly remains the most majestic period in the Club's history. It was the time when success, as the Club had never before known it, was experienced.

But what you are about to read in this book by Don Warters is a history of the Club dating back to 1919. It is always fascinating to learn of earlier times, and in this particular case, the difficult years experienced by those devoted men who formed the Club and those who succeeded them and kept it going despite the odds being against them.

There is no doubt in my view that Don Warters qualifies to write this book because he was associated with the Club through his journalistic work during those memorable and successful years.

During my time at the Club I came to know him well and respected his ability as a fair-minded writer. His match reports in the *Evening Post* always reflected, in my view, a true balance. When praise was due it was duly given, when criticism was included it was constructive.

I know he has put in a tremendous amount of research to present as full a picture as possible of the earlier years of Leeds United. His research and his knowledge of the Club combine to present a story of Leeds United that I am sure you will find interesting reading.

BILLY BREMNER

Formation: United rise

The soccer world was stunned in October 1919 when the Football Association took the unprecedented step of putting Leeds City out of existence following accusations of improper payments made to players during the war years of 1914-18 and the refusal of the Elland Road club to offer its books for inspection and answer the allegations.

It was in the wake of this sensational and embarrassing demise that Leeds United came into being, but only after fervent pleadings by no less a person than the Lord Mayor of Leeds had failed to find favour with those in power at F.A. Headquarters.

The initial crack in the structure of Leeds City first appeared in July 1919 when, according to reports at the time, one of the club's old players—said to be angered at not being re-signed—took the treacherous step of writing to the Football League alleging illegal practices by the club during wartime in paying excessive expenses and bonuses to some of the players who had assisted them.

International matches had been suspended during the war, the competition for the F.A. Cup was not held, and the Football Association had closed the register for professional players and ruled that no wages should be paid to any person for playing football.

Soldiers on leave, and other people who, through various reasons, were not called away to fight for their country, were able to play but

from ashes

under no circumstances were they to be paid.

A joint commission of the Football Association and the Football League investigated the allegations against City, the outcome of which gave the club until the 6 October to produce their books for inspection and scrutiny. These were not forthcoming, however, and City were duly put out of existence.

Sir Frederick Wall, Secretary of the Football Association from 1895 to 1934, later wrote of the affair: 'The books were never placed on the table. They were not obtained. The inference was that Leeds City had in a broad sense carried on as though no embargo had been placed on their action. It was felt that improper payments had been made and that the books would prove this. The F.A. decided to suspend the club, the directors and the officials for ever.'

Not surprisingly the downfall of Leeds City caused an uproar in Leeds and there were many who believed City's only crime was that, of all the League clubs, they had had the misfortune to be the one found out.

Even the President of the Football League in 1919, Mr J. McKenna, must have had this thought at the back of his mind when he said, 'Perhaps others have escaped being found guilty of malpractices but if they are found out now we shall not stand on ceremony or sentiment.'

Mr Joseph Henry, the Lord Mayor of Leeds during those crisis days, did his utmost to save Leeds City in its death throes, by leading an appeal to the F.A. in person and offering to take over control of the club from the Directors, Messrs J. Connor, J. C. Whiteman, S. Glover, and G. Sykes, who had offered their resignations, and to carry it on until a new company could be formed.

Though he was allowed to put his case before the Commission, the refusal of the club to hand over its documents was an insurmountable obstacle and the appeal failed.

One appeal that did succeed, however, was that of Herbert Chapman, the man who was to become what many critics were later to describe as the greatest manager of all time.

He was Secretary of the Leeds City Football Club at the time of its downfall but his argument that he was away on munitions work at the time of the alleged affair and could not be held responsible for any indiscretions found favour with the authorities, and his ban was lifted.

It paved the way for him to carve his name in soccer's history with his outstanding ability as manager—first at Huddersfield Town and later with the mighty Arsenal.

While the death—some might argue suicide—of Leeds City was mourned by many footballing enthusiasts in Leeds, Port Vale were quick to benefit from the event. They took over Leeds City's fixtures in the Second Division of the Football League for the remainder of the 1919-20 season.

Equally rapid and determined efforts to restore professional soccer to the city of Leeds were made and a public meeting held in Salem Central Hall, Leeds, on Friday, 17 October 1919 conceived Leeds United.

Alf Masser, a Leeds solicitor and a highly respected figure of his day, was elected to take charge of the meeting and a proposal that a

The start of it all—Leeds United's first squad of players, assembled mainly as a result of the efforts of Hilton Crowther and Arthur Fairclough to begin their Football League campaign in 1920/21.

Left to right: (back row) M. Barker, Hilton Crowther, Duffield, Cooper, Hart, Brown, Jacklin, Down, Coope, Walton, Jefferies, Stead (assistant trainer), Fairclough (secretary manager), D. Murrel (trainer). Middle row: Frew, Spencer, Lyons, Elson, Thompson, Stuart, Goldthorpe, Reynolds. Front row: Armitage, Mason, Baker, Tillotson, Musgrove, McGee, Best.

professional football club be formed in Leeds immediately, was carried unanimously. A committee of seven was formed: Masser, Joe Henry jun., Mark Barker, C. Morgan, Dick Ray, Charles Snape, and R. E. H. Ramsden.

At a meeting the following day held at Mr Masser's residence in Roundhay it was resolved that Harry Meek, of 120 Harehills Lane, Leeds, and Mr N. D. Booth, of Belle Vue, Hill End Road, Armley, be appointed Joint Secretaries along with Joe Henry jun. as Chairman and Mr Barker as Treasurer.

Tom Coombs and Mr Kaye Aspinall were invited to join the committee and the fight was on in earnest for the re-establishment of professional soccer in Leeds.

Arrangements were eventually completed to take over Leeds City's Elland Road ground and advertisements were inserted in local papers and the *Athletic News* for players—but there was a rocky road to be travelled. It was in these days of hope and uncertainty that a suggestion that might seem completely unacceptable in present-day football was made, and in all seriousness, too.

Huddersfield Town were experiencing financial difficulties after the war years. There was poor support from the public for Association Football at a time when Huddersfield Rugby League Club were a major force and there was a growing reluctance on the part of Mr Hilton Crowther to continue helping to finance a badly supported club.

As a result of these circumstances the suggestion was made to move the Huddersfield Town Club lock, stock, and barrel to Elland Road!

The committee fighting to establish Leeds United resolved to ignore the whole question of the transfer of Huddersfield Town to Leeds but it was later to change its mind after talks with Mr Crowther and the proposals for the move were eventually accepted.

Then, an ironical twist, the citizens of Huddersfield suddenly awoke to what they were going to lose and rallied round strongly to keep their club at Leeds Road.

The Huddersfield team was beginning to achieve success and this inspired interest to such an extent that the required capital was raised and Mr Crowther was bought out. He had, however, made such promises to Leeds in his bid to restore professional football to the city that he felt duty bound to do all he could for the benefit of Association Football in the city.

Fuelled by the desire to succeed he worked feverishly to further the aims of a new club to replace the ill-fated Leeds City. His first job was perhaps the most important—that of finding a man who could build a team to lift Leeds United off the planner's drawing-board and back into the Football League.

He chose wisely—and he did not have to look too far. The problem of the day was solved when he turned to Arthur Fairclough—a man steeped in Soccer tradition both as a player, secretary, and manager. Fairclough took on the role of Secretary-Manager on 26 February 1920.

He was a colourful character with a broad smile who liked a wee dram or two. His waistcoat, slashed across by the then fashionable watch chain, covered a broad expanse.

Above all though he was a man with immense knowledge of the workings of a football club and one who became regarded as a leading authority in the highest circles associated with the game.

A son of Barnsley, Fairclough's record as a team-builder was a remarkable one. He raised Barnsley to the pinnacle of football fame, taking them to the Final of the F.A. Cup in 1910, had the satisfaction of seeing the team he had built get to the Final again in 1912 and win the Trophy. Later he built at Huddersfield a side that won promotion to the First Division and ran through to the Final of the F.A. Cup. Now he was in Leeds and faced with the tremendous challenge of building a team from scratch.

Ask most football followers to name the manager they associate with Leeds United more than any other and it is odds on that Don Revie, who took the Club through its most successful and memorable period in the later 1960s and early 1970s will be the name volunteered.

Yet Fairclough's contributions all those years ago were just as significant in their own way. He proved to be the man who made it all possible for Revie to perform his wonders in later years.

Fairclough's link-up again with Hilton Crowther had brought renewed hope to Leeds but it was hard graft for both men in those early days. Their mission was to get Leeds United elected to the Second Division of the Football League and both men spent a lot of time travelling the country in that first year soliciting votes for the Club.

It was not an easy task. After all they were asking people to vote for a club that barely existed and had not yet got a team together so

Leeds United owe a tremendous debt to this partnership. Mr J. Hilton Crowther (right) was said to have used tens of thousands of pounds of his own money to get Leeds United going after the sad downfall of Leeds City. Arthur Fairclough was the man he selected as the club's first secretary-Manager. Together they spearheaded the establishment of the Club in the uncertain days of its infancy.

at the same time the search for players to fill the side also had to be undertaken.

Hard work and dedication brought its reward. United began to play in the Midland League and at the end of the season the new Leeds United had, along with Cardiff City, won sufficient support to be elected members of the Second Division of the Football League.

The difficult and uncertain days between the demise of Leeds City and the emergence of the new club to succeed it, were over. League football had returned in Leeds.

As with his previous clubs Fairclough insisted on being Secretary-Manager at Leeds. His motives for making such a demand were far from secret. 'I have always had it this way and it has been a big advantage to me. I have been able to control both departments,' he declared.

Having worked closely with Mr Crowther in the past, Fairclough held a great admiration for the man who showed such a great interest in Yorkshire sport in those days and who was prepared to back that interest with big money from his own pocket.

It was widely accepted that Mr Crowther had backed Leeds United in those early formative years with tens of thousands of pounds.

'He has lost a lot of money but he has never been out to make money. He has been out to promote the sport and he has risked any amount of money to advance the game,' Fairclough once said of his friend.

'Many a man with the same amount of wealth and with an inclination towards sport would have set up a racing stable. He would have risked a lot of money but would also have stood a good chance of winning a lot,' he added.

Naturally, Mr Crowther became one of the original Directors of Leeds United being appointed along with Alf Masser and William Henry Platts (chartered accountant) in December 1920. A month later they were joined on the Board by Kaye Aspinall and Mark Barker.

First Division in four years

Leeds United's professional staff at the time the club first qualified for Division One football in 1923-24. Back row (left to right) Murrell (trainer), T. Bell, W. A. Coates, W. Robson, J. E. Armand, W. J. Menzies, J. J. Flood, A. Gordon, A. Noble, B. Duffield, A. Ure (assistant trainer). Second back row—L. H. Baker, J. Frew, L. Smith, E. Hart, M. J. Morris, A. Bell, J. Swann, A. Baker, T. Gascoigne, J. Harris. Third back row—F. Whalley, W. Johnson, H. Shirwin, W. I. Poyntz, W. L. Norman (team manager), J. Hilton Crowther (chairman), A. Fairclough (secretary-manager), J. Richmond, S. Powell. Front row—R. Fullam, W. Down, J. Lambert, R. Mason, J. W. Baker (captain), J. Allen, P. Whipp, G. Speak.

Arthur Fairclough needed only four years to take Leeds United into the First Division and they went up in style as Champions of the Second Division with fifty-four points—three more than Bury, the runners-up.

That memorable first success came in the 1923-24 season and was the result of the shrewd management of Fairclough who had been determined to prove to those people who had supported United's application for election to the Football League that their votes had not been wasted.

Having gained entry to the Second Division for the 1920-21 season United were eager to prove their worth. Fairclough had hurriedly assembled a first team squad of players which he expected would establish the Club in its first season. He did not disguise the fact though that he felt it would take more than one season to secure a side capable of winning promotion.

He confidently believed he had already obtained the nucleus of a good side with players of undoubted class such as Jim Baker, the ex-Huddersfield Town centre-half, whom he appointed first Captain of Leeds United, Ernest Goldthorpe who joined him on a free transfer from Bradford City, and J. H. Frew the ex-Heart of Midlothian full-back.

Among the players Fairclough had hurriedly signed for the new Club were several from the old Leeds City Midland League side. These included the elegant Ernie Hart, an attacking centre-half. He developed into one of the game's top players and is still regarded in some quarters as one of United's best and that after taking into account the stars that were to grace Elland Road in later years under Revie, such as Allan Clarke, Johnny Giles, Bobby Collins, and Mick Jones.

Hart was with the Club for sixteen years as a player during which time he played a prominent part in the promotion-winning teams of 1924, 1928, and 1932. He also won eight full England caps.

As the opening of the 1920-21 season drew near, Fairclough made three more signings—Harold Jacklin, goalkeeper for Blackpool's Central League side, P. Reynolds, an outside-left from Cudworth, and F. Waterhouse, an outside-left from Horsforth who had been with Huddersfield Town.

The full list of players on United's books for the start of that historic season was as follows:

Goalkeepers: H. Jeffrey, W. Down (Ashington), and H. Jacklin (Blackpool).
Full-backs: J. H. Frew (Heart of Midlothian),

B. Duffield (Castleford Town), A. Tillotson (Castleford Town), A. Smelt (Mexborough), and D. Coope.

Half-backs: R. Musgrove (Durham City), J. W. Baker (Huddersfield Town), J. Walton (West Stanley), G. E. Stuart (Dundee), E. Hart, G. F. Cooper (Kimberworth Old Boys, Rotherham), and J. McGee (a Scottish junior who was in business at Ripon).

Forwards: R. Thompson (Durham City), centre; L. Armitage (Sheffield Wednesday), centre; Ernest Goldthorpe (Bradford City), centre or inside; J. Lyon (Hull City), inside-left; E. Elston, inside-right; G. Mason, outside-right; G. Hill (Rotherham Town), outside-right; J. Best (Newcastle United), outside-left; P. Reynolds (Cudworth), outside-left; and F. Waterhouse (Huddersfield Town), outside-left.

The new Club's colours were blue and white striped shirts—a strip retained until 1934 when they changed to shirts of blue and gold halves.

Optimism was high when the first season began—but not too high. Fairclough and his skipper Baker both boldly predicted that it would take three years to achieve their objective of promotion to the top division!

In that first season of 1920-21 United won twelve and drew ten of their forty-four League games with Hart playing only five games. Their first match in the League was on 28 August 1920—and ironically it was against Burslem Port Vale, the club who had replaced the expelled Leeds City in the previous season.

United fielded Down, Duffield, Tillotson, Musgrove, Baker, Walton, Mason, Goldthorpe, Thompson, Lyon, and Best. A crowd of 15,000 welcomed United to League football watching the game in glorious summer weather. United were beaten 2–0.

A gate of 16,958, paying £1,016 saw United play their first game at Elland Road on Wednesday, 1 September 1920. South Shields provided the opposition but defeat was again in store for the League newcomers, who went down 2–1. The distinction of scoring the first League goal for the new Club went to Lyons, the former Hull City inside-left, who scored following a centre from Armitage, an ex-Sheffield Wednesday attacker. There was, fittingly, very much a Yorkshire flavour about the goal.

Victory was not much longer delayed, however, and when Port Vale visited Elland Road three days later the new Club's first victory—and League points—were gained with a 3–1 success, Elson scoring twice and Best getting the single.

United had to be content with fourteenth place at the end of that season—a satisfactory situation—but the second season saw the Club make further progress, as Fairclough's side finished in eighth position having earned forty-five points from sixteen wins and thirteen draws. One position higher was the Club's position in the season of 1922-23.

Progress had been encouraging to say the least and though hopes that First Division football would be realized inside three years had not materialized First Division football did come to United in the 1923-24 season when they won the Second Division Championship—thus achieving in four years what the Leeds City Club had failed to do in its fifteen-year history.

Fairclough had linked up again with Willie Norman, renewing a partnership which had already achieved success with Barnsley and Huddersfield Town. United ended the campaign having lost fewer matches than any other team in the Second Division and they took the coveted Championship with fifty-four points from twenty-one victories and twelve draws.

Former Huddersfield Town centre half Jim Baker had the distinction of being Leeds United's first ever captain when the club embarked on its first season in the Second Division in 1920. He was captain of the promotion winning side of 1923-24 and when he was photographed many years later still cherished the gold championship medal presented to him.

It was as cheap and efficient a team as ever won promotion the *Yorkshire Evening Post* reported at the time. A matter of £500—no more—had been spent on transfers in the season!

Hart was a regular member of the United defence by now and he and Baker played a big part in helping the side achieve a fine defensive record, only thirty-five goals being conceded in the promotion battle—a feat matched only by Bury, the runners-up.

Willis Edwards, who was later to become a member of one of the finest half-back lines in football—alongside Hart and Wilf Copping—made his first appearances with United in their first season of top-grade soccer, after moving from Chesterfield. He developed into a half-back of steely determination and immaculate control, yet his first season with United was not to be the happiest or most memorable of campaigns.

United struggled hard to establish themselves in higher company but the solid-looking defence that had repeatedly kept Second Division attacks at bay the previous season let in fifty-nine goals as the team finished fifth from the bottom—above Arsenal incidentally who just preserved their First Division status by finishing third from the bottom, and also above relegated Preston North End, but well below Huddersfield Town who clinched the First Division Championship for the second successive season.

When Huddersfield set up a record by winning the Championship of the First Division in the season of 1925-26 for the third time in a row, United were again struggling to survive. That season they were fourth from the bottom, only one point away from relegation.

Relegation & Recovery

Willis Edwards, a member of United's famous half-back line of the mid-1930s, developed into one of the most immaculate and accomplished players of his era. After his playing days were over he remained at the club for many years helping in various capacities including coaching and, for a brief spell, managing.

The threat of relegation which had haunted Leeds United in the previous two seasons became reality when they finished second from the bottom of the First Division in 1927 and went down along with West Bromwich Albion.

United's shaky defence had conceded eighty-eight goals and twenty-three of the forty-two League games had been lost. To complete a season of misery their Manager, Albert Fairclough, tendered his resignation.

His successor as Secretary-Manager was Dick Ray, manager of Doncaster Rovers, a former Leeds City player who had seen professional service on the field also with Macclesfield, Burslem Port Vale, and Manchester City.

Taking on this extremely important role was just reward for the sterling work Ray had put in during United's early days. He was an active member of the committee formed to get the new Club off the ground after the suspension of

Leeds City. Indeed he exercised managerial control before Hilton Crowther came on the scene with his protégé Fairclough.

While associated with Leeds City, Ray had run the Midland League side on a weekly wage bill of just £11 and several of the players under his control had subsequently been taken on by Leeds United.

During an eventful eight-year period in control of United, Ray enjoyed a reasonably successful reign, taking the side to promotion on two occasions. His first year at the helm was a particularly memorable one for all concerned at Elland Road.

Promotion was achieved at the first attempt and in the grandest manner. No fewer than ninety-eight goals were scored as United battled through to the runners-up spot behind Manchester City who, incidentally, had bettered the goals-for total by reaching the century mark.

One of Ray's signings that season was Charlie Keetley, a member of the famous Keetley family of Derby who made soccer history in the late 1920s and early 1930s by having at one time five members playing League football. Tom, Frank, Joe, and Harold were the others, all of whom played for Doncaster.

The signing of Charlie Keetley proved a good stroke of business for the Club. He played a big part in the clinching of promotion by scoring three hat-tricks on his way to a goal tally of eighteen from the last fifteen games of the season.

He wasn't, however, United's leading scorer. That honour fell to Tom Jennings, who had been bought from Raith Rovers two seasons earlier. He notched twenty-two.

United were not short on support either in 1927-28 season. There was an attendance of 30,000 to see Keetley score twice in the 3–0 win over Wolverhampton Wanderers and a similar figure for the visit of Port Vale when two goals from Tommy Jennings and one from Russell Wainscoat earned United a 3–0 victory. Biggest crowd at Elland Road that season saw a record 49,799 spectators pack into the ground to see United go down by the only goal of the game to arch promotion rivals Manchester City.

Keetley proved himself to be a prolific scorer for United and was with the Club throughout the eight-year reign of Ray. He was credited with well over 100 goals in that time.

United stayed in the First Division for another three seasons after Ray had taken them up but had another season in the Second Division in 1931-32. It was not more than a short interruption to their top division standing and United were back among the élite the following season when they finished in seventh place—the highest First Division slot the Club had enjoyed since its formation.

That season was also memorable for a new attendance record of 56,988 being set for the Elland Road stadium. The attraction was a Christmas-time League clash with the ever-popular Arsenal. Spectators began arriving at the ground four hours before the kick off and immense crowds boarded the fleet of tramcars which departed from Sovereign Street.

The gates had to be locked with hundreds unable to get in and the crowd overflowed on to the roof of the newly covered part of the popular side where hundreds found a commanding, if precarious, perch, while scores of other people were watching the match from the roof of an inn overlooking the ground.

So great became the crush inside the ground that the gates had to be opened to let some of the fans out and relieve the pressure. The nearby Beeston Pit heap became packed with people eager to get a glimpse of the action which at the end of the ninety minutes left United and Arsenal all square at 0–0.

United remained in the First Division for the seven years leading up to the outbreak of the Second World War, which brought a halt to League football in 1939.

The fifteen-year period from 1925 was a notable one in the history of the Club, not so much in relation to the side winning honours—though they did win promotion to the First Division twice in this period—but in relation to the Club beginning to develop an identity.

Some of the finest players of the day saw service with United and that famed and feared half-back line of Willis Edwards, Ernie Hart, and Wilf Copping first saw the light of day on a football field.

Edwards had joined the Club in March 1925 and yet but for one of those curious chances which crop up in football he might never have moved to Yorkshire. At the time United were struggling to avoid relegation in their first season in the First Division and had decided to scrape the bottom of their cash box in a desperate mad March spending spree.

They bought Tom Jennings from Raith Rovers, Russell Wainscoat from Middlesbrough, and, to improve their middle line, they invested £1,500 in Edwards of Chesterfield on 16 March

The United side in which the Milburn brothers, Jack and George made their mark in the early 1930s. Back row (left to right)— O'Grady, G. Milburn, Potts, Hart, J. Milburn, Copping. (Front)— Hydes, Keetley, Furness, Cochrane.

1925—the last day for transfers in that season.

Edwards did not take long to make up his mind. He signed on the dotted line without trouble but the ink had scarcely time to dry when Aston Villa representatives walked through his doorway in a late—and vain—bid to sign him.

When interviewed some twenty-five years later Edwards admitted that he still did not know what he might have done had the Villa people arrived five minutes earlier than they did. Nevertheless he could have had few regrets at moving to Leeds for he developed a distinguished career with United.

Inside twelve months he was capped for England against Wales for the first time and a month later against Scotland. Down the years, as his hair thinned, his footballing craft grew.

Eleven times in all he played for England and six times he turned out for the Football League against the Scottish League. It was said—and reported—that he would have won more national honours but for Football League disapproval of the fact that he had contracted to give newspaper forecasts of the following week's games, even though he omitted the matches involving Leeds United.

Apart from that slight unwitting indiscretion, Edwards was never in trouble with soccer authority. Not once did he have his name taken or receive a caution from a referee. In Club life he was the perfect model of the professional player. In fair days and foul he always gave of his best.

Superb control of the ball and accuracy in passing were assets which served him well in his career at Elland Road and when he and Hart eventually teamed up with Copping in 1932 the three of them quickly became one of the most feared and famous half-back lines in the country.

Copping was the original 'Iron Man' of Leeds—beating Norman Hunter to this home-spun title, by some thirty-five years. Fearsome in everything he did, Copping made such an impact with United that after three years at the Club his totally committed, tenacious approach had won him such a reputation that Arsenal paid £8,000 to take him to Highbury, and that was big money in those days.

Like his half-back partners at Elland Road, Copping earned International recognition with England. He first appeared for his country in 1933 against Italy and Sweden and in all won twenty caps.

Behind this formidable trio in the early 1930s was another player remembered with admiration by older supporters. His name? Bert Sproston. Signed from Sandbach Ramblers in the later 1920s Sproston stayed at Elland Road for thirteen years. Originally, however, he was a wing-half but converted so successfully to full-back that he won eight England caps before moving to Tottenham Hotspur and later to Manchester City where he added further International honours to his name.

With such formidable figures in their defence, particularly in the early 1930s, it was small wonder that United—apart from one lapse in 1931-32—camped in the First Division.

Defensively they were extremely sound. They owed much to their all-International half-back line and when, more recently, Billy Bremner, Jackie Charlton, and Alan Hunter came on to the scene arguments inevitably developed among older supporters as to which trio formed the better combination.

Those of us who thrilled to the performances of the Bremner–Charlton–Hunter combination find it difficult to accept that any other partnership could be better for when this trio went through their paces United were fighting for honours on more fronts than in the older days—the League Cup and European matches having been added to the fixture list.

Because so many years separate them it can never be known for certain which deserved top billing. Suffice it to say that both were the best in their day and United were indeed fortunate to have two such half-back lines. Great half-back lines like that do not cross the football stage more than once in any generation. More's the pity.

The famous footballing name of Milburn was synonymous with Leeds United when Jack and George partnered each other in the 1930s at full-backs. They were joined some time later by a third member of the family, younger brother Jim, who arrived at Elland Road in 1936-37 and worked his way up through the Club's Yorkshire League and Central League teams. He was about to step into a permanent first team place when war broke out.

After the war Jim returned to Elland Road and later on a nephew of the Milburn brothers was to appear in the United side, Jackie Charlton, of course, being the man in question.

Another player to make his mark with United in the late 1930s was Tom Holley, son of George Holley, who was an England and Sunderland inside-left in his playing days. Tom had joined Barnsley when his father went to Oakwell as trainer but in June 1936 he was transferred to Elland Road and although playing as a wing-half he was quickly to be converted into a centre-half. Standing six feet one and a half inches tall and weighing thirteen and a half stones it was no great surprise.

Tom served United admirably for many years and though he was not to emulate his father by gaining International honours he was highly regarded as a 'stopper' type of centre-half.

Before his playing career ended in 1950 Tom took up part-time journalism with the *Yorkshire Evening Post* and when he finished playing became a full-time member of the sports department of that newspaper, later moving on to Sunday-paper sports journalism.

Now retired Tom follows the fortunes of his old Club from his home in Majorca and one of the first places he visits on his frequent visits to Yorkshire is Elland Road.

Other discoveries were Gordon Hodgson, a South African-born centre-forward who also played with Liverpool and Aston Villa and who was reported to have scored his 300th League goal while with the Elland Road Club; inside-forward William Furness, and Eric Stephenson who sadly had his career ended by the war when he lost his life serving in Burma.

War, Decline and the Major

Billy Hampson, a former player with Leeds City, who became manager of Leeds United for a five year spell starting in the mid 1930s.

The mid 1930s had seen Leeds United appoint their third Manager, Dick Ray having resigned after an eventful eight years. Billy Hampson, the man who took over, had, like Ray before him, seen service with the Leeds City Club.

Indeed, he had been a member of the all-conquering City side which in the wartime tournaments of 1914-18 when Herbert Chapman managed the side, won the competition for two seasons and were runners-up in the third.

Hampson kept United ticking over steadily, if not too successfully, in First Division football until his management spell was interrupted by the Second World War.

Chairman of the Club during the war years was Ernest Pullan, who saw his top priority in those dark and difficult days of uncertainty and anguish that of striving to keep the Club going. With almost all the Club's playing staff serving in the Forces, Pullan and his Board had a difficult task.

The Boardroom at Elland Road, the tea-rooms and dressing-rooms were requisitioned for military administration purposes but for a couple of hours on Saturday afternoons the ground—by kind permission of the War Office—reverted to its original purpose. Guest players and local youngsters managed to keep some football going.

When League football thankfully got into full swing again after the war, Hampson, who in his previous managerial position at Carlisle had 'discovered' Bob Batey and none other than Bill Shankly, was nearing the end of his spell at Elland Road.

While at the Club Hampson had been

Edwards in his coaching days.

responsible for bringing Jim Twomey, David Cochrane, and Bobby Browne—who all won International caps for Northern Ireland while playing for United—into English football. But the first season of League activity after the war proved to be quite the most disastrous in the Club's history.

Failure after failure sent the Club hurtling down the First Division and into the Second, having won only six of their forty-two League games in the process of establishing an unwanted First Division record for the lowest number of points in a season—just eighteen.

Queens Park Rangers were later to 'earn' the right to share this doubtful distinction with United when they finished the 1968-69 season with eighteen points on their way down to the Second Division.

By the end of that disastrous season for United, Hamspon was no longer Manager of the Club. Instead he held the title and role of Chief Scout—a title he was to relinquish himself eight months later when he went freelance.

Willis Edwards, who when he ceased to play for United, became one of the Club's Assistant Trainers and coaches and who had been in charge of the Central League side immediately after the war, was appointed Team Manager in April 1947, shortly before the end of that terrible season.

Hope was high that matters would improve but the success which had followed Edwards on the field as a player did not unfortunately accompany him as a Manager. Having hurtled from the First Division there was to be no instant remedy for the Club's ills. They finished eighteenth in the Second Division with thirty-six points. It simply was not good enough.

Edwards's reign as Team Manager was brief. In April 1948, only a year after United had appointed him to the job they took on his successor and fifth Manager—Major Frank Buckley.

Major Buckley was considered a 'prize catch' for United and no one was more delighted at his decision to join Leeds than Sam Bolton, who was Chairman at what was a critical period in the Club's history.

The Major's playing career had been spent with Aston Villa, Birmingham City, and Derby County before the First World War and he had gained International honours against Ireland in 1914 as a centre-half. During the war he held the rank of Major in the Footballers' Battalion.

Norwich City were the first club to engage him as Manager back in 1919 but in 1920 he joined Blackpool. When he moved to Wolverhampton Wanderers in 1926, the club was struggling at the bottom of the Second Division but by 1932 he had taken them back to the First Division and wiped out all their outstanding debts.

Major Buckley had a tendency to sell star players and produce replacements from within the Club's reserve ranks and in the four-year period from 1935 he netted Wolves £110,658 in transfer fees.

He was given a life contract in January 1938 with the Molineux club, the first manager ever to receive this recognition, but in February 1944 he joined Notts County at a salary stated to be between £4,000 and £4,500 a year—the highest ever paid in football up to that time.

He surprised the football world again though when he severed his connection with County

at his own request. He joined Hull City where he stayed for four years before resigning after the club had taken on Raich Carter, the England inside-forward from Derby County as player and Assistant Manager and dismissed Frank Taylor as his Assistant after the two of them had been together in football for many years.

Major Buckley was not every soccer fan's cup of tea. It was once said about him that no man in football had been more cheered or jeered than he. Yet he did things very much his own way. Criticism had little or no effect on him.

One of the first things he did after his appointment at Elland Road was to introduce his own mechanical kicking machine to aid training. The machine, built of tubular steel, had the look of a rocket-firing machine and was loaded with half a dozen footballs at once and when a mechanical foot depressed by springs was released the balls were shot singly at an adjustable height.

Any type of shot at which a goalkeeper may have been weak could be produced at will and it was also used to improve the heading ability of players, and also their first-time kicking and trapping.

The Major had caused a sensation when, while at Wolverhampton, he treated some of his players with monkey gland extract in the belief that it would sharpen up their thinking and make them better and more decisive players. In 1951 he introduced a similar but more advanced form of treatment for players at Elland Road.

'Only a few players are having the glandular tonic, some by injection some by capsule,' he explained to interested reporters.

An executive of the Hertfordshire firm who supplied the treatment said the effect was to improve the intelligence quotient of the player and enable him to think and act a split second faster. No one could ever prove, however,

Leeds United considered themselves to have made a top class 'signing' when they appointed Major Frank Buckley manager in February 1949. Looking on— Sam Bolton (Chairman of the club), left, and Harold Marjason (Finance Director).

whether it did the players any good at all . . . or for that matter any harm.

It is not understating the case to say that Leeds were in a poor way when Buckley joined them. They had become run-down during the war and the first thing the new Manager did was to advise the Board at Elland Road to get £30,000 worth of debentures paid off as it was a millstone round the Club's neck.

'You are giving them football on the cheap in Leeds,' he was quoted as saying, and then proceeded to rail off the popular side of the ground and put up the prices on the Lowfields Road terraces. He continued to seek out his talent on the park pitches, in minor football and colliery welfare grounds, but the tide was beginning to turn against him.

There were no longer thousands of football-playing youths on the dole and only too eager to become part of what seemed to them to be the luxurious life of a Football League player. Society was becoming more affluent.

Major Buckley was no stranger to criticism and he came under fire very early on in his five-year reign at Elland Road. United had an abysmal record in the F.A. Cup, never once managing to get through three rounds of the competition.

In his first season with the Club United had been drawn at home to Newport in the third round but were humiliated by a 3–1 defeat. Thousands of angry fans streamed away from the ground in disgust long before the end while others stayed behind to applaud the visitors.

Leeds United during Major Buckley's days. Left to right (back)—Ingham, McCabe, Charles, Dunn, Searson, Milburn, Burden, Kerfoot, Browning, Roxburgh (trainer). Seated—Mr S. L. Blenkinsop (director), Mr H. Marjason (director), Mr P. A. Woodward (vice chairman), Mr S. Bolton (chairman), Major F. C. Buckley (manager), Mr J. Bromley (director), Mr Hilton Crowther (director), Mr C. A. Crowther (secretary). On ground—Cochrane, Iggleden, McMorran, Dudley, Williams.

Lesser men might have wilted. But not Major Buckley.

He had faced far more hostile criticism than that when at Wolverhampton. Though he had transformed Wolves from a quiet little provincial club into one of the most feared teams in the game there was a time when the crowd invaded the pitch (yes, it happened in those days) after a game and tore up the goalposts in their wrath because he had been transferring star players.

His reply was to promote youngsters to their places, Wolves took thirteen points out of the next sixteen games and his policy was vindicated.

In the teeth of the storm of criticism at Elland Road he prophesied: 'In twelve months' time the people of Leeds will be acclaiming Leeds United and me.' To many it seemed he had gone too far out on a limb with that bold statement but, not for the first time in his remarkable career, he was proved right in his prophecy.

The side enjoyed a much-improved season in the 1949-50 campaign, finishing fifth in the Second Division and reaching the quarter-finals of the F.A. Cup—the furthest the Club had ever progressed in this popular and strongly contested competition.

His most vociferous critics on the popular side at Elland Road had swung firmly behind him by now and the chant 'Come on the Buckley Boys' was frequently shouted with enthusiasm.

United's F.A. Cup exploits, not surprisingly in view of the relative lack of success and active interest in the competition in years gone by, captured the public's imagination more than ever before.

They set off in style at Carlisle where goals from Len Browning, Northern Ireland winger Dave Cochrane, Welsh winger Harold Williams, and a couple from Frank Dudley, helped United to a 5–2 third round success.

A crowd of 51,000 saw Williams hit the target in a fourth round home draw with First Division Bolton Wanderers and though the Lancashire side were very much favourites to win the replay at Burnden Park, United brought off one of those giant-killing acts the competition is noted for.

Two more goals from Dudley and one from Browning earned a 3–2 success and set United up for a fifth round home tie with Second Division Cardiff City.

Cup fever gripped the City but when the Club decided to sell tickets for the Cardiff game at a Central League game—the idea being that each supporter could buy a Cup ticket as he moved through the turnstiles into the ground—the plan came under fire from fans. But the Club stuck to their guns on the issue and when United's reserve side took on Derby County reserves on 5 February 1950 no fewer than 31,000 people had passed through the turnstiles.

When the Cup tie was played Elland Road housed a 50,000 crowd and United did not disappoint. They sent their followers home in high spirits with a 3–1 success over the Welshmen, the goals that mattered came from Williams, Cochrane, and Ray Iggleden.

The reward for that success was a quarter-final visit to Arsenal. There was a big rush to book up buses, 'planes, and trains for the journey to Highbury but there was to be no

happy ending this time for the Buckley Boys. Arsenal went through on the narrowest of margins in front of a crowd of 62,573, disposed of Chelsea 2–0 in the semi-final, and lifted the coveted trophy with a win over Liverpool by the same score in the Final.

United's form of upsurge could be looked upon with satisfaction not only by Buckley and his players but by the United Board and in particular by its Chairman, Sam Bolton, who was then fifty-five and just as much a son of Holbeck as he was when he had a trial for Leeds City many years before.

He was one of the few soccer club chairmen who had graduated from the 'bobside'—a reference to the days when admission to the popular side could be gained for just one shilling (or 5p these days)—to the Board, which he had joined in 1945 and of which he was still a member at the time of his death in December 1976 at the age of eighty-one.

The Major's five-year managerial spell ended in April 1953 when he left to take up a similar appointment with Walsall. But his reign at Elland Road was notable for one thing, perhaps, above all else.

He was the man who first gave a chance to the great John Charles—the Welsh colossus who went on to become one of the greatest players the game has ever known.

Raich Carter who took over from the Major.

Welsh winger Harold Williams (right) shows his paces for United.

All the power and determination Welsh international John Charles brought to his game is mirrored in this action shot during his Leeds United days.

The legendary John Charles

John Charles is undoubtedly the one player above all others—including those who rose to International stardom when Don Revie took Leeds United through its most memorable and successful era—Leeds people still delight in talking about.

The towering Welshman—he stood six feet one and a half inches and weighed thirteen stone and ten pounds at the peak of his illustrious career—carved such a huge niche for himself in the Club's history that it remains difficult to put into words just how great an impact he made on Leeds fans or indeed the game.

Big John, went on to become known as the 'Gentle Giant of Elland Road' and later, as his deeds increased, 'King John'. But like all footballers he started at the bottom.

The Charles story began, so far as United were concerned, when he moved to Yorkshire from his home town near Swansea to seek fame and fortune at the tender age of fifteen. At that time he was not the powerfully built figure he later became but the talent and know-how was evident from the word go and it quickly became apparent that United's Welsh scout Jack Pickard, who was later to discover Gary Sprake, Terry Yorath, and Byron Stevenson, had found a winner.

Charles became a full professional just over a year after moving to Leeds when he was seventeen and almost galloped through the third and second teams and in April 1949 he was promoted to centre-half in the first team for a friendly match against Queen of the South. He made a sound enough début in a goalless draw.

His opponent in that match was Billy Houliston, one of the most formidable centre-forwards of his day, who had jumped with unusual speed from the comparative obscurity of Second Division football to Scotland's International side. Ten days before coming up against Charles, the Scottish attacker had led his country's front line in a 3–1 triumph over England at Wembley and had given a defender of the calibre of Neil Franklin plenty to think about.

Yet after the game against Leeds, Houliston could not conceal his admiration for the young Charles. 'He's the best centre-half I have ever come up against,' he said.

Charles had not yet grown to six feet and his weight was about eleven and a half stones but, unlike many promising players today who are nursed along gradually, he was not allowed to develop his talents in the relative tranquillity of the second team.

Two weeks after playing against Houliston, he embarked on his League career when he made his Second Division début against Blackburn Rovers. Jimmy Dunn and Harold Williams were scorers for Leeds on that memorable day in a 2–1 success.

United's Manager, Major Frank Buckley, an England centre-half before the First World War prematurely concluded a brilliant playing career, rarely lost an opportunity to talk freely about the Elland Road boy wonder and Charles frequently made the headlines.

His continued impressive form resulted in his being selected to play for Wales in his first year as a professional. At the age of eighteen he became his country's youngest International.

Ireland were the visitors to Wrexham but Charles surprisingly had a far from memorable game. The *Yorkshire Post* later said of his display: 'Charles was a complete failure in that game. Whereas in Leeds United's matches he had never been hesitant to dictate terms to opponents double his age and experience, here he was neither prepared to go in and tackle nor to stand off and wait. He started to tackle, withdraw, and was lost in helpless decision.'

Hardly the most flattering or encouraging of remarks to have made about the player who went on to become, arguably, the best to grace football grounds in England and Wales since the war.

Back in the United side, however, Charles continued to develop at a rapid rate into an accomplished centre-half. His decisiveness, determination, and ball control was a delight to see and it was not surprising that he became the top attraction with the Elland Road side.

Other clubs began to sit up and take notice of the star man and offers were received on several occasions for him; one club making it clear they were prepared to part with £35,000—a tidy sum in those days—even though Charles still had to undergo his two-year period of National Service.

United were having none of it. They were intent on sticking to their prodigy. Inquiring clubs were politely but sternly informed of the fact.

National Service with the Royal Tank Regiment and two operations inside two years for the removal of a cartilage from each knee, did little to hinder his career which took a surprising twist in 1952.

United were struggling again in the Second Division and finding goals exceptionally hard to come by. Major Buckley's plan to solve this worrying deficiency was to bring the height, power, and skills of Charles into his forward line and the move proved to be a resounding success.

Charles adapted to his new mission with incredible success. He started out by scoring against Barnsley in a 4–1 win at Elland Road in a game in which Albert Nightingale scored twice and Don Mills got the fourth and in his first six consecutive completed League games the magical Welshman notched no fewer than eleven goals!

In fourteen matches his goal tally had reached nineteen and by the end of the season the Welsh wonder had knocked in twenty-seven goals, many of them ferocious headers, to become one of the most feared strikers in the country. He was well ahead of United's second highest scorer, Iggleden, who had scored twelve. George Meek was in third place with eight goals.

Much to his delight—and relief—his success as a forward also attracted the attention of the Welsh selectors and he was chosen to play inside-right in the Wales side against Ireland in Belfast on 15 April 1953, three years after he had won his first International cap as a starry-eyed eighteen-year-old centre-half.

United, however, finished in a mid-Table position—tenth to be exact—that season and at the end of the term Major Buckley resigned the managership and took on the onerous task, and that at the age of seventy, of managing Walsall who were facing the indignity of having to apply for re-election to the old Third Division South.

Former England, Sunderland, and Derby County inside-forward Horatio 'Raich' Carter stepped into the Major's shoes at Elland Road, just as he had done at Hull City five years earlier.

The thirty-eight-year-old silver-haired maestro of football, as newspapers had a habit of calling him, had been a firm favourite with fans and players and had achieved a distinguished career as a player. Cup medals came his way with Sunderland and Derby County, and he won more than a dozen England caps. He was very much a soccer strategist.

At Hull he had been player-manager and though he took them to the Championship of the Third Division he was handicapped in his recruitment for the club because he was unable to look for players himself because of time spent playing.

As a result a number of his signings for Hull did not prove too successful. Don Revie was bought from Leicester City, Ackerman came from Clyde, Neil Franklin from Stoke City, and Moore from Chesterfield—all good players in their own right, but only Franklin stayed.

Carter's appointment at Elland Road was solely as Manager. The change at the top had little effect on John Charles who continued to play at centre-forward. Indeed so successful was Charles in the 1953-54 season that he scored forty-two League goals in thirty-nine appearances to set up a Club record that still holds good today and seems unlikely ever to be surpassed.

No other striker in the Football League could match that total and if there were any doubts as to Charles being the most feared attacker in the country they were well and truly dispelled.

Nightingale had chipped in with seventeen League goals while Forrest, Williams, and Iggleden added twenty-three between them to help United reach a goal total for the season of eighty-nine. Yet things were at a standstill. United again had to settle for tenth place in the Second Division.

Next season proved to be much more encouraging though the Club's Directors had to fight off a shock transfer request from the great Charles, who, eager to put his skills to the test of First Division football, had sent ripples of fear running through United followers by writing out his request.

For three hours the United Directors discussed Charles's request before Sam Bolton emerged to tell the waiting soccer world that it had been turned down. 'Why should we sell a brilliant player like Charles. Our aim is to get United into the First Division and we cannot do that by selling our star player,' the Chairman explained, no doubt to the nodding approval of all United fans.

The Board's decision greatly disappointed Cardiff City manager, Trevor Morris, who after making it clear his club would pay almost

any price to get Charles, had travelled to Elland Road and sat outside the Boardroom while United deliberated the Welshman's future.

Arsenal, too, were frustrated at the outcome for though they were not present at Elland Road they had asked to be notified immediately if United were willing to part.

It was widely believed that had United decided to sell they could have netted between £40,000 and £50,000—easily topping the record fee of £35,000 which Sheffield Wednesday had paid out for Jackie Sewell.

United had added to their first team strength by signing Sheffield United's Harold Brook, amusingly referred to in Football Annuals of the time as a 'goal-snapper'. He lived up to that description, by topping the Elland Road goal-chart that season with sixteen, closely followed by the dependable Nightingale who had scored thirteen. Charles still managed to score eleven goals even though he had reverted to the role of centre-half.

Though they had scored nineteen goals fewer than the previous season United only narrowly missed being promoted, having finished only one point adrift of the three leading clubs, Birmingham City and Luton Town, who were promoted with a superior goal average, and Rotherham United.

Raich Carter's men had better luck the following season when nine years in the relative obscurity of the Second Division came to an end. Fittingly for Carter, promotion became a reality at Boothferry Park, the home, of course, of Hull City, where seven years earlier he had been chaired off the field when the City side he captained and managed won promotion to the Second Division.

Having pressed encouragingly for promotion all season United moved into second place on 21 April 1957 when they thrilled the vast majority of a 49,274 crowd at Elland Road who saw them defeat promotion rivals Bristol Rovers 2–1.

A champagne occasion. Silver-haired Soccer maestro Raich Carter (Manager at Elland Road from 1954-58) pours out the bubbly for big John Charles after Leeds United had clinched their return to the First Division in April 1956 with a 4-1 success at Hull City, Carter's previous club. Enjoying the celebrations are (left to right) Mr H. Marjason (director), Carter, Jimmy Dunn, Eric Kerfoot, Bob Roxburgh (trainer), Charles, Grenville Hair, Keith Ripley, Albert Nightingale, Harold Brook and, in front, George Meek.

Rovers had brought whoops of delight from their following among the crowd by taking the the lead after only three minutes of the game but United overcame that initial blow and were level after seventeen minutes. George Meek's tenacity won the chance and Charles dashed in through a hesitant Rovers defence to head a brilliant goal.

Ten minutes later Elland Road erupted when Brook and Charles linked well for the big Welshman to loop a shrewd pass across the Rovers cover defence for Jackie Overfield to slam the ball home from the underside of the bar.

Promotion was nearer for United now than at any other time in the previous nine years and the *Yorkshire Evening Post* duly acknowledged the part Charles had played. 'He showed true genius, true captaincy and superb fitness,' their report said.

United had two away games left in which to clinch promotion and a 2–0 win at Rotherham (Nightingale scoring twice from passes given to him by Meek) two days after the win over Rovers, sent United on to Boothferry Park needing just one point to secure their return to the First Division.

An estimated 15,000 Leeds fans made the journey to Boothferry Park on the following Saturday and they were not to be disappointed. Charles scored after only six minutes when he climaxed a superb run with a brilliant left-foot shot and although Hull were level in the thirteenth minute when Martin raced in to meet an accurate low centre from Fraser, United were in front again when Charles scored from the penalty spot after sixty-two minutes.

Harold Brook got United's third goal after seventy-eight minutes after Charles and Meek had done the spadework and Brook set the seal on a memorable afternoon by adding the fourth goal a minute later.

Fittingly for Manager Raich Carter promotion was clinched on a ground where he was remembered as the man who had helped Hull to promotion some few years earlier.

Predictably Charles had played a key part in his side's long-awaited return to the First Division. He led the challenge from the start and finished with thirty goals as United secured second place with eighty goals and fifty-two points to go up with their great Yorkshire rivals Sheffield Wednesday.

Disaster: Charles departs and fire

The big question on the lips of soccer fans up and down the country was how John Charles would fare in the more demanding confines of the First Division—a league widely accepted as the toughest in the world of football.

Charles was an awesome figure of a man and he had been an undisputed King in Second Division football. Now his power and skill were to be put to the long-awaited major test.

There was to be no let down. The big Welshman took the First Division by storm and crashed in thirty-eight goals with typical power and determination to finish as leading First Division scorer in his first season in the top flight. His nearest challenger in the division was Jackie Mudie who notched thirty-two goals for Blackpool that season, and Nat Lofthouse who managed twenty-eight for Bolton Wanderers.

Charles's feat that season was bettered by only one player in the entire Football League, Arthur Rowley scoring forty-four League goals for Leicester City, and was equalled by one of today's most prominent soccer figures, Brian Clough whose thirty-eight goals helped Middlesbrough to a respectable sixth place in the Second Division.

The New Look. Leeds United kicked off the 1955-56 season at Barnsley wearing a newly-designed strip —a darkish blue shirt with gold collar and white shorts in preference to the previous strip of old-gold jersey with blue sleeves and collar and black shorts, which had brought some criticism from the Elland Road side's female fans. The side that days was: (left to right) back row—Kerfoot, Dunn, Wood, Gibson, Hair. Front—Williams, Nightingale, Brook, Charles (captain), Henderson, Meek.

EVENING POST
EVENING POST

United, not surprisingly with such a bold and prominent figure as Charles in their line-up, restarted their First Division life in the most devastating fashion. Their team for the first match at home to Everton showed only one change from that which had clinched promotion with victory at Hull in the last game of the previous season—Archie Gibson coming in for Keith Ripley—but United hammered their Goodison opponents 5–1—and scored all their goals in a rip-roaring first thirty-four minutes of the game.

Overfield scored after only two minutes, when Charles—predictably—provided the chance and nine minutes later Charles scored his first goal in the First Division with a thundering header after a good run on the left and a cross from Brook.

Brook then scored a hat-trick with efforts in the thirteenth, seventeenth, and thirty-fourth minutes before Farrell hit a consolation goal for the Merseysiders eight minutes from the end.

It was the best possible beginning but while Charles and his team-mates were busily adjusting to the more sophisticated style of First Division football disaster struck the Elland Road Club when a night-time fire on 18 September 1956 completely destroyed the main West Stand.

All the Club's equipment went up in flames, including jerseys, balls, boots, stockings, and the Club's valuable records. It was indeed a cruel blow to United who had adjusted so superbly to the First Division in those early weeks of the season that they were lying second with thirteen points from their first nine games.

Crowds at the early games had increased by leaps and bounds and there was every prospect of a crowd of 50,000 for the Club's next match, at home to popular Aston Villa.

An appeal went out immediately to residents in Elland Road to open their homes to the players and provide emergency changing accommodation. As Chairman Sam Bolton declared defiantly: 'The game against Villa will go on as planned.'

The cost of the damage caused by the fire was put at £100,000 and while arrangements were immediately put in hand for a new stand to be built, United's players faced the problem of overcoming the upheaval and preparing to meet the challenge of Villa four days later.

Naturally the magnitude of the cruel blow was not lost on them but the main topic of conversation was boots—the most important

Top: John Charles leads out his men through the charred and twisted remains of the West Stand when United played Aston Villa only a few days after the fire. In the foreground, hanging over the debris is Charles' old No. 8 jersey. United won the game 1-0 with a goal from Charles.

Below left: The heat-buckled girders of the West Stand at Elland Road present a skeletal picture after the disastrous fire of September 1956. The club lost everything—its equipment, dressing rooms, strip, footballs, club offices and all records relating to the running of the club since its formation.

Below Right: Manager Raich Carter (centre), Willis Edwards (assistant trainer) right, and Mr H. Lunn (assistant secretary) survey the immense damage done by the fire.

Top: Leeds United's £130,000 new stand which opened its turnstiles to the public for the first time at the start of the 1957-58 season.

Below: United lost no time in setting the wheels in motion for a replacement stand and as workmen were busy removing the last remains of the burned out stand others were already hard at work preparing the foundations for the new stand.

part of a footballer's kit and to which most players become very attached.

Manager Raich Carter took instant steps to get new footwear and forty pairs of boots were delivered to Elland Road shortly after the players reported for training on the morning after the fire. The order went out for his men to wear their boots on every possible occasion until the week-end, and doubtless to sleep in them if they thought fit to do so.

The charred remains of the burnt-out stand were duly fenced off, United took the field as planned on the Saturday, and kept up their challenge with a 1–0 victory over Villa, John Charles—who else?—scoring the all-important goal.

Meanwhile efforts were being made to have the stand replaced and eventually the Lord Mayor of Leeds, who at that time was Alderman T. A. Jessop, launched a public appeal for £60,000, the figure being the difference between the insurance payment the Club were to receive and the cost of a new stand to seat 4,000 spectators and provide additional facilities underneath such as dressing-rooms and offices.

'It is a challenge and we have to meet that challenge. The prestige of the city is at stake,' said the Lord Mayor.

United continued to fulfil their commitments at Elland Road that season but slipped slightly from their encouraging early season placing. But eighth position in their first season back among the country's top clubs was satisfying enough though they would have done far better had they not failed badly at the end of the term.

Nine of the last twelve points available to them had been squandered.

The new West Stand—which cost £130,000—was ready at the beginning of the 1957-58 season and brought a much classier look to the Elland Road stadium, once more in keeping with the Club's First Division status.

Main contractors for the stand scheme were the Leeds building firm of Robert R. Roberts and the architect Mr Brian Jackman of the Leeds firm of Braithwaite and Jackman and it provided accommodation for 4,000 seated spectators and 6,000 more in terracing at the front.

It was in use for the first time on 24 August, the first Saturday of the season and as United were playing at Blackpool that day, United's reserve side was the first to be watched by fans using the new structure.

When United played their first League game of the season the following week, 27,000 fans were at the game to see Leicester City beaten 2–1.

Unfortunately for United and their followers there was no John Charles to help them in their chase for honours this season. Though the Club had turned down numerous attempts from other clubs to get them to part with the Welsh International, the Charles story had taken a dramatic turn when overseas interest in him developed shortly before the end of the 1956-57 season.

Signor Umberto Agnelli, son of the Fiat motor millionaire and President of Juventus of Turin, had seen Charles playing for Wales against Ireland and had decided the Welshman was just the man needed to make Juventus, who were having a lean season, tick again.

Agnelli fought off interest from several other clubs including Internationale of Milan and reported interest from Real Madrid the wealthy Spanish club and European Cup holders at the time, and also from the Rome club Lazio.

After some particularly hard bargaining on both sides United and Juventus reached agreement. Charles was happy with the terms, the deal was duly struck, and the lad from Swansea who had signed for United for just £10 became the costliest British footballer.

The fee was said to be £65,000, with Charles receiving £10,000, a salary of between £60 and £70 per month plus £25 for an away win and £15 for a home win, a car, a flat of his own choice in Turin and a contract covering two years.

It was too good to be true. These were staggering rewards indeed for twenty years ago and presented a wonderful opportunity for the player. But it was a sad day for United. 'Naturally we shall be sorry to see Charles go. But we did not want to stand in his way,' lamented Mr Bolton.

Though the deal was agreed on 20 April 1957 Charles played a game for United two days later watched by Juventus scout Gigi Peronace who was there to take delivery of Charles after the match.

A crowd of nearly 30,000 was there to bid a fond farewell to the King of Elland Road and the Welshman made it a night to savour by scoring twice in a 3–1 win over Sunderland.

On his arrival in Turin, the final piece of the Charles transfer slotted into place without trouble. 'Charles is the fittest man I know playing football. I have never seen a better human machine in a lifetime of medicine,' Professor Amilcare Bosatti, the doctor who examined Charles, reported.

How Don Revie became Manager

Without the services of a player widely regarded as the most famous footballer since the war, it was perhaps not surprising that United should find it a struggle to overcome the departure of John Charles.

They dropped to seventeenth place in the First Division and at the end of the season United decided not to renew the contract of their Manager Raich Carter when it expired at the end of May 1958.

It was a decision which came as a major surprise to Carter who was not slow to point out that in his five-year management he had taken the Club from a mid-Table position in the Second Division to fourth place and then to promotion and eighth place in the First Division.

'The past season we were seventeenth, after the Directors had sold Charles the greatest player in the world and given me far less than half his transfer fee to spend on replacing him. This last season could never be any more than a holding season once a player like Charles had gone,' Carter reasoned.

He was succeeded by Bill Lambton, who, after undertaking a period as Acting Manager, was given the managership in December 1958, seven months after Carter's departure, but his reign was brief. Three months after his elevation to Manager, he resigned saying: 'I have considered this course of action for some time owing to interference from Directors in my training methods.'

In his short time with the Club Lambton, who had originally been taken on to work under

Opposite Page: Don Revie prepared for his first game in Leeds United's colours following his transfer to Elland Road in November 1958.

Above: The start of Don Revie's climb to success in November 1958—when he signed as a player for Leeds United. Watching on are (left to right) Harold Marjason (finance director), Cyril Williamson (secretary) and Bill Lambton (chief trainer-coach who became manager).

Leeds United in 1960. Back row (left to right)—Ashall, Cameron, Humphreys, Charlton, Hair, Goodwin. Front—Murray, Peyton, Revie, McCole, Grainger.

Carter as a disciplinarian and fitness expert, had had a large say in the departure of Scottish centre-forward Hughie Baird back to Scotland and in the signings of Alan Humphreys, a right-winger from Northern Ireland and Alan Shackleton a centre-forward from Burnley.

There was another signing during his time, the man who was later to play such a huge and memorable part in the development of the Club's most successful period of history—Don Revie.

Revie—incidentally it's pronounced Reevy—joined United in a £12,000 deal which brought him from Sunderland in November 1958. It was described at the time as one of the most exciting signings of the season and it greatly disappointed Middlesbrough who had high hopes of being able to take him to Ayresome Park to let him finish his playing days with his home-town club.

He was not to know it then, of course, but Revie made the best possible decision when he agreed to move to West Yorkshire. As a player he had wandered far and wide but he was a greatly valued individual.

Hull City paid Leicester City £20,000 for him in 1949-50; Manchester City handed Hull £25,000 in 1951-52; Sunderland paid out £23,000 in 1956-57 to Manchester City, and United's contribution in 1958 took the total outlay on him to £80,000—a record total involving any player at that time.

At thirty-one and with six International appearances for England to his credit, Revie had the kind of experience United were looking for to take charge of a team of hard-trying individuals and mould them into a first-rate side.

He made his début on 29 November 1958 in a 3–2 win over Newcastle United and less than two months later, six weeks to be exact, following a slump in the Club's on-the-field activities, five matches including a Cup-tie being lost out of the last six matches, he took over the Club captaincy.

Wilbur Cush, the Northern Ireland International, had resigned because he felt the duties were affecting his play. Lambton hurriedly held a players' meeting and it was by unanimous vote that Revie got the job.

'I feel honoured and will give the job all I can on the field and off it,' Revie said. United's fortunes, however, did not improve. They finished fifteenth in the First Division and the following season were relegated.

Shortly after the start of the 1960-61 season Revie followed in the footsteps of Cush and relinquished the captaincy but for a different reason. As became more and more apparent later when he was Manager of the Club, Revie was of a superstitious nature and his reason for handing over the captaincy was purely and simply that he did not feel he was a lucky captain.

Freddie Goodwin, the burly ex-Manchester United central defender took on the job but an improvement in United's fortunes were not immediately apparent. The side continued to struggle and with a placing in the bottom half of the Second Division facing them Yorkshireman Jack Taylor, who had left the managerial chair at Queens Park Rangers to succeed Lambton at Elland Road resigned.

Taylor, who was United's sixth Manager in the sixteen years since the war, took this step even though his £2,000 a year contract still had more than a year of its three-year span to run.

His resignation was handed in on 13 March 1961. Four days later the decision that was eventually to transform the Club was made. Don Revie was given the job of Team Manager.

Sam Bolton still occupied the position of Chairman of the Club but it was Harry Reynolds, a bold, bluff Yorkshireman and self-made millionaire who was directly responsible for Revie becoming Team Manager at Elland Road.

Invited on to the Board six years earlier by Mr Bolton, he had a dream of building United into one of the most successful clubs in the country; a dream that was to be realized in due course after a great deal of hard work and the usual disappointments strewn along the way.

Harry Reynolds, a vastly interesting character who held a variety of jobs from flour boy with the Co-operative Society in Leeds to railway cleaner and fireman before making his money out of steel, was clearly looking ahead when he paved the way for Revie's appointment.

Revie had made a big impression on Mr Reynolds initially when the two of them travelled, at the then Manager Jack Taylor's request, to look at a player at Bolton. On the journey to Burnden Park, Reynolds expounded his ideas for the Club's future and to his surprise and satisfaction the coincided a lot with those of Revie. 'Don Revie came to my house a lot after that and we talked about many things connected with football. I liked him,' Mr Reynolds once revealed.

The pathway to the United Manager's chair began when Chester inquired about the possibility of Revie going there as a player coach and though Jack Taylor was willing to let him move Revie did not fancy it.

At that time Bournemouth were on the look out for someone to become their manager and Mr Reynolds wrote to them outlining Revie's qualifications only to realize that if the man in question had such capabilities as he himself had outlined then he was good enough to manage Leeds United.

A Board meeting was called at Elland Road, Jack Taylor was seen and told by Mr Reynolds that he was going to recommend he and the Club parted company. The Directors agreed and three days after Taylor's departure Revie was unanimously named as his successor.

Nine months after Revie's appointment Mr Reynolds took over as Chairman when Sam Bolton resigned and the partnership which began on that relatively short journey to Bolton began to work in earnest for the Club.

Many miles were covered looking for young players and though numerous youngsters who were to help the Club in the future were found and signed, Mr Reynolds never lost sight of the fact that the youth policy had been introduced before Revie took over.

It had been put into operation in Bill Lambton's time and carried on during Taylor's reign, and in the early 1960s there were clear signs that United had a wealth of promising young players battling through towards the first team. Success in a European youth tournament in Holland gave Mr Reynolds one of his most memorable moments in the game, the Championship of the Northern Intermediate League and prominent displays in the F.A. Youth Cup added to the belief that United were destined to go places.

Revie's impact on the managerial scene was neither immediate nor, for that matter, too encouraging. In his first full campaign as Manager, United came perilously close to dropping into the Third Division. Only by a whisker did they manage to steer clear of what could easily have been the kiss of death to United as a professional club.

It was said later that United might easily have folded had they been relegated for with debts said to be something in the region of £150,000 and only the prospect of lower division gates to rely on the future at best would have been a constantly mountainous battle to stay afloat.

In a mediocre first season for Revie, United found themselves needing victory at Newcastle in their last game of the season to be sure of staying in the Second Division. It seemed a forlorn hope that they would achieve their objective for they had won only two away games all season.

Revie, however, had his men suitably motivated and United surprised almost everyone by winning 3–0. Albert Johanneson, the coloured flying winger from South Africa whose skills and speed earned him the affectionate title of the 'Black flash' among Elland Road fans, got a goal, so too did Billy McAdams while an own goal from Newcastle defender Keith completed the scoring to provide United with an escape act Houdini at his peak would have been proud of.

Confidence and decisiveness are attributes Revie never lacked. Though he breathed a huge sigh of relief at that result at St James's Park he was convinced he had the blueprint for success at Elland Road largely in the shape of two of football's smallest players.

Billy Bremner the tenacious little Scot from Stirling was a youngster Revie rightly believed he could build a team around and in the greatly experienced Bobby Collins, another tiny Scot who arrived at Elland Road towards the end of that worrying season, Revie felt he had the basis for survival and success.

Collins had thrown in his lot with United in March 1962 when in his third season with Everton after having joined the Goodison Park club in a £25,000 deal from Celtic. The decision caused surprise on both sides of the coin.

Firstly there were people who thought the little inside-forward crazy to leave the First Division to join a club at the bottom of the Second Division as United were at the time of his signing while there were grave doubts in other quarters as to the wisdom of hard-up United paying out a record £25,000 fee for a player who was all of thirty years old.

If it was a two-sided gamble it paid rich dividends all round in the years ahead. Collins played his part in helping to stave off relegation in 1961-62 as indeed did Bremner, and both players figured prominently in the emergence of

United as a force in the game not only in this country but on the Continent.

Having shown himself prepared to take chances in the transfer market Revie took another in the summer of 1962—one which after protracted negotiations saw a return to Elland Road of Welshman John Charles following a five and a half year spell in Italy with Juventus.

The Italian club paid United a reported fee of £65,000 when they plucked him from his promising career at Elland Road and it cost United a record fee of £53,000 to buy him back. It was a move which captured the imagination of all United followers particularly those so fond of the big Welshman in his first spell with the Club.

Unfortunately it was a move which did not work out as well as everybody hoped. Big John did not make the necessary impact. He made less than a dozen appearances, scoring three times, and it became obvious that he was not the player he had been.

Out of the disappointment came a satisfactory conclusion. United, who had temporarily, and unwisely in the view of many of their followers, put up their admission charges to help pay the transfer fee, recouped their outlay—and a little more—when Roma moved in to whisk Charles back to Italy.

United had made a poor start to the season, losing three and drawing one of their opening six matches but Revie, with slender playing resources to fall back on, was slowly but surely adopting a blueprint for the future. This was apparent to even the less discerning followers of the Club's fortunes when he surprised many by 'blooding' several teenagers in a Second Division match at Swansea in September 1962.

Paul Reaney, Norman Hunter, and Rod Johnson all got a taste of first team action that day in a United side that also had a youthful Gary Sprake making his second appearance in goal. A 2–0 win was Revie's reward for his gamble.

While Harry Reynolds was spearheading off-the-field activity with his behind-the-scenes enthusiasm, Revie was looking ahead with optimism and a dedication that was to stamp him in the years ahead as one of the most thorough of soccer managers.

United picked up in the 1962-63 season but Revie and his men had to be content with fifth placing. Next season it all began to happen for United as they surged to the Championship in an exciting campaign which saw them edge out Sunderland from top spot to return to the First Division after four seasons' absence.

Left Top: The legendary Stanley Matthews meets a boyish looking Billy Bremner.

Left Bottom: Fearless Bobby Collin, the 'wee midfield general'.

Above: There are one or two likely lads in this picture taken in May 1961 Can you pick out the faces of Billy Bremner, Norman Hunter, Paul Reaney and Terry Cooper? The full list of players, pictured with club chairman Harry Reynolds (extreme right), is—back row, left to right— D. Roper, P. Cooney, R. Blackburn, T. Cooper, P. Metcalfe, M. Addy, E. Thompson, N. Hunter. Front—P. Reaney, D. Schofield, S. Silverwood, T. Lloyd, B. Bremner, H. Ryden, T. Casey and R. Johnson.

Foundation for success

Gary Sprake as a young looking 16-year-old chats to Scottish international goalkeeper Tommy Younger in September 1961. Sprake was an apprentice professional who had just made his Central League debut and Younger was the man he eventually replaced as first choice.

Don Revie had worked slowly but surely towards building a side capable of restoring First Division football to Elland Road and his team at the outset of the 1963-64 promotion campaign clearly possessed the exuberance of youth and the skills and valuable know-how of more experienced players.

Like most managers, Revie—who had the full backing of the Directors who had chipped in £10,000 from their own pockets to help the Club in the bid for fame and glory—was only too well aware of the need to have younger players around and he had clearly demonstrated his faith in two of them when he gave first team baptisms to Gary Sprake and Peter Lorimer.

Sprake, the blond Welshman who was soon to play for Wales—even before he established a regular place at Elland Road—made just about the most dramatic Football League début in the history of the game when he was rushed at speed by taxi and plane to play against Southampton at the Dell in a Second Division match on 17 March 1962 when United's Scottish International goalkeeper Tommy Younger was taken ill hours before the kick off.

Revie made an immediate request for reserve goalkeeper Alan Humphreys to be rushed to the South Coast but he was found to be unfit. Attention was focused on Sprake who lay in bed at his Leeds lodgings, not far from Elland Road, resting in readiness for a junior team game that afternoon.

The Football League gave special permission for the start of the game to be delayed as Sprake was taken by taxi to board a specially chartered plane—at the cost of about £80—for the flight to Southampton.

It landed some six miles from Southampton and there followed another dash by taxi. The youngster arrived at the ground minutes before 3 p.m. The match started about fifteen minutes late during which time Sprake recovered from air sickness.

At sixteen—as he then was—Sprake became

the youngest player ever to wear the United first team strip. He was beaten four times when United lost 4–1 but the youngster had performed commendably and had given some indication that he was destined to reach the top.

Six months later Sprake lost the distinction of being United's youngest débutant when Lorimer, at the ripe old age of 15 years and 289 days, was called into first team action, because of injury to Billy Bremner, for a Second Division home game, coincidentally against Southampton.

The youngster from Dundee was pushing a broom along the steps of the Lowfields Road stand at Elland Road, doing his bit to tidy up the ground, when the news was broken to him. He was delighted of course and amazed. Yet Revie had carefully weighed up the situation before making his decision.

Only four months had gone by since Lorimer joined the Club but in that relatively short period he had succeeded in impressing United's back-room staff. He possessed a reputation for coolness—having played for Scotland schoolboys in front of a 30,000 crowd—and also for scoring goals.

He had played only six games in the Central League game and had scored only one goal when his first team chance came along but he had a tremendous pedigree in schoolboy football where he had been dubbed 'The Cannonball Kid' because of his ability to shoot with a power not generally associated with players of that age.

The season before joining United's ground staff he notched the massive total of 176 goals playing for his school on Saturday mornings and for the local Y.M.C.A. in the afternoon. It was the sort of record that brought no fewer than twenty-eight professional clubs in hot pursuit of his signature, including Manchester United who were considered to be favourites.

Elland Road is one of the few grounds protected against the icy temperatures by under soil heating. But it was very different in the winter of February 1963. Leeds United turned to straw and braziers in a bid to keep their pitch fit for play.

Strangely, perhaps, Lorimer turned down the chance to link up with Matt Busby and one of Europe's glamour clubs, as the Old Trafford side then was, to join Second Division Leeds who by no stretch of the imagination could be regarded in those days as one of the country's more fashionable clubs.

Just why the youngster had taken the decision was a mystery to many but, in fact, he made his decision to settle in Yorkshire rather than Lancashire because of one man—Revie. 'There was something about him that impressed me greatly. Even though the club had been struggling in the Second Division at the time, he had a firm belief that Leeds were going to succeed and I decided to go along with him,' he said later.

Paul Madeley, Terry Cooper, and Jimmy Greenhoff made their first team débuts in United's promotion season though they could not be described as regular members of the team. The eighteen-year-old Sprake was in goal to start the season, Younger having been forced into retirement with back trouble, and at right-back was Paul Reaney, then a relatively inexperienced nineteen-year-old.

Billy Bremner was a couple of years older and

Top: United's Under 18 side of 1964. Back row (left to right)—Terry Hibbitt, Jimmy Lumsden, Bobbie Sibbald, David Harvey, John Price, Mick Bates, Dennis Hawkins. Front—Graham Smith, Eddie Gray, Jimmy Greenhoff, Barry Wright (captain), Peter Lorimer, Nigel Davey, Derek Ryder and Rod Belfitt.

Below: South African born winger Albert Johanneson, who delighted Elland Road fans with his speedy runs and delicate ball control skills over a nine year period from 1961.

alongside the more mature Jack Charlton at the centre of the defence was nineteen-year-old Norman Hunter. Willie Bell was the regular choice left-back.

Bobby Collins, Jim Storrie, Ian Lawson, and Don Weston brought a more experienced look to the front line though at outside-left Revie fielded the speedy and tricky Albert Johanneson, a twenty-one-year-old South African.

Johanneson was 'making good' after arriving at Elland Road from Johannesburg in 1961 with his modest belongings packed into a suitcase. He was given a trial with United on the recommendation of a South African schoolmaster who had spent hour upon hour teaching him the skills of the game until he could control a tennis ball with his bare feet almost as easily as he could walk.

Johanneson impressed United sufficiently to be taken on as a full-time professional after making a fine début in a League game against Swansea Town in April 1961 when he made his mark almost immediately, measuring a centre perfectly for Jack Charlton to ram home a header.

Teamwork and dedication to duty were vitally important factors in Revie's guide to management and they played a major part in United's Second Division Championship success, but not before two shrewd sorties into the transfer market gave them the extra fillip they needed to clinch the award.

The first of these was to prove one of soccer's best-ever bargain buys—Johnny Giles, the skilful Irishman who went on to become a kingpin in the most successful team United have ever had. Revie handed over £33,000 to Manchester United for the Dublin-born Giles when, after seven years with the Old Trafford club, the player had suddenly become uneasy about his future.

'I don't mind one bit having to drop down to the Second Division. And who knows, I may be playing in the First Division again quite soon,' said Giles, almost as if he knew what was about to happen.

Giles, who had joined the Old Trafford club on leaving school, played on the wing for the Reds and within forty-eight hours of signing for Leeds was in action at Elland Road against Bury wearing the No. 7 shirt. Though he failed to find the net, it was a winning start for the Irishman with Collins, Storrie, and Johanneson scoring goals.

He missed only one match all season as he put his undoubted skills to good use helping United along the way as their promotion challenge gathered momentum. Around the turn of the year, however, United were suffering badly from a lack of punch in their attack and in the hope of rectifying this failing, Revie turned to his home-town club Middlesbrough—the attraction being twenty-six-year-old Alan Peacock, the former England centre-forward.

The fee of £50,000 was the highest ever received by the Ayresome Park club for a player, easily beating the £42,000 they took from Sunderland in July 1961 for Brian Clough, whom Peacock succeeded as centre-forward, when he switched from an inside-left position.

It was the highest fee United had paid to another English club and the figure rose by another £5,000 when promotion was clinched, the agreement with Middlesbrough being for that amount to be added to the original total if Peacock help United to gain the Championship.

Although Peacock had had an unlucky season, injuries restricting his appearances with Middlesbrough, for whom he had scored 126 goals in the Second Division, to a mere nine, United were hopeful he would add impetus to their run-in for promotion.

Some questioned the wisdom of spending so much money on a player who had been troubled by a knee injury and, indeed, had had a cartilage removed from his left knee, but Revie went ahead after a specialist had given the player a clean bill of health. Peacock duly went on to play a key role as United won promotion and then clinched the Second Division Championship.

There were fourteen games to go in the hectic tense finish to the 1963-64 campaign and Peacock played in them all. He wasted no time in getting down to business and scored his first goal for his new club in his first game—a 2-2 draw at Norwich on 8 February 1964.

Peacock had the satisfaction of scoring one of his new club's three goals in a vital 3-1 away win at the home of his old club. He scored in the next game, a 3-1 home win over Grimsby Town and when United picked up five precious points out of six available to them in a hectic Easter programme of three games in four days it was Peacock who scored a point-clinching goal in a keen match at Derby.

Giles and Don Weston earned two more precious points with a home win over Leyton Orient to take the points total for the season to fifty-seven—a record for United in any season—and send them on to Swansea needing one point to secure promotion.

United were three points ahead of their nearest rivals, Sunderland, and five in front of Preston North End, the only other team seriously in with a chance of promotion from the Second Division, when they went to Swansea who were expected to 'fight to the death' as they sought points to help them in their fight against relegation.

Revie made one change—and a surprising one, too—to the side that had beaten Leyton in the previous game by giving a League début to nineteen-year-old Cooper, a Yorkshire lad from Brotherton, near Pontefract. He played at outside-left in place of Albert Johanneson, the side's leading scorer.

Confidence was high in the United camp and they went on to clinch promotion in fine style sweeping Swansea aside with a 3-0 victory. Peacock did the greatest damage by scoring two of the goals inside a tremendous four-minute spell of action.

Only fifteen minutes had gone when Cooper crossed from the left for Peacock to sweep the ball in with his right foot and the cheering from happy United followers had hardly died down when the tall lean striker struck again, this time turning the ball in after Giles had touched on a corner from Collins.

A happy and fruitful afternoon was completed when Giles scored in the thirty-fourth minute with an accurate and crisply struck shot following a Cooper corner.

Having got promotion the next target was, naturally enough, the Second Division Championship. Cooper had impressed greatly on his début but Johanneson was back for the last home game of the campaign, against Plymouth Argyle. United slipped a little and were held to a 1–1 draw, a thirty-yard goal from Willie Bell having been equalized by Jennings.

Cooper was back for the final game of the season at Charlton as Revie fielded the team that had clinched promotion at Swansea two weeks' earlier—Sprake, Reaney, Bell, Bremner, Charlton, Hunter, Giles, Storrie, Peacock, Collins, Cooper.

With their rivals Sunderland—now promoted along with them—playing at Grimsby, United had to aim for a victory at Charlton and they duly achieved their objective. Two goals from the lively Peacock giving them a 2–0 success and himself a satisfying total of eight goals in the fourteen games he had played since his move from Middlesbrough.

United's final total of points was sixty-three—the highest by any Second Division side since Tottenham Hotspur were promoted in 1920 with seventy. It was also the best achievement by any team in any of the four divisions that season. Their record of having lost only three away games was also the best in the four divisions as was their record of having won twelve games away. There was tremendous satisfaction among United followers who had seen their team go undefeated at home in twenty-one League games.

United were 'champs' in every sense of the word and Revie and his men were standing on the threshold of what was to become the most successful and memorable period in the history of the Club.

The faith placed in Revie had brought its reward and the dream of Chairman Harry Reynolds that United would become one of the country's leading clubs was about to come true.

Though the most meticulous of managers, Revie had not altered his side much by the time the 1964-65 season got under way. The United side which began the term was the same as that which Giles appeared in for the second game of the promotion campaign, namely Sprake, Reaney, Bell, Bremner, Charlton, Hunter, Giles, Weston, Storrie, Collins, and Johanneson.

As seems to be the case with most clubs when they first return to the top flight, United were expected to struggle to stay above water but those critics who predicted a hard time ahead could not have been wider of the mark. Revie's men took the division by storm.

Their first game was at Aston Villa and inside three minutes Phil Woosnam had dashed their spirits by scoring the first goal in the First Division against Revie's side. As Villa fans sat back in the expectation of seeing more go by Sprake they had not reckoned on the never-say-die spirit of the lads from Leeds.

Villa were unable to add to that early goal and United hit back to win with goals from Albert Johanneson, who got the equalizer, and Jack Charlton.

Liverpool, holders of the First Division Championship, were United's first visitors to Elland Road, their line-up in those days being Lawrence, Byrne, Moran, Milne, Yeats, Stevenson, Callaghan, Hunt, Chisnall, Wallace, and Thompson.

They were well beaten, however, as the Second Division Champions put one over the First Division title-holders by winning 4–2. Ron Yeats had the distinction of scoring the first goal in a home game for Revie's men when he put through his own goal after sixteen minutes and though Roger Hunt equalized Don Weston netted United's second five minutes before half time. A goal from Billy Bremner in the fifty-second minute quickly followed by one from Johnny Giles in the fifty-fifty completed United's total while Gordon Milne scored a second for the Merseysiders.

United made it three wins in a row when two goals from Jim Storrie and one from Charlton, brought them a home victory over Wolverhampton Wanderers and the stage was set for them to make an amazingly sustained, and completely unexpected, assault on the First Division Championship.

Not content with that Revie's capable outfit took the F.A. Cup competition by storm, too, and reached Wembley for the very first time in their history. Cruelly, however, both trophies

Left Top: Second Division champions 1964. Left to right (back row)—Willie Bell, Paul Reaney, Fred Goodwin, Gary Sprake, Brian Williamson, Norman Hunter, Ian Lawson. (Front row)—Johnny Giles, Billy Bremner, Jim Storrie, Bobby Collins (captain), Don Weston, Jimmy Greenhoff, Jack Charlton. Inset—Albert Johanneson (left) and Alan Peacock (right). The trophy on the left is the West Riding Senior Cup.

Left Below: First taste of success for Don Revie's Leeds United side. The Second Division Championship trophy is on the left and in the centre is the local West Riding Senior Cup. In the front row are (left to right) Wright, Bell, Hawksby, and Reaney.

It's 1965 and there is plenty for Leeds United's Directors to smile about. Happy in the knowledge that the team are back in the First Division and doing well are, left to right, (standing)—Mr Robert R. Roberts, Mr Sydney Simon, Mr Sam Bolton, Mr Manny Cussins (sitting), Alderman Percy Woodward, Mr Harry Reynolds (chairman) and Mr Albert Morris.

eluded them at the final hurdle.

Progress in the Cup was gained at the expense of Southport, Everton after a fourth round replay, Shrewsbury Town, and Crystal Palace to reach a semi-final clash with Manchester United. A capacity 65,000 crowd at Hillsborough saw the two Uniteds locked in goalless combat for ninety minutes and it was on to Nottingham Forest's City ground for a replay.

Again a closely fought battle ensued but it was the tenacious little Scot Billy Bremner who settled the issue by scoring the only goal two minutes from the end following a tremendous goalmouth scramble. Against all odds Leeds had triumphed. The men who did it were Sprake, Reaney, Bell, Bremner, Charlton, Hunter, Giles, Storrie, Peacock, Collins, and Cooper.

The defeated Manchester United side fielded P. Dunne, Shay Brennan, Tony Dunne, Pat Crerand, Bill Foulkes, Nobby Stiles, Connelly, Bobby Charlton, David Herd, Denis Law, and George Best.

Liverpool were to provide the opposition for Leeds in a disappointing 1965 Final but before that eagerly awaited date at Wembley, United had to get through a hectic fixture list. There could be no letting up in their efforts as they were front runners, along with Manchester United, for the First Division title.

Victories at home against West Ham United and Stoke City and a 2–0 success at West Bromwich kept United well in the running but then came two set-backs—a 1–0 defeat at home to Manchester United and 3–0 away defeat to Sheffield Wednesday.

Hopes picked up with a home victory over Wednesday and success against Sheffield United at Bramall Lane, but a 3–3 draw at Birmingham meant they finished level on points with Manchester United—and the title went to Old Trafford because Matt Busby's side had a fractionally better goal average.

Revie took his disappointed men to London for the Cup Final five days later and though they succeeded in forcing Liverpool into extra time they went down 2–1 to miss out on their second major trophy.

Roger Hunt got the first goal for Liverpool and when Bremner equalized it seemed as though United might live to fight another day. Ian St John dashed that hope by scoring the winner three minutes from the end of extra time.

Disappointment was immense for United

Far Left: Defeat in the 1965 F.A. Cup Final at Wembley brings dejection for tireless Leeds United midfield man Billy Bremner.

Top: A high spot for Leeds United and Billy Bremner in the 1965 F.A. Cup Final. Bremner hammers in a shot to equalise Roger Hunt's opening goal for Liverpool. But Ian St John got the winner for the Reds.

Below: There's no cup to show off but Leeds United were given a tremendous reception on their return from the 1965 F.A. Cup Final at Wembley.

who had done so much in their first season in the top flight and come so close to achieving the minor miracle of the League Championship and F.A. Cup double. But to have confounded their critics to the extent they did could be considered something of an achievement.

They could feel additional satisfaction in that just before the end of the season the Football Writers' Association had named Collins as Footballer of the Year. The tiny Scot was such a convincing winner that he polled 50 per cent of the votes cast and his margin over runner-up, Jack Charlton, who had 16 per cent, was one of the widest since the award was inaugurated in the 1947-48 season.

As a matter of interest Jimmy Dickinson of Portsmouth was third while Manchester United's Bobby Charlton came fourth and Liverpool's Peter Thomson fifth.

The award crowned a wonderful season for Collins who, at the age of thirty-four, had played brilliantly to lead Leeds so near to that major double and who had regained his place in the Scotland side after having been discarded six years previously.

When Collins received his award he became the third individual at Elland Road to win it. Don Revie was given the honour in 1955 when a player with Manchester City and Syd Owen, United's Chief Coach, received the award when he captained Luton Town at Wembley in 1959.

Taking everything into account Revie's United could feel well satisfied with their first efforts in the top flight which had qualified them for something entirely new to Elland Road—European competition.

Glory, glory Leeds United

Teamwork was the basis of Don Revie's management during the successful days of the late 1960s and early 1970s. He is pictured here (middle) with his famous backroom staff (left to right)—Cyril Partridge (second team trainer), Bob English (physiotherapist), Syd Owen (chief coach), Les Cocker (first team trainer-coach).

Leeds United came to possess one of the finest English club sides of all time during the glory years of the late 1960s and early 1970s during which Don Revie ran the Club on family lines.

Nothing was too much trouble for Revie, regarded as 'father' of the United 'family', as he succeeded in making everyone at Elland Road, from the laundry ladies and newest groundstaff boy right through to the Board, feel they had a vital part to play in the continued success of the Club.

One particular section, however, was constantly singled out for praise by Revie—his 'back-room team' who had the responsibility not only of finding players for the Club but developing them into top-class players.

Les Cocker, a qualified F.A. coach who had for twenty years played with Stockport County and Accrington, joined United after a spell as coach at Luton and formed a partnership with Revie that grew and grew as the years went by and continued later when Revie left to become England Manager and then moved on as soccer supremo with the United Arab Emirates.

Full of confidence and ideas, and not afraid to put them forward, Cocker coached and trained United's first team throughout Revie's successful years at Elland Road.

Another valuable member of the back-up team was Syd Owen, Chief Coach at Elland Road and a man highly respected in football for his extensive knowledge and dedication to the game.

One of the most feared scouts in the business was how Revie once described Maurice Lindley, who was promoted from Chief Scout in 1965 to the post of Assistant Manager and whose loyalty to the Club over the years has been admirable and never more so than when he several times stood in as caretaker manager to help the Club through difficult times.

Bob English, a former Army physical trainer instructor, held the important post of physiotherapist and the 'back-room team' was completed by Cyril Partridge who had charge of the second team.

Everyone played his part to the full and just how successful United were under Revie can perhaps be judged from the fact that in the ten years they were in the First Division under his management United never finished outside the top four.

Having narrowly failed to pull off the F.A. Cup and League Championship double in their first season back in the First Division in 1964-65, United had to be content again the following season to finish in second place, this time behind Bill Shankly's Liverpool, though Revie had succeeded in leading his men to the semi-final of the European Fairs Cup where they lost out to Real Zaragoza.

Peter Lorimer had made his mark in this season finishing as leading scorer with eighteen League and Cup goals to his name and he was again to lead United's score-chart in the 1966-67 season which saw Revie's men again going well in the League Championship race but which was more notable for the Club's Cup exploits.

United reached the Final of the Fairs Cup where they eventually lost to Dinamo Zagreb and made another sterling showing in the F.A. Cup—the trophy their Chairman, Harry Reynolds, wanted as much as any other.

After disposing quite comfortably of League Cup opponents Newcastle United and Preston North End, United went to Upton Park for a fourth round confrontation and were promptly clobbered 7–0. It was their biggest ever Cup roasting and one particularly memorable for winger John Sissons, who scored a hat-trick. Geoff Hurst chipped in with two more goals, Martin Peters got one, and Paul Reaney completed the scoring with an own goal.

Undaunted by their massive defeat United turned in some splendid displays in the F.A. Cup. Goals from Mike O'Grady, Willie Bell, and Albert Johanneson gave them a 3–0 third round success against Crystal Palace and there were more goals for United followers to savour in the fourth round 5–0 hammering of West Bromwich Albion. Lorimer scored twice, so did Rod Belfitt, and Paul Madeley was credited with the other.

The fifth round saw United locked in a titanic struggle with Sunderland, arch rivals since they both returned to the First Division together after United had pipped the Roker Park men for the Championship.

The first clash was at Roker Park and Martin gave Sunderland the upper hand when he scored after twenty-two minutes but eight minutes later Charlton had levelled the scores and that's how it stayed until the end. The replay at Elland Road attracted a record crowd of 57,892, thousands of whom were in their places two hours before the kick off.

Soon after the start, however, crash-barriers broke on the Lowfields Road terrace side and the game had to be halted for a quarter of an hour while the crowd were reseated. There followed a memorable and keenly fought Cup tie. O'Hare gave Sunderland a thirty-fifth minute lead but Johnny Giles put United level again two minutes later. Extra time could not find a winner so it was off to Hull City's Boothferry Park five days later for a third attempt.

United were in front for the first time in the tie after eight minutes when Belfitt scored but the Roker men fought tigerishly and got their reward after seventy-nine minutes when Gauden equalized. The game seemed destined to reach full time with the scores level when United were awarded a penalty a minute from the end.

It was a decision that Sunderland did not take kindly to but the referee, Stokes of Newark, had decided Irwin had fouled Greenhoff in the area. Herd and Mulhall were ordered off after the penalty award and Giles, displaying great calm amid the upheaval, slotted the ball home to send United into a home quarter-final clash with Manchester City.

Charlton's fiftieth-minute goal saw off the men from Maine Road but United were to be frustrated—and beaten in the semi-final at Villa Park. Chelsea provided the opposition and though Hateley put the Pensioners ahead after forty-four minutes United firmly believed they should have had at least a draw out of the game.

Terry Cooper had a 'goal' disallowed for offside but the most frustrating aspect of their defeat was another disallowed 'goal'. United were awarded a free kick and though Lorimer rocketed the ball past Bonetti and into the goal a minute from the end, the referee, Ken Burns, ordered the kick to be retaken because Chelsea defenders had not moved ten yards back. United argued that they had been penalized for an infringement committed by their opponents

but the referee was adamant that the kick should be taken again. It was, Chelsea cleared the danger and United were out of the Cup in a disappointing fashion.

Consistency had been the keynote of United's first three seasons in the First Division but it was the fourth term that really proved to be the big breakthrough for them. It was a notable season in many ways and it began with a big disappointment when Harry Reynolds, the man whose vision had put Revie in the driving-seat, was forced to resign as Chairman of the Club and also from the Board of the Club.

His six-year period as Chairman had seen the Club rise from the relative obscurity of Second Division football to a place of prominence among Europe's top clubs. Average gates had risen to over 30,000, debts of near £150,000 had been cleared, and profits in his last two years in office had reached £138,000.

United rewarded his services to the Club by making him a Life Vice-President of the Club and Albert Morris, a Leeds businessman took over as Chairman. Ironically the major honour Harry Reynolds longed to see his side win came in the season of his resignation.

Though they had undoubtedly been one of the best teams in the country United had nothing to show for their efforts in the way of silverware since their promotion. United again had to be satisfied with fourth place in the League Championship race but there was triumph awaiting them at long last in the League Cup.

Luton Town, Bury, Sunderland, Stoke City, and Derby County had been disposed of on the route to Wembley and when United stepped out in front of 100,000 fans on 2 March 1968 it was Arsenal who provided the final obstacle.

The Final had little to commend it as an outstanding spectacle but Revie was not unduly concerned at that. To him, and his side, the important thing on this occasion was to win the trophy and crack the hoodoo that had wrecked previous efforts to win Cup competitions.

In a generally dull and defensive game Arsenal spoilt their chance by poor finishing and the game was settled by full-back Terry Cooper who blasted home a twenty-yard effort after eighteen minutes. It was indeed a dream come true for the likeable Yorkshireman. In conversation before the game Cooper had revealed that had had dreamed for three successive nights up to the Final of scoring the winning goal.

Revie was delighted and so, too, was one man

Left Top: Billy Bremner holds the League Cup aloft after the 1968 Final at Wembley.

Left Below: Leeds United full-back Terry Cooper, holding the League Cup aloft, dreamed for three successive nights before his side played Arsenal in the 1968 League Cup Final at Wembley that he would score the winning goal—and his dream came true.

Above: Don Revie and Bertie Mee (right) lead out Leeds United and Arsenal at Wembley for the League Cup Final in 1968.

Below: The scene outside Leeds Town Hall as Skipper Billy Bremner shows the League Championship trophy to the fans.

Above: This was the feverish scene in February 1969 when Leeds United fought and won a battle against the weather before their First Division game against Chelsea.

Right Top Left: A boyish looking Allan Clarke is greeted at Elland Road by skipper Billy Bremner after he had signed for Leeds United from Leicester City for £160,000 in July 1969.

Right, Top Right: Gary Sprake (left) and Paul Madeley show off the Football League championship trophy after their triumph in the 1968/69 season.

Right Below: Another page in Soccer's history book was written when Johnny Giles scored this goal in the 1-0 victory over Nottingham Forest in 1969. The win gave Leeds United a record breaking 67 points in the First Division

who had had to sit and watch United's progress from the sidelines. He was Mick Jones, the tireless front man who had joined the Elland Road Club earlier in the season when Revie paid out a Club record fee of £100,000 to Sheffield United to secure his transfer.

Jones, who went on to become one of the best-known and most successful of First Division forwards with United, scored a couple of vital goals to aid United's F.A. Cup bid that season but for the second season in succession United's hopes were to end in semi-final defeat.

An error of judgement by Gary Sprake put United in trouble. The Welsh International goalkeeper miskicked straight to Husband whose lobbed shot was bound for goal until Charlton handled the ball to stop it. Morrissey made no mistake with the resultant penalty kick in the forty-fourth minute and that proved sufficient to put Everton into the Final.

Success in the League Cup was the springboard United were looking for, however. They followed up by winning the delayed 1967-68 Fairs Cup by beating Hungarian side Ferencvaros and by the end of the 1968-69 season they had succeeded in winning the First Division Championship—the achievement the players cherished more than any other.

United had the satisfaction of clinching the title by earning a goalless draw at the home of their only real Championship rivals, Liverpool, after which the Anfield Kop gave Revie's men a tremendous salute in admiration of their success. Such a fine sporting gesture was very much appreciated by United and the players and Revie never forgot it.

With one game left—at home to Nottingham Forest—United, who had lost only two League games all season, both of them away, needed victory to set up a new record for the First Division of sixty-seven points. Forest were struggling in the lower reaches of the Division at that stage but they provided stern opposition and it was not until five minutes from the end that Giles got the goal that gave them the record.

United's commitments in the 1969-70 campaign provided the most hectic season the Club have ever had. In addition to battling to the semi-finals of the European Cup, where they lost to Celtic, they finished runners-up to Everton in the League, and reached the F.A. Cup Final.

Some said at the time United had too much on their plate and that may well have been true but it was nevertheless a season to be remembered with pride even though United missed

GS
PM

out on silverware.

Three titanic semi-final clashes with Manchester United must have sapped a lot of energy from United players, who had got that far by knocking out Swansea Town 2–1, the Isthmian League side Sutton United 6–0, Mansfield Town 2–0, and Swindon Town 2–0.

A goalless draw in the first clash with the Old Trafford Reds at Hillsborough was followed by another scoreless game at Villa Park before a solitary goal from Bremner settled the issue in the second replay at Burnden Park, Bolton.

Having failed twice to 'turn on the style' in their previous appearances at Wembley, United were keen to impress when they took on Chelsea in the Final on a pitch that had had 100 tons of sand spread on it.

Surprisingly, perhaps, in such circumstances, United played magnificently. Eddie Gray was in superb form and gave Chelsea defender David Webb a very trying afternoon. Yet the game ended all square at 2–2, Charlton's opening twenty-second-minute goal having been equalized by Houseman in the forty-third minute and Hutchinson giving Chelsea a replay chance when he scored three minutes from time to

Left Top: Celebration time at Elland Road. Terry Cooper (left) and Johnny Giles show off the Charity Shield after they had beaten Manchester City 2-1 in August 1969.

Left Below: Eddie Gray turned in a superb display of controlled football to give Chelsea defender David Webb one of the most trying afternoons of his career in the 1970 F.A. Cup Final which was drawn at Wembley 2-2, Chelsea won the replay at Old Trafford 2-1.

Top: Wembley goal for Jack Charlton. Jubilant United players, Charlton (extreme left) Mick Jones, Paul Madeley and Allan Clarke salute the goal in the 1970 F.A. Cup Final against Chelsea.

equal an eighty-fifth-minute goal from Jones.

A hard-fought replay at Old Trafford saw United awarded twenty-four fouls and Chelsea eleven, but it was not to be United's night. Jones's thirty-sixth-minute goal was equalized by Osgood in the seventy-ninth and when the replay went into extra time Webb knocked in the winner.

United had missed out again but there was plenty to encourage their followers. Billy Bremner and Johnny Giles had become one of the most respected midfield duos in the business and another swoop into the transfer market by Revie before the start of the campaign had paved the way for the development of one of English football's most feared attacking spearheads.

Having brought Jones from Bramall Lane for £100,000 the previous season, Revie went to Leicester City and paid £162,000 for Allan Clarke, a lean boyish-looking attacker who had skills and knowledge that belied his appearance. They were to become one of the most productive of First Division partnerships. In the first season they were together Clarke notched twenty-six League and Cup goals while Jones

Below: Leeds United's F.A. Cup Final clash with Chelsea in April 1970. Peter Bonetti foils striker Allan Clarke.

WAY OUT
WAY OUT

had twenty-five. In a season which saw United play sixty-three competitive matches Lorimer had twenty and Giles ten.

Finishing runners-up in the First Division suggests a fair measure of achievement in what is regarded as the toughest league of its kind in soccer and though United occupied this position in the 1970-71 campaign it was a season that had a particularly sad finale.

United ended up winning the European Fairs Cup at the expense of Juventus, but there were huge disappointments for Revie's men in the F.A. Cup and towards the close of the League Championship battle.

United's F.A. Cup efforts were going well, victories over Rotherham United, after a replay, and at home to Swindon Town sent them to Fourth Division Colchester for a fifth round tie —and disaster.

Revie had confessed to being a little concerned about this particular pairing ever since the draw was made and his worst fears were

Left: Another Wembley goal for Leeds. This time Mick Jones (socks rolled down) puts United ahead for the second time in the 1970 F.A. Cup Final. Giles, Lorimer and Clarke are the other Leeds players in the picture.

Above: A familiar sight for Leeds United fans during the successful days of Don Revie's reign. This triumphant salute from Allan Clarke heralds another goal for the tall lean striker and United.

Above: Hot-shot Scot Peter Lorimer failed by only two goals to equal the aggregate goal scoring record for Leeds United
Right: Eddie Gray, whose dedication as a youngster with Leeds United was an object lesson to any junior wishing and hoping to make the grade.

realized when little Colchester went three up before United could pull themselves together. Crawford, with two goals, and Simmons with one, had put United into an acute state of embarrassment and though Norman Hunter and Johnny Giles scored goals later, Colchester held out for the shock result of the competition.

United sought consolation in their battle for the League title but a disastrous mid-April Saturday afternoon put paid to their aspirations when West Bromwich Albion visited Elland Road. Lincolnshire referee Ray Tinkler made himself very unpopular by allowing a goal from Jeff Astle to stand when another Albion player Colin Suggett was several yards offside.

An invasion of the pitch by some United followers incensed at the decision made it necessary for the match officials to seek police protection after the game and Revie voiced the feelings of many supporters when he described the decision as being the worst he had ever seen and one that had undone almost ten months of hard work.

United made strenuous efforts to recover the ground lost by that defeat. Two goals from Jones and an own goal from Hollywood gave them a 3–0 win at Southampton in their next match, an eighty-ninth-minute goal from Charlton earned them a 1–0 success over Arsenal, and they went on to beat Nottingham Forest 2–0 in their last League game of the season.

Their title rivals, Arsenal, who had games in hand, went from strength to strength and clinched the title from United by one point.

But the aftermath of those sensational scenes when spectators invaded the pitch at the West Bromwich match was to have serious repercussions for United. The F.A. Disciplinary Commission held an inquiry into the stormy scenes and considered remarks made after the game by Revie and by Alderman Percy Woodward, who had succeeded as Chairman of the Club on the death of Mr Morris in 1968—and meted out unprecedented punishment.

The Elland Road ground was ordered to be closed for three weeks from the beginning of the 1971-72 season and the Commission went on to fine the Club £500, and ordered them to compensate visiting clubs for the loss of receipts during the period of the ground closure.

Revie was severely censured and warned as to his future conduct for remarks made on television and Alderman Woodward was also severely censured, though apologies from both men were accepted by the Commission.

United were due to undertake four home League games during the period of the closure of their ground and they switched games against Wolverhampton Wanderers and Crystal Palace to neighbouring Leeds Road, the ground of Huddersfield Town, took on Tottenham Hotspur at Hull City's Boothferry Park, and Newcastle United at Sheffield Wednesday's Hillsborough stadium. In terms of results

CA

Above: Allan Clarke (left) and Mick Jones, one of the most feared of First Division attacking partnerships during the successful years of Leeds United, get together for a round of golf. **Right:** Mick Jones in action.

Right: Don Revie's efforts at Leeds United were suitably rewarded by the Manager of the Year trophy.

United did well, taking six points from a possible eight, but attendances were well down and the cost to the Club in financial terms was put at many thousands of pounds.

In spite of a punishment which caused United to give up home advantage on four occasions, Revie's indomitable side came within a point of clinching the League and F.A. Cup double that season—a performance that illustrated to the more discerning football follower the strength and talent within the Club.

Jones, Clarke, Lorimer, and Giles—the Club's leading goalscorers over the successful seasons—played major roles in getting United to the F.A. Cup Final, Clarke having one of his most memorable games for United in the fourth round replay against Liverpool when he scored both the goals that gave his side a fully deserved 2–0 win.

It was Centenary Year for the F.A. Cup and, as had been the case in the 1968 League Cup Final, Arsenal were United's opponents. Having lost in their two previous Finals, United at last rewarded their fans with the F.A. Cup.

Not a classic Final by any means but one in which United deserved their victory. Clarke and Jones were the heroes of the afternoon, the former for his superb header which brought the only goal of the game after fifty-three minutes and the latter because of the right-wing centre which made the goal possible, though at the expense of an excruciatingly painful dislocated elbow.

United fans had been treated to some scintillating football in League games during the season as Revie's side approached its peak of effectiveness and two games in particular stood out as arguably the best ever seen on the Elland Road ground.

Manchester United were hammered 5–1 in mid-February with a delightful display of football which saw Jones knock in three goals, Clarke one, and Lorimer the other, and when Southampton followed them to Elland Road for

the next home game there was more ecstasy for home fans.

Southampton were taken apart in breathtaking style as United ran out 7–0 winners, Lorimer getting three, Clarke two, Jones one, and Charlton one. Nottingham Forest were beaten 6–1 in a later game at Elland Road but the hectic season caught up with Revie's revellers, the result being that one outstanding League game had to be rearranged for just two days after the F.A. Cup Final.

United were not happy at having to play the game so shortly after the Wembley date but they could do nothing about it. The fixture had to be fulfilled so Revie cut short the celebrations of his players and took them to Wolverhampton on Sunday in readiness for the game.

It was a crucial one, too, for United needed only a point and the Championship would be theirs to add to the F.A. Cup success. A crowd of 53,379 packed into Molineux and United were beaten 2–1, after having had one seemingly clear-cut claim for a penalty for hand ball denied them. Derby County, who were enjoying an

end-of-season break in Spain, were left as Champions.

Revie guided his men back to Wembley the following season but there was to be no repeat success for his side; only acute embarrassment as they went down to Second Division Sunderland who took the Cup against all the odds with a well-taken goal by Ian Porterfield and some superb saves from goalkeeper Jim Montgomery helping in the unexpected triumph.

Despite the continued lengthy involvement in most of the domestic competitions Revie and his men still longed for another crack at the European Champions' Cup and in the 1973-74 season they set themselves first and foremost to win the League Championship—and they succeeded.

Liverpool were their only rivals as the battle reached its closing stages and when the Anfield Reds were surprisingly beaten at home by Arsenal in the last week of the season, United were Champions before they undertook their final game against Queens Park Rangers, which they duly won with a cracking goal from Clarke.

Left Top: The goal that gave Sunderland the F.A. Cup in 1973. Ian Porterfield (striped shirt on left) knocks the ball past David Harvey, despite the close attention of Norman Hunter (No. 6).

Left Below: It's only half time during the 1973 F.A. Cup Final at Wembley but it's obvious from the look of dejection on the faces of Leeds United players. They were trailing to a 31st minute goal from Ian Porterfield and that's how the scoreline stayed.

Right Top: Trevor Cherry hammers the ball into Sunderland's net as Leeds United fight for an equaliser but the effort was disallowed for a foul on goalkeeper Jim Montgomery by Allan Clarke (No. 8).

Right Below: Wembley is a lonely place when you end up on the losing side, especially to a Second Division side. Billy Bremner and Don Revie reflect the gloom felt in Leeds United's camp after they had been beaten

The Battlefields of Europe

European football was to become an accepted part of life for Leeds United over the next ten years but in the season of 1965-66 it was very much a new and intriguing venture for the Elland Road Club.

No one knew just what to expect for sure when they began their quest for the European Fairs Cup—forerunner of the present day U.E.F.A. Cup—with a two-leg tie against the Italian side Torino.

United had proved in their first season back in the First Division that they could be counted on to give nothing less than 100 per cent effort all down the line and they succeeded in tipping the Italians out of the competition. But their success was to be tinged with tragedy.

The rain was pouring down as a crowd of 33,852 welcomed competitive European soccer to Elland Road for the first time on the night of 29 September 1965, and it was the little man with the big heart, Billy Bremner, who brought the crowd to their feet by scoring the first goal after twenty-five minutes.

Bremner, whose tireless efforts in United's cause the previous season had earned him International recognition with Scotland, scored with a touchline shot which saw the wet ball fly into the net off the shoulder of the Torino goalkeeper and when Peacock put Revie's side 2–0 up in the forty-eighth minute United had every cause to be well satisfied with their European baptism.

Orlando's seventy-seventh minute goal for the Italians did not dampen Revie's admiration for the way his side had fought. 'The team have never played better since I became manager. They were splendid in their skill and determination. I am the proudest manager in Britain,' Revie remarked.

United took their 2–1 advantage to Italy for the second leg, adopted a defensive policy, and reached half time with a goalless scoresheet, which was all in their favour.

A few minutes into the second half, however, and Collins, their dynamic little midfield 'general' fell victim to a desperate scything tackle from a Torino defender and was carried from the field with a broken left thighbone. With no substitutes allowed, United were faced with holding Torino for nearly forty minutes with only ten men. They stuck manfully to their task, the scoreline stayed goalless, and they went through to a second round game against F.C. Leipzig.

Mid-winter had descended with a vengeance when United flew to East Germany for a 24 November clash with Leipzig. The new £5,000,000 stadium where the game was being staged had a six-inch covering of dry snow but the game went on after the snow had been rolled flat.

Bremner again led the way for United with a sterling performance matched in the defence by Jack Charlton and Paul Reaney. Three goals came in the last few minutes with Peter Lorimer scoring in the eightieth minute, Bremner two minutes later, and Frenzel getting one for Leipzig in the eighty-third.

Snow lay thick on the Elland Road pitch for the return leg and the game went on only after a massive snow-clearing operation. A goalless draw was sufficient to see United reach a third round game, the home leg of which erupted into a brawl the like of which Elland Road had never seen before.

Valencia were the opponents and when the brawl broke out a dozen policemen dashed on to the field to help Dutch referee, Leo Horn, restore peace. He took both teams off the field for ten minutes to allow tempers to simmer down during which time he visited both dressing-rooms.

Three players were sent off in the game, Jack Charlton and Valencia full-back Videgany for fighting, and then Lage was given his marching orders after fouling Storrie.

In between the skirmishes both sides had shown they could play good football. Munoz had given Valencia the lead after sixteen minutes but Lorimer, who made his mark as a goalscorer by topping United's score chart with nineteen in all games during the season, replied in the sixty-sixth minute with a thunderous shot that was to become his trademark in the fruitful days ahead.

United had not been too active in the transfer market since their return to the First Division, Revie believing he had a number of very talented youngsters waiting in the wings but he did make one sortie to sign Leeds-born Mike O'Grady, who had risen to prominence as a winger with neighbouring Huddersfield Town

European football was an accepted part of Leeds United's fixture list under Don Revie's astute management. The men from Elland Road had competed for ten successive seasons when this picture of Norman Hunter was taken. Big Norm cannot conceal his delight after United had beaten Barcelona in a two-leg tie to reach the 1976 European Champions' Cup Final.

Leeds born Mike O'Grady (right) moves in to score a goal against Coventry in a League game in 1969.

and been rewarded for his efforts with recognition by England.

He cost £30,000 when signed in October 1965 and he helped to pay back a large slice of that fee when he shrugged off a double tackle to unleash an angled shot after seventy-five minutes to give his new club a 1–0 second leg victory in Valencia which was enough to see them into the quarter-finals. Happily there had been no repetition of the unsavoury incidents witnessed in the first game.

United waltzed through the quarter-final tie against the Hungarian side Ujpest Dozsa, with Terry Cooper, Jim Storrie, Bremner, and Willie Bell helping to give their side a 4–1 first leg scoreline and when Lorimer scored in the second leg in Hungary, United went through on a 5–2 aggregate.

One of the most skilful youngsters ever to come out of Scotland, Eddie Gray made his first European appearance, along with Barnsley-born Jimmy Greenhoff and Johanneson, in the first leg of the semi-final against Real Zaragoza in Spain on 20 April.

Unfortunately for United, defeat was tasted for the first time in Europe, Lapetra scoring from the penalty spot. But United were often at their most dangerous when pinned with their backs to the wall and against a very talented and direct side fought back to win the second leg 2–1, Johanneson and Charlton scoring to take the tie to a play-off.

Charlton delighted Revie and his team-mates by winning the toss for a home play-off but it was a disastrous game for Europe's newcomers. The brilliant Spaniards rammed in three goals in a blistering fourteen-minute opening and United were doomed. Charlton scored after eighty minutes but it was no more than a consolation goal and Revie was big enough to admit his side had been beaten by a superior team.

'We gave all we had but it was nowhere good enough,' said Revie, who dubbed Zaragoza's front line—Canario, Santos, Marcellino, Villa, and Lapetra—'The Magnificent Five'.

United's first season of European football had proved a tremendous experience for Revie's emerging side and no one could say that they had been disgraced. The foundations had been well and truly laid for further adventures on the football battlefields of Europe.

Largely through their superbly consistent efforts in the ensuing League campaigns, United remained very much involved in one or other of the major European competitions for a further nine years during which they became one of the most feared of all British sides.

After their semi-final failure in the 1965-66 Fairs Cup United went a step further the following season, reaching the Final in another eventful European escapade.

D.W.S. Amsterdam was United's first port of call this time and there was a worry for Revie when Bremner had to link up with the party late. The Scot had lost his passport and was forced to make the extra journey to Liverpool to get another one before catching a later plane for Holland.

The upheaval made little difference to the tenacious Scot's play. His name was on the scoresheet after only twelve minutes. Johanneson added another after twenty-seven minutes and Greenhoff a third in the forty-seventh before Boogaard pulled one back in the last minute. The return game at Elland Road was even more decisive for United, Johanneson scoring three times, Giles once from the penalty spot, and Paul Madeley chipping in with his first goal in Europe for the Club in a 5–1 romp.

United accounted for Valencia in the next round with a memorable away display after being held to a 1–1 draw at Elland Road. The odds were stacked high against them as Reaney, Cooper, Greenhoff, Johanneson, and O'Grady were all absent through injury.

Nineteen-year-old Bradford-born Terry Hibbitt, a promising outside-left in those days, whose only taste of first team football had been as second half substitute at Nottingham Forest the previous season, was flung in at the deep end.

He took his place in a forward line—made up of Lorimer, Rod Belfitt, Giles, Lorimer, and Gray—with an average age of scarcely twenty. But United triumphed by winning 2–0—Giles and Lorimer scoring—and went through to the quarter-final where another nail-biting climax was in store for them.

A three-match fifth round F.A. Cup-tie with Sunderland was settled in United's favour 2–1, in a second replay at Hull City's Boothferry Park ground, only hours before they flew to Bologna.

They stayed in Hull overnight but began the journey to Italy at 5.30 a.m. Bologna beat them 1–0 but when the return leg had been in progress only eight minutes United were level.

Janich fouled Greenhoff and with a lot resting on the penalty Giles, as cool a customer as could be found on a football field, slotted the ball

home. That was how it remained and when extra time failed to produce a winner it was left to the toss of a disc to decide who went through.

Bologna's Captain, Bulgarelli, called red and when the disc landed, white was showing, much to United's delight. Only Kilmarnock now stood between United and their first appearance in a European Final. The first leg clash was memorable for a hat-trick inside the first thirty minutes of the game by Belfitt, who beat Scottish International goalkeeper Bobby Ferguson, who was due to join West Ham United, in a £60,000 transfer after the competition, with two superb headers and a telling shot.

McIlroy scored twice for the 'Killies' and Giles got his name on the scoresheet to give his side a 4–2 advantage which proved good enough to get United through, the second leg ending in a goalless draw.

United's big breakthrough to a European trophy had not yet arrived, however, for when the Final was played—at the start of the following season—they were beaten on a 2–0 aggregate by Dinamo Zagreb.

The 1967-68 Fairs Cup competition changed all that as United at last got their name inscribed on the handsome-looking trophy.

United, in the main, 'took the high road' to European success for they disposed of three Scottish clubs—Hibernian, Glasgow Rangers, and Dundee—to reach the Final after trouncing the part-timers Spora of Luxembourg 16–0 and Partizan Belgrade on a 3–2 aggregate.

Of these victories United's 2–0 success over Rangers was probably the most memorable

Top Right: The year is 1968 and Billy Bremner shows off the European Fairs Cup after his side's first triumph in the competition.

Top Left: Thirst-quenching . . . Billy Bremner relaxes with a 'Coke' after Leeds United had won the Fairs Cup in Budapest.

United playing some good football in the home leg when a penalty from the ice-cool Giles and a thirtieth minute goal from Lorimer sealed Rangers' fate.

A crowd of 50,498 saw the game, after 80,000 spectators had watched Rangers held to a goalless draw in the first leg by United's resolute defence. Once again United faced a lengthy wait for the Final, the game being held over to the start of next season. This time Revie's men faced Ferencvaros, the crack Hungarian side.

Mick Jones, that fairest and hardest trier of them all, was United's hero scoring the only goal of the first leg at Elland Road after forty-one minutes of dour, hard football.

The Hungarians clearly fancied their chances of pulling the Final round in the second game but they had reckoned without the brilliantly effective skills of Welsh International keeper Gary Sprake who was in superb form.

One of the most exciting matches United have ever figured in came at the start of the 1968-69 Fairs Cup competition. United had held Standard Liège to a goalless draw in the away leg of the tie and were confidently expecting to coast through comfortably in the return clash. But after fifty-one minutes they were trailing 2–0.

It looked all over for them, but a magnificent rally saved the day, Charlton pulling a goal back in the fifty-second minute, Lorimer equalizing in the seventy-second, and Bremner getting the all important goal two minutes from time.

United progressed as far as the fourth round before going out to Ujpest Dozsa of Hungary.

The major European club competition is, of course, the Champions' Cup and United had the honour of playing in this competition during the 1969-70 campaign following their first-ever First Division Championship success.

Right: That great feeling again . . . Mick Jones holds the Fairs Cup high as he and his teammates do a lap of honour following the 1971 success. Paul Reaney is on the right and Billy Bremner on the left.

Above: The European Fairs Cup belongs to Leeds United for the second time. This is the 1971 celebration at Elland Road after they had beaten Juventus on the away goals rule. Left to right: Billy Bremner, Allan Clarke, Johnny Giles, Terry Cooper, and Mick Bates.

Mick Jones was reaching the peak of his career as one of the best club centre-forwards in the game and though he scored many goals for United he was also highly regarded as a maker of goals for others—in particular, for his attacking partner Allan Clarke. But it was as goalscorer that he took the eye in United's progress to the semi-finals of the Champions' Cup.

Four times he found the net as part-timers Lyn Oslo were slaughtered 16–0, his second round total in the 6–0 rout of Ferencvaros was four. Giles and Lorimer got the goals in the 2–0 aggregate success at the expense of Standard Liège to take United through to an all-British semi-final clash with the pride of Scottish football, Glasgow Celtic.

Jock Stein, a big friend of Revie's, was guiding the Glaswegians to honour after honour and the semi-final clash was eagerly awaited and billed as an unofficial British club championship battle.

Not one solitary goal had been put past United in their six games in the competition up to the semi-final but inside sixty seconds of the first leg at Elland Road Celtic broke the spell and scored.

Celtic winger Connelly unleashed a good shot but the ball took a deflection off Terry Cooper and went past Sprake. It was a set-back from which United never recovered. The goal was all that stood between the two sides when the second leg was played in front of the biggest crowd ever to watch United in action.

A total of 134,000 fans were packed into Hampden Park for the game. The noise was terrific. It was not a night for the faint-hearted. Nerves of steel were needed, if you were an Englishman.

Celtic played some superb football but Bremner, a player who never seemed to know the meaning of the word defeat, hammered in a fine goal after fourteen minutes to put the aggregate scores level and those of us who would not have minded an English victory began to think it a possibility after all, if only a slight one.

But it was not to be. Hughes put Celtic in front after forty-seven minutes, beating Sprake with a well-taken effort and when the Welshman had to go off injured, just after the goal, David Harvey came on only to be beaten almost immediately, Murdoch putting the issue beyond doubt by scoring Celtic's third goal of the tie.

Disappointment was enormous but United had got over it by the next season when they went through to win the Fairs Cup for the second time in three seasons, disposing of Liverpool in the semi-final with the help of a goal from Bremner, scored at Anfield, before beating the skilful and capable Italian side Juventus on the away goals rule after the aggregate scores stood at 3–3.

The Fairs Cup was superseded by the U.E.F.A. Cup in the 1971-72 season when United were surprisingly beaten in the first round by the Belgian side Lierse. United had had little trouble, even without six of their Internationals, in taking a two-goal lead in the first leg game in Belgium with goals from Chris Galvin and Lorimer.

For the return, Revie rested Charlton and Hunter and allowed teenage goalkeeper Peter Shaw to make his début, but it was a move which backfired. Lierse were 3–0 up in thirty-eight minutes with Shaw suffering from first-night nerves. Sprake was sent out for the second half and Hunter was in the defence but the wounds had been too deeply inflicted. Lierse went on to score another goal and United had suffered their biggest defeat in seven years of European commitment.

United hit back strongly the following season

to reach the Final of the Cup-winners' Cup by disposing of the Turkish side Ankaragucu, Carl Zeiss Jena of East Germany, Rapid Bucharest of Romania, and Hajduk Split of Yugoslavia.

Sunny Salonika was the setting for the Final and the Italian club A.C. Milan were United's opponents. Defeat was in store for Revie's men who found themselves victims of some puzzling refereeing decisions, to say the least, by the Greek referee who controlled the match.

United could do little right for the official, were repeatedly penalized, and had what they considered three genuine penalty claims brushed aside.

If you think it sour grapes on United's part to moan about the decisions afterwards they had thousands of allies in the predominantly Greek crowd which stood and applauded Revie's men off the field, obviously feeling the Yorkshire side had been hard done by.

Revie's last season with the Club he had yanked by its bootlaces from the doldrums to a position of dominance at home and abroad, ended after the 1973-74 campaign in which United progressed to the third round of the U.E.F.A. Cup before going down to Vitoria Setubal of Portugal.

Brian Clough was in charge when United took on and beat F.C. Zurich 4–1 in the home leg of the 1974-75 Champions' Cup but he had departed when the team travelled under the leadership of caretaker boss Maurice Lindley for the second leg where a 2–1 reverse was not sufficient to put them out of the competition.

One-time England full-back Jimmy Armfield got his first taste of managing a side in Europe when he took United to Hungary for a second round clash with Ujpest Dozsa in a game that was marred by the sending off of Duncan McKenzie.

The irrepressible McKenzie, who had been bought by Clough for £250,000 from Nottingham Forest during his forty-four day reign at Elland Road, was given his European début by Armfield but inside fifteen minutes he was back in the dressing-room having been ordered off for retaliating after being fouled.

Even down to ten men, however, United proved too good for the Hungarians. Lorimer had lashed in a goal before the dismissal to equalize a second-minute penalty from Fazekas and Gordon McQueen's goal after twenty-two minutes enabled United to start the second game at Elland Road with a clear advantage.

Another goal from McQueen, one from

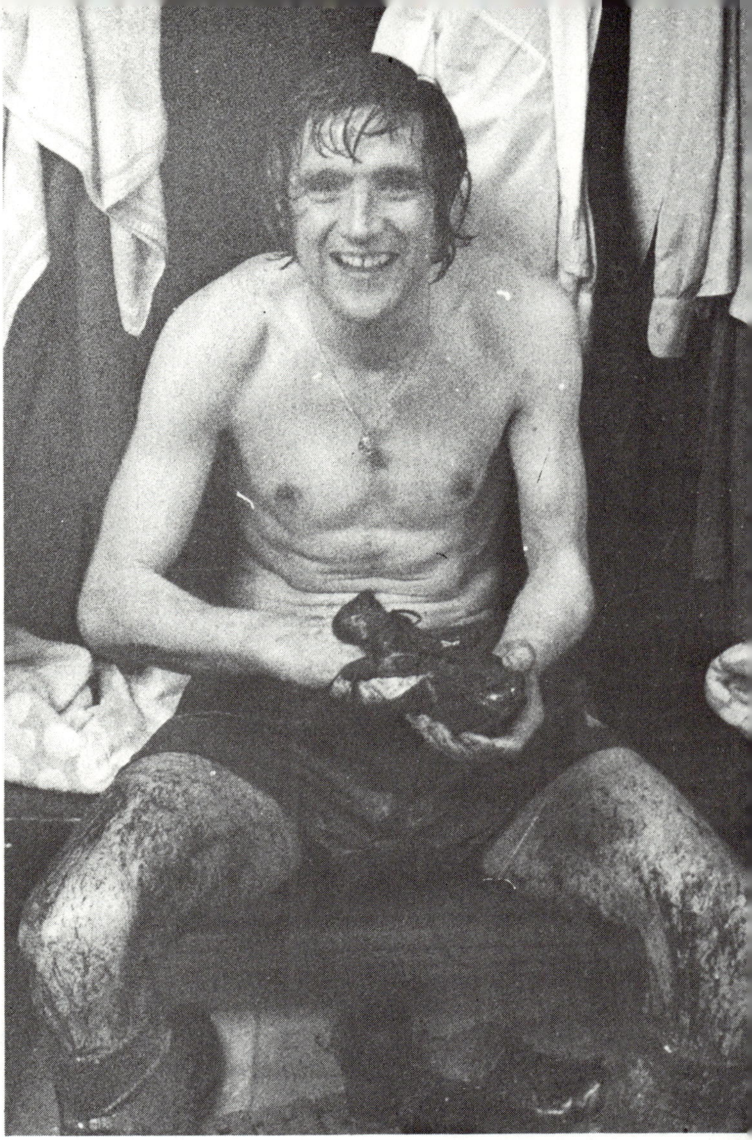

Left: Leeds United's European Cup quarter final tie with Anderlecht went on despite the atrocious conditions of the pitch in Belgium but it turned out to be mud, glorious mud as far as United were concerned.

Above: A job well done. Norman Hunter is all smiles after the successful battle in the mud of Anderlecht's ground.

Below: Mud-spattered Allan Clarke with manager Jimmy Armfield after the success in Anderlecht.

Leeds United have just qualified for the 1975 European Cup Final by beating Barcelona and there can be no mistaking the joy of Paul Madeley, chairman Manny Cussins and Allan Clarke.

Right: Paul Madeley and Billy Bremner (arms raised) and Allan Clarke have that good to be alive feeling after disposing of Barcelona to reach the final of the Champions' Cup in 1975.

Bremner, and a third from Terry Yorath made United emphatic winners. There was another clear-cut victory to enjoy in the quarter-finals when Joe Jordan, McQueen, and Lorimer scored in a 3–0 first leg win over Anderlecht.

This game was notable also for Armfield's decision to substitute skipper Bremner eighteen minutes from the end for the first time in the Scot's long and illustrious career. He was back, however, for the next game—a League clash at Ipswich—and he was in the side that opposed Anderlecht on one of the worst rain-affected pitches United have ever played on.

Massive pools of water were standing on the surface long before the start but United survived wonderfully well and Bremner set the seal on their performance by scoring the only goal of the game.

Winning the Champions' Cup was the honour United yearned for more than any other. Barcelona, Johan Cruyff, and Johann Neeskens included, stood between them and their first-ever appearance in the Final. It was a memorable tie.

Armfield left out Norman Hunter and Lorimer from the first leg game at Elland Road but Bremner, scorer of the first ever goal in Europe for United, put his side ahead after only ten minutes and a crowd of 50,393, the biggest for nearly six years, went wild with excitement.

The Spanish side was a good one, however, and it was no great surprise when Asensi equalized after sixty-six minutes, Allan Clarke revived United with a goal in the seventy-ninth minute and United went off to Spain with the slender lead of one goal.

Would it be sufficient? That was the big question. Cruyff who had not shown too prominently at Elland Road was expected to make a greater contribution in the return match. Few people would have risked much money on the outcome.

A crowd of 110,00 wildly cheering fans, the vast majority of them Spanish, were convinced Barcelona would carry too much power for United on their own ground. But they had not anticipated United's early burst of attacking power.

Only seven minutes had ticked by when Lorimer scored one of the most important goals of his career. Clares equalized in the seventieth minute and then came a huge set-back—McQueen was sent off and United were left to hold out for twenty nerve-jangling minutes with only ten men.

Trevor Cherry, the former Huddersfield Town defender had done a remarkably effective job in keeping Cruyff relatively ineffective and he continued to do so while the rest of the United side pulled together to offset McQueen's absence and prevent Barcelona entering the Final.

McQueen, who had allowed his temper to get the better of him by striking Clares, missed the Final as an automatic punishment and United suffered the greater all-round disappointment of failing, at the final hurdle, to lift the most coveted of all the European club trophies.

Ill-luck dogged United's final effort against Bayern Munich in Paris when having threatened to run the Germans into the ground they fell to goals in the seventy-second and eighty-second minutes from Roth and Muller. United saw a fierce shot from Norman Hunter crash against the bar, a 'goal' from Lorimer disallowed on what must have been the closest of decisions, and a strong claim for a penalty turned down after Beckenbauer had brought Clarke down.

Worse than the defeat for United, however, was the rioting of the hooligan element of their so-called 'fans' which brought shame on the Club and led to U.E.F.A. banning United from European competitions for four seasons, a ban subsequently halved after an appeal launched and conducted by a painstakingly efficient Armfield.

Eyes on the future

Don Revie's one remaining ambition at Elland Road was to lead his men to triumph in the Champions' Cup but when he had the opportunity to take his side into Europe's premier club competition in the 1974-75 season he passed it up. There had to be a good reason for doing so—and there was, the managership of England.

His enviable record of achievement and consistency over a thirteen-year stint as Manager of United had impressed many and, finally, the powers at Lancaster Gate. The F.A. wanted Revie and after much heart-searching he decided to take his managerial know-how and use it to the benefit of England.

He left Elland Road in the summer of 1974 with, of course, many regrets and United were, on their part, extremely sorry to see him depart. But after making their admiration for him known they reluctantly agreed it would have been unfair to stand in the way of such a tremendous honour.

Revie's memorable reign, which had seen United to the Second Division Championship, twice, the F.A. Cup, the League Cup, and the Fairs Cup twice, in addition to three other Cup Finals and numerous semi-finals, and to a top four placing in all ten years of his First Division Managership, was at an end.

United had much to thank him for. His successful efforts in building one of the best club sides in the land had brought sufficient money into Club funds to enable Directors to make colossal improvements to the Elland Road stadium. Indeed United were clearly one of Europe's foremost clubs in every respect.

Revie was also responsible for changing United's colours to all white—a strip associated with Real Madrid, who in the early days of Revie's management were the team every soccer supporter knew and admired. Revie wanted his men to be associated with success, to become as well known and admired as the Spanish side were, and it was one of his biggest disappoint-

Left: A smiling welcome from Leeds United chairman Manny Cussins (right) for Brian Clough and his two sons Simon (left) and Nigel in July 1974 after Clough had been appointed manager in succession to Don Revie. Clough however was on his way 44 days after beginning his duties.

Above: If ever two men had plenty to talk about it's Don Revie, former Leeds United and England manager and Les Cocker, the man who was at his side at all times.

Above: Brian Clough (centre), trainer Jimmy Gordon (left) and John McGovern pictured at Elland Road during their short stay with Leeds United.

Left: Chairman Manny Cussins (left) and assistant manager Maurice Lindley (right) in conversation with Jimmy Armfield after the former Bolton Wanderers' boss had taken on the manager's job with Leeds United.

ments that during their lengthy escapades in Europe, United were never drawn against Real Madrid.

United's switch to all white was the Club's fourth change of strip since its formation back in 1919. Blue and white stripes were the Club's first colours until 1934 when they switched to shirts of blue and gold halves. In October 1948 Major Frank Buckley introduçed a jersey of old gold with blue sleeves and collars and black shorts, but these were changed in Raich Carter's days in 1955 to dark blue jerseys and gold collar with white shorts.

Revie's departure left United in a state of shock. Replacing a man of his calibre was not going to be easy for the United Board, now headed by furnishing millionaire Manny Cussins, who had succeeded Percy Woodward two year's previously. At first it seemed Johnny Giles was to be the man for the job—he was certainly Revie's choice and recommendation to the Directors—but the position was left vacant for a while as the Board gave further thought to the matter.

Maurice Lindley, the ever-faithful Assistant Manager took over as caretaker boss before Brian Clough was appointed Manager in July 1974. Clough breezed in amid suggestions he would make sweeping changes in playing personnel. Clough seemed a strange choice to many. After all he had not been too complimentary about United on a number of previous occasions. But he was, all the same, a manager who had got results at Derby.

John O'Hare and John McGovern, both with Clough in his days at the Baseball Ground, were brought to Elland Road and the decisive Yorkshireman promptly spent £250,000 to bring the lively and extrovert Duncan McKenzie from Nottingham Forest.

A sensation was just round the corner however. Forty-four days after taking up office United parted company with Clough amid reports of player power and, though no contracts had been signed, paid the ex-Derby County boss compensation which was reported to be a tax-free £20,000. It cost United much more than that, though, for with tax the cost to the Club was said to be over £100,000.

After another spell as caretaker manager, Lindley handed over the managerial reins to former Blackpool defender and England captain Jimmy Armfield, regarded then as one of the most promising young managers, having done well in his only previous managerial task with Bolton Wanderers.

Leeds United marked Billy Bremner's 500th League appearance with a gift from the club. Making the presentation is chairman Manny Cussins.

An extremely likeable man and a knowledgeable one, Armfield had taken on one of the most difficult tasks in English football. He faced the prospect of dismantling Revie's ageing side but at the same time he knew he needed experience in his team if they were to stand a chance of becoming the second English club to win the Champions' Cup.

He had no alternative but to wait a season before attempting to replace players of undoubted world-class ability and it so very nearly paid handsome dividends, too, United reaching the Final before losing to Bayern Munich.

Armfield had sold O'Hare and McGovern to Nottingham Forest in February 1975 for a combined fee of £35,000 and Terry Cooper departed a month later to Middlesbrough for £50,000. The summer of 1975 saw the cultured Giles end his Elland Road career when he moved to become player-manager—and successfully as it was to turn out for West Bromwich Albion—in July for £45,000.

The break-up of Revie's wonder team continued the following year with Terry Yorath moving to Coventry City for £140,000, Mick Bates to Walsall for £25,000, Billy Bremner joining Hull City for £30,000, and a cheque for £40,000 taking 'iron man' Norman Hunter to Bristol City.

In addition, Armfield sold McKenzie, who was keen to try his luck on the Continent, to Belgian club Anderlecht for £200,000.

Incoming talent saw that most gifted of midfield players, Tony Currie, leave Sheffield United for Elland Road for a fee of £240,000, burly attacker Ray Hankin make the short ourney from Burnley to Leeds for £172,000, to be followed a year later by Aberdeen's tricky and speedy winger, Arthur Graham, who cost £125,000, and another Burnley player, midfield man Brian Flynn, for £175,000.

While steering United to the Champions' Cup Final in 1975, Armfield saw United's League form suffer and the Club finished in ninth position—the first time they had been out of the top four since winning promotion to the First Division in 1964. The following season, as some of Armfield's signings were beginning to make their mark, United wound up in fifth position but narrowly missed qualifying for Europe.

So far as Cup football was concerned the promise of success had not materialized. They lost in the quarter-final of the F.A. Cup to Ipswich Town in a third replay in 1975 and were beaten in the semi-final in 1977 by Manchester United.

In the League Cup, Armfield took his side to the semi-finals in 1977-78 where they were defeated on a two-leg basis by Nottingham Forest, managed now by Clough, who must have taken a great deal of satisfaction in the result. Yet by most standards, Armfield's record at Elland Road was far from poor. No one could call him a failure yet he was not a roaring success.

Changes had taken place in the make-up of the United Board in the summer of 1976 when younger men were added in the persons of Brian Roberts, Rayner Barker, Jack Marjason, and Brian Woodward, all men of substance and with family ties to present or past members of the Board.

On the playing side, however, Armfield was to face further problems when, in the early months of 1978, he suffered the undoubted blows of losing Scottish Internationals Joe Jordan and Gordon McQueen to Manchester United, the former moving for £350,00 and the latter bringing in a transfer fee of £500,000.

The departures did Armfield's planning no good whatsoever, though the fact that the sale of both men had 'made' the Elland Road Club a handsome profit, Jordan having cost only £15,000 when signed as an eighteen-year-old from Morton and McQueen costing in the region of £30,000 from St Mirren—both incidentally in Revie's days—went some way to softening the blows.

Eventually Armfield replaced the powerful

In the thick of the action. Allan Clarke gets in a shot at goal as anxious West Bromwich Albion defenders look on.

Scots by paying Blackpool £330,000 for defender Paul Hart and bringing John Hawley from Hull City for the relatively small fee of £85,000.

Paul Reaney departed to Bradford City—becoming the first player in the country to transfer himself following the newly agreed freedom of contract policy—and Allan Clarke took on the new challenge of player-manager with Fourth Division Barnsley where he succeeded in taking the Oakwell club to promotion in his first term of office.

In 1976-77 United slumped to tenth position, a new First Division 'low' for them in their present spell of higher grade football and there was only a marginal improvement the following season when they had to be content with ninth placing.

At the conclusion of the 1977-78 season rumour was rife that Armfield's spell at Elland Road was about to be ended by the Board and in July 1978 rumour became fact.

Armfield had had his critics, who labelled him indecisive, and though it was often said, with some degree of accuracy, that he was too nice an individual to be a success at top-level soccer management, he had tackled a job at Elland Road which Don Revie had always maintained he would have found near impossible.

Yet Armfield was not to be allowed the

opportunity to see all his signings blend together and that, not surprisingly, was a major disappointment to him.

Replacing him was a far from easy task for the United Board. Top men such as Lawrie McMenemy, Ron Saunders, and Don Howe who had gone through a spell as Chief Coach to Armfield, could not be tempted to Elland Road and as the search went on United went into the 1978-79 season with the faithful Maurice Lindley in another spell of caretaker managership.

Yet with the season only one match old, United found a successor to Armfield in Jock Stein, the former Glasgow Celtic supremo who had not been too happy at being pushed into a back seat job with Celtic. Stein was a man in many respects similar to Revie. He was big in stature, knew the game inside out, and he had an aura of success about him after his glorious years with Celtic during which the Champions' Cup went to Celtic Park.

Stein impressed greatly and would have done the job of restoring former glories to Elland Road. It was not to be as Scotland made him their target to manage the national team. He found the honour too great to turn down, and a desire on the part of his wife to stay living in Scotland doubtless helping him in his decision,

Top Left: All mine . . but not for long. Former Glasgow Celtic supremo Jock Stein is happy enough on his arrival at Elland Road in August 1978 but he was on his way back North of the Border 44 days later when Scotland succeeded in tempting him to manage the national side.

Below: Ray Hankin (centre) receives the congratulations of Byron Stevenson (left) and Gordon McQueen after the Leeds United striker had scored a goal against Manchester United in September 1977.

Top Right: Ray Hankin (left) and Arthur Graham (right) in action against Liverpool during the 1977/78 season.

and he returned to Scotland after only forty-four days at Elland Road.

Lindley duly entered his fourth spell as caretaker boss and though there were suggestions that he might well make the ideal successor, the Club eventually tempted Jimmy Adamson away from Sunderland to take up the challenge other top men had seen fit to shy away from.

A man steeped in soccer experience, Adamson saw lengthy service as a player with Burnley, then became coach and later manager of the Turf Moor side before moving to Roker Park as manager.

During his days at Burnley, Adamson, highly regarded in the game for his coaching abilities, struck up a partnership with Dave Merrington, another former Burnley defender and the partnership was formed again at Elland Road when Merrington, having demonstrated his admiration for Adamson by turning down the chance to manage Sunderland followed him to Elland Road. Another Roker departure was Chief Scout Dave Blakey who now holds a similar vital post with United.

United ended up having their best season

Left Top: Welcome to Elland Road. Director Bob Roberts and manager Jimmy Adamson

Left Below: Leeds United manager Jimmy Adamson paid Blackburn Rovers £357,000 to bring full-back or midfield Kevin Hird, to Elland Road.

Top: Leeds players (left to right) defending their goal are Frank Gray, Paul Madeley, Eddie Gray and Ray Hankin.

Bottom Left: Determination is the name of the game here as Leeds United striker Ray Hankin darts between two Ipswich defenders.

Bottom Right: Former Hull City player John Hawley (right) was Leeds United's leading scorer with 17 goals during the 1978/79 season.

IM BANANAS
UNITED

since Don Revie's departure, finishing fifth in the League and at last qualifying again for Europe, their high placing putting them among England's contenders for the 1979-80 U.E.F.A. Cup.

Having been forced to play their F.A. Cup-ties away from Elland Road last season, United went out of the competition when they were beaten by West Bromwich Albion, one of the country's best teams in this campaign, in the fourth round. They did much better in the League Cup before losing out again in the semi-finals, this time to Southampton.

The end of the season saw another of Revie's men depart—Scottish hot-shot, Peter Lorimer, who failed only by two goals to equal the aggregate League scoring record of 154 for United by John Charles. He left to play North American League football with Toronto Blizzard.

The future, however, is the important thing for any club and particularly so for Leeds United who, not having won a trophy since the days of Don Revie, are thirsting for success again.

Adamson is determined to give the Club that success. He spent £357,000 on full-back/midfield player Kevin Hird from Blackburn Rovers shortly before the end of his first season and in the summer months he broke United's record pay-out fee when he splashed £400,000 on Swansea's Welsh International striker Alan Curtis.

The Board are sure that in Adamson they have the right man to spearhead the Club's return to its former high standing in the game. All followers of United will wish him well in his task.

Welsh international striker Alan Curtis, signed from Swansea for £400,000 in May 1979 makes no secret of the joy he feels at having joined a First Division club. 'I'm bananas over Leeds United' is the message on his bowler.

Paul Hart (left) and Paul Madeley in action against Aston Villa.

First team squad at Elland Road at the start of the 1978/79 season. Left to right back row—John Hawley, Paul Madeley, Paul Hart, David Stewart, Ray Hankin, David Harvey, Keith Parkinson, Tony Currie, Byron Stevenson. Front row—Frank Gray, Eddie Gray, Peter Lorimer, Brian Flynn, Trevor Cherry, Carl Harris, Arthur Graham, Peter Hampton.

Statistical Appendix

EUROPEAN MATCHES

1965-66 FAIRS CUP

FIRST ROUND

FIRST LEG

Leeds 2 (Bremner, Peacock); Torino (Italy) 1. Att: 33,852
Sprake, Reaney, Madeley, Bremner, Charlton, Hunter, Giles, Lorimer, Peacock, Collins, Cooper.

SECOND LEG

Torino 0, Leeds 0
Sprake, Reaney, Madeley, Bremner, Charlton, Hunter, Giles, Lorimer, Peacock, Collins, Cooper.
Leeds won on aggregate 2-1

SECOND ROUND

FIRST LEG

SC Leipzig (East Germany) 1, Leeds 2 (Lorimer, Bremner)
Sprake, Reaney, Charlton, Madeley, Bremner, Hunter, Storrie, Lorimer, Bell, Giles, O'Grady.

SECOND LEG

Leeds 0, Leipzig 0. Att: 32,111
Sprake, Reaney, Bell, Bremner, Charlton, Hunter, Storrie, Lorimer, Peacock, Giles, O'Grady.
Leeds won on aggregate 2-1

THIRD ROUND

FIRST LEG

Leeds 1 (Lorimer); Valencia 1. Att: 34,414
Sprake, Reaney, Bell, Bremner, Charlton, Hunter, Storrie, Lorimer, Belfitt, Giles, O'Grady.

SECOND LEG

Valencia 0, Leeds 1 (O'Grady)
Sprake, Reaney, Bell, Bremner, Charlton, Hunter, Storrie, Lorimer, Madeley, Giles, O'Grady.
Leeds won on aggregate 2-1

QUARTER FINAL

FIRST LEG

Leeds 4 (Cooper, Bell, Storrie, Bremner); Ujpest Dozsa (Hungary) 1. Att: 40,462
Sprake, Reaney, Bell, Bremner, Charlton, Hunter, O'Grady, Lorimer, Storrie, Giles, Cooper.

SECOND LEG

Ujpest 1, Leeds 1 (Lorimer)
Sprake, Reaney, Bell, Bremner, Charlton, Hunter, O'Grady, Lorimer, Storrie, Giles, Cooper.
Leeds won on aggregate 5-2.

SEMI-FINAL

FIRST LEG

Real Zaragoza (Spain) 1, Leeds 0
Sprake, Reaney, Bell, Bremner, Charlton, Hunter, Greenhoff, E. Gray, Storrie, Giles, Johanneson.

SECOND LEG

Leeds 2 (Johanneson, Charlton); Zaragoza 1. Att: 45,008
Sprake, Reaney, Bell, Bremner, Charlton, Hunter, Greenhoff, E. Gray, Storrie, Giles, Johanneson.
Aggregate scores level.

Play off match at Elland Road

Leeds 1 (Charlton); Zaragoza 3. Att: 43,046
Sprake, Reaney, Bell, Bremner, Charlton, Hunter, Greenhoff, Lorimer, Storrie, Giles, O'Grady.

1966-67

SECOND ROUND

FIRST LEG

DWS Amsterdam 1, Leeds 3 (Bremner, Johanneson, Greenhoff)
Sprake, Reaney, Bell, Bremner, Charlton, Hunter, O'Grady, Greenhoff, Madeley, Giles, Johanneson

SECOND LEG

Leeds 5 (Johanneson 3, Giles, Madeley); DWS Amsterdam 1. Att: 27,096
Sprake, Reaney, Bell, Bremner, Charlton, Hunter, Storrie, Madeley, Greenhoff, Giles, Johanneson.
Leeds won on aggregate 8-2.

THIRD ROUND

FIRST LEG

Leeds 1 (Greenhoff); Valencia 1. (Att: 40,644)
Sprake, Reaney, Madeley, Bremner, Charlton, Hunter, Giles, Gray, Greenhoff, Collins, Cooper.

SECOND LEG

Valencia 0, Leeds 2 (Giles, Lorimer)
Sprake, Madeley, Bell, Bremner, Charlton, Hunter, Giles, Lorimer, Belfitt, Gray, Hibbitt.
Leeds won on aggregate 3-1.

FOURTH ROUND

FIRST LEG

Bologna 1, Leeds 0
Sprake, Reaney, Bell, Bremner, Charlton, Hunter, Lorimer, Belfitt, Madeley, Giles, Cooper.

SECOND LEG

United 1 (Giles); Bologna 0. Att: 42,128
Sprake, Reaney, Madeley, Bremner, Bell, Hunter, Giles, Belfitt, Greenhoff, Gray, Cooper.
Leeds went through on toss of disc.

SEMI-FINAL

FIRST LEG

Leeds 4 (Belfitt 3, Giles); Kilmarnock 2. Att: 43,000
Sprake, Reaney, Bell, Bremner, Madeley, Hunter, O'Grady, Lorimer, Belfitt, Giles, E. Gray.

SECOND LEG

Kilmarnock 0, Leeds 0
Sprake, Reaney, Bell, Bremner, Madeley, Hunter, Lorimer, E. Gray, Belfitt, Giles, Cooper.
United won on aggregate 4-2.

FINAL

FIRST LEG

Dinamo Zagreb 2, Leeds 0
Sprake, Reaney, Cooper, Bremner, Charlton, Hunter, Bates, Lorimer, Belfitt, E. Gray, O'Grady.

SECOND LEG

Leeds 0, Dinamo Zagreb 0. Att: 35,604
Sprake, Bell, Cooper, Bremner, Charlton, Hunter, Reaney, Belfitt, Greenhoff, Giles, O'Grady.
Zagreg won on aggregate 2-0.

1967-68

FIRST ROUND

FIRST LEG

Spora Luxembourg 0, Leeds 9 (Lorimer 4, Bremner, Greenhoff 2, Madeley, Jones). Harvey. Reaney, Madeley, Bremner, Charlton, Hunter, Greenhoff, Lorimer, Jones, E. Gray, Cooper.

SECOND LEG

Leeds 7 (Johanneson 3, Greenhoff 2, Cooper, Lorimer); Spora 0. Att: 15,196
Sprake, Reaney, Cooper, Madeley (Bates), Charlton, Hunter, Greenhoff, Lorimer, Belfitt, Hibbitt, Johanneson.
Leeds won on aggregate 16-0.

SECOND ROUND

FIRST LEG

Partizan Belgrade 1, Leeds 2 (Lorimer, Belfitt)
Harvey, Reaney, Cooper, Bremner, Charlton, Hunter, Greenhoff, Lorimer, Madeley, Belfitt, Gray (Bates).

SECOND LEG

Leeds 1 (Lorimer); Partizan Belgrade 1. Att: 34,258
Sprake, Reaney, Cooper, Bremner, Charlton, Hunter, Greenhoff, Lorimer, Madeley, E. Gray, Hibbitt (Johanneson).
Leeds won on aggregate 3-2.

THIRD ROUND

FIRST LEG

Leeds 1 (E. Gray); Hibernian 0. Att: 31,522
Sprake, Reaney (Madeley), Cooper, Bremner, Charlton, Hunter, Greenhoff, Lorimer, Jones, E. Gray, Giles.

SECOND LEG

Hibernian 1, Leeds 1 (Charlton)
Sprake, Reaney, Cooper, Bremner, Charlton, Hunter, Greenhoff, Lorimer, Jones, Giles, E. Gray.
Leeds won on aggregate 2-1.

FOURTH ROUND

FIRST LEG

Rangers 0, Leeds 0
Sprake, Reaney, Cooper, Bremner, Charlton, Hunter, Greenhoff (Belfitt), Lorimer, Jones, Giles, Madeley.

SECOND LEG

Leeds 2 (Giles, Lorimer); Rangers 0. Att: 50,498
Harvey, Reaney, Cooper, Bremner, Charlton, Hunter, Greenhoff, Madeley, Jones, Giles, Lorimer.
Leeds won on aggregate 2-0.

SEMI-FINAL

FIRST LEG

Dundee 1, Leeds 1 Madeley)
Harvey, Reaney, Cooper, Bremner, Charlton, Hunter, Greenhoff, Lorimer, Madeley, Giles, E. Gray.

SECOND LEG

Leeds 1 (GRAY); Dundee 0. Att: 23,830
Sprake, Reaney, Cooper, Bremner, Madeley, Hunter, Greenhoff, Lorimer, Jones, Giles, E. Gray.
United won on aggregate 2-1.

FINAL

FIRST LEG

Leeds 1 (Jones); Ferencvaros 0. Att: 25,268
Sprake, Reaney, Cooper, Bremner, Charlton, Hunter, Lorimer, Madeley, Jones (Belfitt), Giles (Greenhoff), E. Gray.

SECOND LEG

Ferencvaros 0, Leeds 0
Sprake, Reaney, Cooper, Bremner, Charlton, Hunter, O'Grady, Lorimer, Jones, Madeley, Hibbitt, Bates.
Leeds won on aggregate 1-0.

1968-69

FIRST ROUND

FIRST LEG

Standard Liege 0, Leeds 0
Sprake, Reaney, Cooper, Bremner, Charlton, Hunter, O'Grady, Lorimer, Jones, Madeley, Hibbitt.

SECOND LEG

Leeds 3 (Charlton, Lorimer, Bremner); Standard Liege 2. Att: 24,178
Sprake, Reaney, Cooper (Bates), Bremner, Charlton, Hunter, O'Grady, Lorimer, Jones, Madeley, Hibbitt (E. Gray).
Leeds won on aggregate 3-2.

SECOND ROUND

FIRST LEG

Leeds 2 (Charlton); Naples 0. Att: 26,967
Sprake, Reaney, Madeley, Bremner, Charlton, Hunter, O'Grady, Jones, Belfitt, Giles, Lorimer.

SECOND LEG

Naples 2, Leeds 0
Sprake, Reaney, Cooper, Bremner, Charlton, Hunter, O'Grady, Madeley, Jones, Giles, E. Gray.
Leeds wnt through after toss of disc.

THIRD ROUND

FIRST LEG

Leeds 5 (O'Grady, Hunter, Lorimer 2, Charlton); Hanover 1. Att: 25,162
Sprake, Reaney, Madeley, Bremner, Charlton, Hunter, O'Grady (Hibbitt), Lorimer, Jones, Giles, E. Gray.

SECOND LEG

Hanover 1, Leeds 2 (Belfitt, Jones)
Sprake, Reaney, Bremner, Charlton, Hunter, O'Grady, Lorimer, Jones, Belfitt, E. Gray.
Leeds won on aggregate 7-2.

FOURTH ROUND

FIRST LEG

Leeds 0, Ujpest Dozsa 1. Att: 30,906
Sprake, Reaney, Madeley, Bremner, Charlton, Hunter, O'Grady, Belfitt (Lorimer), Jones, Giles, E. Gray.

SECOND LEG

Ujpest Dozsa 2, Leeds 0
Sprake, Bates, Cooper, Bremner, Madeley, Hunter, Lorimer (Yorath), Belfitt, Jones (Hibbitt), Giles, E. Gray.
Ujpest Dozsa won on aggregate 3-0.

EUROPEAN CHAMPIONS' CUP

1969-70

FIRST ROUND

FIRST LEG

Leeds 10 (Jones 3, Clarke 2, Bremner 2, Giles 2, O'Grady); Lyn Oslo 0. Att: 25,979. Sprake, Reaney Cooper, Bremner, Charlton, Hunter, Madeley, Clarke, Giles (Bates), O'Grady.

SECOND LEG

Lyn Oslo 0, Leeds 6 (Hibbitt 2, Belfitt 2, Jones, Lorimer)
Sprake, Reaney, Cooper, Bremner, Madeley, E. Gray, Lorimer, Belfitt, Jones, Bates, Hibbitt.
Leeds won on aggregate 16-0.

SECOND ROUND

FIRST LEG

Leeds 3 (Jones 2, Giles); Ferencvaros 0. Att: 37,291
Sprake, Reaney, Madeley, Bremner, Charlton, Hunter, Lorimer, Bates, Jones, Giles, E. Gray.

SECOND LEG

Ferencvaros 0, Leeds 3 (Jones 2, Lorimer)
Sprake, Reaney, Cooper, Bremner, Charlton, Hunter, Lorimer, madeley, Jones, Giles, E. Gray (Galvin).
Leeds won on aggregate 6-0.

THIRD ROUND

FIRST LEG

Standard Liege 0, Leeds 1 (Lorimer)
Sprake, Reaney, Cooper, Bremner, Charlton, Hunter, Lorimer, Clarke, Jones, Giles, Madeley.

SECOND LEG

Leeds 1 (Giles); Standard Liege 0. Att: 48,775
Sprake, Reaney, Cooper, Bremner, Charlton, Hunter, Lorimer, Clarke, Jones, Giles, Madley.
Leeds won on aggregate 2-0.

SEMI-FINAL

FIRST LEG

Leeds 0, Glasgow Celtic 1 (Connelly). Att: 45,505
Sprake, Reaney, Cooper, Bremner (Bates), Charlton, Madeley, Lorimer, Clarke, Jones, Giles, Gray.

SECOND LEG

Celtic 2, Leeds 1 (Bremner)
Sprake (Harvey), Madeley, Cooper, Bremner, Charlton, Hunter, Lorimer (Bates), Clarke, Jones, Giles, E. Gray.
Celtic won on aggregate 3-1.

1970-71

FAIRS CUP

FIRST ROUND

FIRST LEG

Sarpsborg (Norway) 0, Leeds 1 (Lorimer)
Sprake, Madeley, Cooper, Bremner, Kennedy, E. Gray, Lorimer, Belfitt, Jones, Bates, Hibbitt.

SECOND LEG

Leeds 5 (Charlton2, Bremner 2, Lorimer); Sarpsborg 0. Att: 19,283
Sprake, Madeley, Cooper (Reaney), Bremner, Charlton, Hunter, Lorimer, Clark, Belfitt, Bates, E. Gray.
Leeds won on aggregate 6-0.

SECOND ROUND

FIRST LEG

Leeds 1 (Lorimer); Dinamo Dresden 0. Att: 21,292
Harvey, Davey, Cooper, Bremner, Charlton, Hunter, Lorimer, Clarke, Jones, Belfitt (Galvin), Madeley.

SECOND LAG

Dinamo Dresden 2, Leeds 1 (Jones)
Sprake, Davey, Madeley, Bremner, Charlton, Hunter, Lorimer, Clarke, Jones, Giles, Bates.
Leeds won on away goals rule.

THIRD ROUND

FIRST LEG

Leeds 6 (Clarke, Bremner, E. Gray 2, Charlton, Chovanec o.g.); Sparta Prague 0. Att: 25,843
Sprake, Madeley, Cooper, Bremner, Charlton, Hunter, Lorimer, Clarke, Belfitt (Reaney), Giles, E. Gray.

SECOND LEG

Sparta Prague 2, Leeds 3 (E. Gray, Clarke, Belfitt)
Sprake (Harvey), Reaney, Cooper, Bremner, Madeley, Hunter (Yorath), Lorimer, Clarke, Belfitt, Bates, E. Gray.
Leeds won on aggregate 9-2.

FOURTH ROUND

FIRST LEG

Leeds 2 (Lorimer, Giles); Vitoria Setubal 1. Att: 27,143
Harvey, Davey (Yorath), Reaney, Bates, Charlton, Hunter, Lorimer, Belfitt, Jones (Jordan), Giles, Madeley.

SECOND LEG

Vitoria Setubal 1, Leeds 1 (Lorimer)
Harvey (Sprake), Reaney, Cooper, Bates, Charlton, Hunter, Lorimer, Clarke, Jones, Giles, Madeley.
Leeds won on aggregate 3-2.

SEMI-FINAL

FIRST LEG

Liverpool 0, Leeds 1 (Bremner)
Sprake, Reaney (Davey), Cooper, Bremner, Charlton, Hunter, Bates, Clarke, Jones, Giles, Madeley.

SECOND LEG

Leeds 0, Liverpool 0. Att: 40,462
Sprake, Madeley, Cooper, Bremner, Charlton, Hunter, Bates, Clarke (Reaney), Jones (Jordan), Giles, E. Gray.
Leeds won on aggregate 1-0.

FINAL

FIRST LEG

Juventus 2, Leeds 2 (Madeley, Bates)
Sprake, Reaney, Cooper, Bremner, Charlton, Hunter, Lorimer, Clarke, Jones (Bates), Giles, Madeley.

SECOND LEG

Leeds 1 (Clarke); Juventus 1. Att: 42,483
Sprake, Reaney, Cooper, Bremner, Charlton, Hunter, Lorimer, Clarke, Jones, Giles, Madeley (Bates).
Leeds won on away goals rule.

1971-72

UEFA CUP

FIRST ROUND

FIRST LEG

Lierse (Belgium) 0, Leeds (Galvin, Lorimer)
Sprake, Reaney, Yorath, Bremner, Faulkner, Hunter, Lorimer, Galvin, Belfitt, Giles, Bates.

SECOND LEG

Leeds 0, Lierse 4. Att: 18,680
Shaw (Sprake), Reaney, Cooper, Yorath, Faulkner, Madeley, Lorimer, Mann (Hunter), Belfitt, Bates, Galvin.
Lierse won on aggregate 4-2.

FAIRS CUP PLAY OFF

First winners (Barcelona) v last winners (Leeds) to see who retained the defunct Fairs Cup.

Barcelona 2, Leeds 1 (Jordan)
Sprake, Reaney, Davey, Bremner, Charlton, Hunter, Lorimer, Jordan, Belfitt, Giles, Galvin.

1972-73

CUP-WINNERS CUP

FIRST ROUND

FIRST LEG

Ankaragucu (Turkey) 1, Leeds 1 (Jordan)
Harvey, Reaney, Cherry, Bremner, Ellam, Hunter, Lorimer, Galvin (Yorath), Jordan, Giles, Madeley.

SECOND LEG

Leeds 1 (Jones); Ankaragucu 0. Att: 22,411
Harvey, Reaney, Cherry, Bremner, Ellam, Hunter, Lorimer, Clarke, Jones, Giles, Bates.
Leeds won on aggregate 2-1.

SECOND ROUND

FIRST LEG

Carl Zeiss Jena (East Germany) 0, Leeds 0
Harvey, Madeley, Cherry Bremner, Charlton, Hunter, Lorimer, Clarke, Jordan, Bates, E. Gray.

SECOND LEG

Leeds 2 (Cherry, Jones); Carl Zeiss Jena 0. Att: 26,885
Harvey, Reaney, Cherry, Bremner, Charlton, Hunter, Lorimer, Clarke, Jones, Bates (Giles), Yorath.
Leeds won on aggregate 2-0.

QUARTER FINAL

FIRST LEG

Leeds 5 (Giles, Clarke, Lorimer 2, Jordan); Rapid Bucharest 0. Att: 25,702
Harvey, Reaney, Cherry, Bremner, McQueen (Yorath), Hunter, Lorimer, Clarke, Jordan, Giles, Madeley.

SECOND LEG

Rapid Bucharest 1, Leeds 3 (Bates, Jones, Jordan)
Harvey, Reaney, E. Gray, Madeley, McQueen, Hunter, Lorimer, Jordan, Jones, Giles (Yorath), Bates (F. Gray).
Leeds won on aggregate 8-1.

SEMI-FINAL

FIRST LEG

Leeds 1 (Clarke); Hajduk Split (Yugoslavia) 0. Att: 32,051
Harvey, Reaney, Cherry, Bremner, Yorath, Hunter, Lorimer, Clarke, Jones, Giles, Bates (Jordan).

SECOND LEG

Hajduk Split 0, Leeds 0
Harvey, Reaney, Cherry, Bremner, Yorath, Hunter, Lorimer, Jones, Jordan, Giles, Madley.
Leeds won on aggregate 1-0.

FINAL

in Salonika

Leeds 0, AC Milan 1
Harvey, Reaney, Cherry, Bates, Yorath, Hunter, Lorimer, Jordan, Jones, F. Gray (McQueen), Madeley.

1973-74

UEFA CUP

FIRST ROUND

FIRST LEG

Stroemsgodset (Norway) 1, Leeds 1 (Clarke)
Sprake, Madeley, Cherry, Yorath, McQueen, F. Gray, Liddell, Clarke, Jones, Bates, E. Gray.

SECOND LEG

Leeds 6 (Clarke 2, Jones 2, F. Gray, Bates); Stroemsgodset 1. Att: 18,711
Harvey, Reaney (O'Neill), Cherry, Bremner, Ellam, Yorath, Lorimer, Clarke (McGinley), Jones, Bates, F. Gray.
Leeds won on aggregate 7-2.

SECOND ROUND

FIRST LEG

Leeds 0, Hibernian 0. Att: 27,145
Harvey, Cherry, Madeley, Bremner, Ellam, Yorath, Lorimer, Clarke, Jones, Bates, F. Gray.

SECOND LEG

Hibernian 0, Leeds 0
Shaw (Letheren), Reaney, Cherry, Bremner, Ellam, Yorath, Lorimer, Clarke, Jordan, Bates, F. Gray.
Leeds won 5-4 on penalty tie-breaker.

THIRD ROUND

SECOND LEG

Leeds 1 (Cherry); Vitoria Setubal (Portugal) 0. Att: 14,196
Harvey, Reaney (Davey), Cherry, Bremner, McQueen, Hunter, Lorimer, Clarke, Jordan, Bates, Yorath, F. Gray.

SECOND LEG

Vitoria Setubal 3, Leeds 1 (Liddell)
Harvey, Reaney, Cherry, Yorath, McQueen (Liddell), Ellam, Lorimer, Mann, Jordan, Hampton, F. Gray.
Setubal won on aggregate 3-2.

1974-75

EUROPEAN CUP

FIRST ROUND

FIRST LEG

Leeds 4 (Clarke 2, Lorimer, Jordan); FC Zurich 1. Att: 20,012
Harvey, Reaney, Cooper, Yorath, McQueen, Hunter, Lorimer, Clarke, Jordan, Giles, Madeley.

SECOND LEG

FC Zurich 2, Leeds 1 (Clarke)
Harvey, Reaney, Cherry, Yorath, Madeley, Hunter, Lorimer, Clarke, Jordan, Bates, F. Gray (Hampton).
Leeds won on aggregate 5-3.

SECOND ROUND

FIRST LEG

Ujpest Dozsa (Hungary) 1, Leeds 2 (Lorimer, McQueen)
Harvey, Reaney, Cooper, Yorath, McQueen, Hunter, Lorimer, McKenzie, Jordan, Giles, Madeley.

SECOND LEG

Leeds 3 (McQueen, Bremner, Yorath); Ujpest Dozsa 0. Att: 28,091
Harvey, Reaney, Cooper, Yorath, McQueen, Hunter (Cherry), Lorimer (Harris), Clarke, Bremner, Giles, Madeley.
Leeds won on aggregate 5-1.

QUARTER FINAL

FIRST LEG

Leeds 3 (Jordan, McQueen, Lorimer); Anderlecht (Belgium) 0. Att: 43,195
Stewart, Madeley, F. Gray, Bremner (Yorath), McQueen, Hunter, Lorimer, Clarke, Jordan, Giles, E. Gray.

SECOND LEG

Anderlecht 0, Leeds 1 (Bremner)
Stewart, Reaney, F. Gray, Bremner, McQueen, Hunter, Lorimer, Clarke, Jordan, Yorath, Madeley.
Leeds won on aggregate 4-0.

SEMI-FINAL

FIRST LEG

Leeds 2 (Bremner, Clarke); Barcelona 1. Att: 50,393
Stewart, Reaney, F. Gray, Bremner, McQueen, Madeley, Yorath, Clarke, Jordan, Giles, E. Gray.

SECOND LEG

Barcelona 1, Leeds 1 (Lorimer)
Stewart, Cherry F. Gray, Bremner, McQueen, Hunter, Lorimer, Clarke, Jordan, Yorath, Madeley.
Leeds won on aggregate 3-2.

FINAL

IN Paris

Leeds 1 (Lorimer); Bayern Munich 2
Stewart, Reaney, F. Gray, Bremner, Madeley, Hunter, Lorimer, Clarke, Jordan, Giles, Yorath (E. Gray).

F.A. CUP

1921-22

FIRST ROUND

Swindon 2, Leeds 1 (Swan)
Whalley, Duffield, Rogerson, Sherwin, Baker, Walton, Mason, Armitage, Howarth, Swan, Moore.

1922-23

FIRST ROUND

Portsmouth 0, Leeds 0
Whalley, Duffield, Frew, Sherwin, Hart, Baker, Noble, Whipp, Armitage, Walton, Harris.

Replay

Leeds 3 (Whipp, Armitage, Swan); Portsmouth 1. Att: 25,000
Whalley, Duffield, Frew, Sherwin, Hart, Baker, Noble, Whipp, Armitage, Swan, Harris.

SECOND ROUND

Bolton Wanderers 3, United 1 (Swan)
Whalley, Duffield, Frew, Sherwin, Hart, Baker, Noble, Whipp, Armitage, Swan, Harris.

1923-24

FIRST ROUND

Leeds 1 (Whipp); Stoke City 0. Att: 25,000
Down, Duffield, Speak, Sherwin, Hart, Baker, Armand, Whipp, Richmond, Swan, Harris.

SECOND ROUND

West Ham United 1, Leeds 1 (Coates)
Down, Duffield, Speak, Sherwin, Hart, Baker, Coates, Whipp, Richmond, Swan, Harris.

Replay

Leeds 1 (Whipp); West Ham United o. Att: 32,000
Down, Duffield, Speak, Sherwin, Hart, Baker, Coates, Whipp, Richmond, Swan, Harris.

THIRD ROUND

Aston Villa 3, Leeds o
Down, Duffield, Menzies, Sherwin, Hart, Baker, Coates, Whipp, Richmond, Swan, Harris.

1924-5

FIRST ROUND

Liverpool 3, Leeds 0
Down, Menzies, Speak, Sherwin, Hart, Smith, Robson, Armand, Whipp, Swan, Harris.

1925-6

THIRD ROUND

Middlesbrough 5, Leeds 1 (Armand)
Johnson, Allen, Menzies, Edwards, Townsley, Atkinson, Turnbull, Whipp, Jennings, Armand, Jackson.

1926-27

THIRD ROUND

Leeds 3 (Jennings 2, Duggan); Sunderland 2. Att: 31,000
Potts, Roberts, Allen, Edwards, Townsley, Reed, Turnbull, Duggan, Jennings, Armand, Mitchell.

FOURTH ROUND

Leeds 0, Bolton Wanderers 0. Att: 42,694
Potts, Allen, Menzies, Edwards, Townsley, Reed, Sissons, Wainscoat, Jennings, Armand, Mitchell.

Replay

Bolton Wanderers 3, Leeds 0
Potts, Allen, Menzies, Edwards, Townsley, Reed, Riley, Mears, Jennings, Wainscoat, Mitchell.

1927-28

THIRD ROUND

Manchester City 1, Leeds 0
Potts, Townsley, Menzies, Edwards, Hart, Reed, Turnbull, White, Jennings, Wainscoat, Mitchell.

1928-29

THIRD ROUND

Exeter City 2, Leeds 2 (Keetley, Menzies)
Potts, Townsley, Menzies, Edwards, Hart, Reed, Turnbull, White, Keetley, Wainscoat, Mitchell.

Replay

Leeds 5 (Wainscoat, Reed, Cochrane, Keetley, Lowton o.g.); Exeter City 1. Att: 23,000
Potts, Townsley, Menzies, Edwards, Hart, Reed, Turnbull, White, Keetley, Wainscoat, Cochrane.

FOURTH ROUND

Huddersfield Town 3, Leeds 0
Wilson, Townsley, Menzies, Edwards, Hart, Reed, Turnbull, White, Keetley, Wainscoat, Cochrane.

1929-30

THIRD ROUND

Leeds 8 (Wainscoat 3, Jennings 2, White 2, Turnbull); Crystal Palace 1. Att: 25,000
Potts, Roberts, J. Milburn, Edwards, Hart, Reed, Turnbull, White, Jennings, Wainscoat, Mitchell.

FOURTH ROUND

West Ham United 4, Leeds 1 (Jennings)
Potts, Roberts, J. Milburn, Edwards, Hart, Reed, Turnbull, White, Jennings, Wainscoat, Mitchell.

1930-31

THIRD ROUND

Leeds 2 (Hydes, Furness); Huddersfield Town 0. Att: 41,103
Potts, G. Milburn, J. Milburn, Edwards, Hart, Copping, Turnbull, Furness, Hydes, Wainscoat, Mitchell.

FOURTH ROUND

Leeds 4 (Furness, Wainscoat 2, Mitchell); Newcastle United 1. Att: 40,261
Potts, G. Milburn, J. Milburn, Edwards, Hart, Copping, Turnbull, Furness, Keetley, Wainscoat, Mitchell.

FIFTH ROUND

Exeter City 3, Leeds 1 (Mitchell)
Potts, G. Milburn, J. Milburn, Edwards, Hart, Copping, Turnbull, Furness, Hydes, Wainscoat, Mitchell.

1931-32

THIRD ROUND

Queen's Park Rangers 3, Leeds 1 (J. Milburn)
Moore, J. Milburn, Menzies, Edwards, Danskin, Copping, Duggan, Firth, Keetley, Bennett, Cochrane.

1932-33

THIRD ROUND

Newcastle United 0, Leeds 3 (Hydes 3)
Potts, G. Milburn, J. Milburn, Edwards, Hart, Copping, Mahon, Hydes, Keetley, Furness, Cochrane.

FOURTH ROUND

Tranmere Rovers 0, Leeds 0
Potts, G. Milburn, J. Milburn, Edwards, Hart, Copping, Mahon, Hydes, Keetley, Furness, Cochrane.

Replay

Leeds 4 (J. Milburn, Mahon, Cochrane, Hydes); Tranmere 0. Att: 25,000
Potts, G. Milburn, J. Milburn, Edwards, Hart, Copping, Mahon, O'Grady, Hydes, Furness, Cochrane.

FIFTH ROUND

Everton 2, Leeds 0
Potts, G. Milburn, J. Milburn, Edwards, Hart, Copping, Duggan, Hydes, Keetley, Furness, Cochrane.

1933-34

THIRD ROUND

Leeds 0, Preston North End 1. Att: 29,158
Moore, G. Milburn, J. Milburn, Hornby, Hart, Copping, Duggan, Firth, Keetley, Furness, Cochrane.

1934-35

THIRD ROUND

Leeds 4 (Hydes 2, Furness, Mahon); Bradford 1. Att: 35,444
Moore, Sproston, J. Milburn, Edwards, McDougall, Neal, Mahon, Duggan, Hydes, Furness, Cochrane.

FOURTH ROUND

Norwich City 3, Leeds 3 (Mahon, Duggan, Cochrane)
Moore, Sproston, J. Milburn, Hart, McDougall, Neal, Mahon, Duggan, Hydes, Furness, Cochrane.

Replay

Leeds 1 (Hydes); Norwich City 2. Att: 27,000
Moore, Sproston, J. Milburn, Hornby, Hart, Copping, Duggan, Firth, Keetley, Furness, Cochrane.

1935-36

THIRD ROUND

Wolverhampton Wanderers 1, Leeds 1 (McDougall)
McInroy, Sproston, J. Milburn, Edwards, McDougall, Browne, Duggan, Brown, Kelly, Furness, Cochrane.

Replay

Leeds 3 (Kelly, Cochrane, Duggan); Wolves 1. Att: 35,000
McInroy, Sproston, J. Milburn, Edwards, McDougall, Browne, Duggan, Brown, Kelly, Furness, Cochrane.

FOURTH ROUND

Leeds 3 (Brown 2, Duggan); Bury 2. Att: 19,633
McInroy, Sproston, J. Milburn, Edwards, McDougall, Browne, Duggan, Brown, Kelly, Furness, Cochrane.

FIFTH ROUND

Sheffield United 3, Leeds 1 (Furness).
McInroy, Sproston, Milburn, Edwards, McDougall, Browne, Armes, Brown, Kelly, Furness, Cochrane.

1936-37

THIRD ROUND

Chelsea 4, Leeds 0
Savage, Sproston, G. Milburn, Edwards, Kane, Mills, Powell, Ainsley, Trainer, Hydes, Buckley.

1937-38

THIRD ROUND

Leeds 3 (Armes, Buckley 2); Chester 1. Att: 37,155
Savage, Sproston, Milburn, Makinson, Kane, Mills, Armes, Ainsley, Hodgson, Stephenson, Buckley.

FOURTH ROUND

Charlton Athletic 2, Leeds 1 (Hodgson)
Savage, Sproston, Milburn, Makinson, Kane, Mills, Armes, Ainsley, Hodgson, Stephenson, Buckley.

1938-39

THIRD ROUND

Leeds 3 (Stephenson, Hargreaves, Cochrane); Bournemouth 1. Att: 10,114
Savage, Milburn, Gadsby, Edwards, Holley, Parry, Cochrane, Powell, Hodgson, Stephenson, Hargreaves.

FOURTH ROUND

Leeds 2 (Hodgson, Cochrane); Huddersfield Town 4. Att: 43,702
Savage, Milburn, Gadsby, Edwards, Holley, Parry, Cochrane. Powell, Hodgson, Stephenson, Hargreaves.

1946-47

THIRD ROUND

West Bromwich Albion 2, Leeds 1 (Ainsley)
Twomey, Jim Milburn, Gadsby, Henry, Holley, Martin, Cochrane, Powell, Ainsley, Short, Grainger.

1947-48

THIRD ROUND

Blackpool 4, Leeds 0
Twomey, Milburn, Gadsby, Bullions, Martin, Willingham, Cochrane, Powell, Holley, Wakefield, Hindle.

1948-49

THIRD ROUND

Leeds 1 (Browniing); Newport County 3. Att: 30,000
Fearnley, Dunn, Milburn, Bullions, Depear, McCabe, Cochrane, Burden, Browning, Marsh, Heaton.

1949-50

THIRD ROUND

Carlisle United 2, Leeds 5 (Browning, Dudley 2, Williams, Cochrane)
Searson, Dunn, Milburn, McCabe, Charles, Burden, Cochrane, McMorran, Browning, Dudley, Williams.

FOURTH ROUND

Leeds 1 (Williams); Bolton Wanderers 1. Att: 51,000
Searson, Dunn, Milburn, McCabe, Charles, Burden, Cochrane, McMorran, Browning, Dudley, Williams.

Replay

Bolton Wanderers 2, Leeds 3 (Dudley 2, Browning)
Searson, Dunn, Milburn, McCabe, Charles, Burden, Cochrane, Iggleden, Browning, Dudley, Williams.

FIFTH ROUND

Leeds 3 (Williams, Cochrane, Iggleden); Cardiff City 1. Att: 50,600
Searson, Dunn, Milburn, McCabe, Charles, Burden, Cochrane, Iggleden, Browning, Dudley, Williams.

SIXTH ROUND

Arsenal 1, Leeds 0
Searson, Dunn, Milburn, McCabe, Charles, Burden, Cochrane, Iggleden, Browning, Dudley, Williams.

1950-51

THIRD ROUND

Leeds 1 (Browning); Middlesbrough 0. Att: 45,583
Searson, Dunn, Milburn, McCabe, Charles, Burden, Harrison, Miller, Browning, Dudley, Williams.

FOURTH ROUND

Manchester United 4, Leeds 0
Searson, Dunn, Milburn, McCabe, Charles, Burden, Harrison, Iggleden, Browning, Dudley, Williams.

1951-52

THIRD ROUND

Rochdale 0, Leeds 2 (Kirk 2)
Searson, Dunn, Hair, Kerfoot, Charles, Burden, Kirk, Mills, Fidler, Iggleden, Williams.

FOURTH ROUND

Leeds 2 (Milburn, Iggleden); Bradford 0. Att: 50,645
Searson, Dunn, Hair, Kerfoot, Charles, Burden, Kirk, Stewart, Milburn, Iggleden, Williams.

FIFTH ROUND

Leeds 1 (Milburn); Chelsea 1. Att: 52,500
Searson, Dunn, Hair, Kerfoot, Charles, Burden, Kirk, Mills, Milburn, Iggleden, Williams.

Replay

Chelsea 1, Leeds 1 (Kirk)
Searson, Dunn, Hair, Kerfoot, Charles, Burden, Williams, Stewart, Kirk, Iggleden, Hughes.

Second replay at Villa Park

Leeds 1 (Mills); Chelsea 5
Searson, Dunn, Hair, Kerfoot, Charles, Burden, Williams, Mills, Kirk, Iggleden, Hughes.

1952-53

THIRD ROUND

Brentford 2, Leeds 1 (Charles)
Scott, Dunn, Hair, Kerfoot, McCabe, Burden, Meek, Nightingale, Charles, Iggleden, Tyrer.

1953-54

THIRD ROUND

Leeds 3 (Iggleden, Charles, Ramsey o.g.); Tottenham 3. Att: 42,000
Scott, Dunn, Hair, Kerfoot, Marsden, Burden, Williams, Nightingale, Charles, Iggleden, Tyrer.

Replay

Tottenham 1, Leeds 0
Scott, Dunn, Hair, Kerfoot, Marsden, Burden, Williams, Nightingale, Charles, Iggleden, Tyrer.

1954-55

THIRD ROUND

Leeds 2 (Kerfoot, Charles); Torquay United 2. Att: 28,000
Wood, Dunn, Hair, Ripley, Marsden, Kerfoot, Williams, Nightingale, Charles, Brook, McCall.

Replay

Torquay United 4, Leeds 0
Wood, Dunn, Hair, Ripley, Marsden, Kerfoot, Williams, Nightingale, Charles, Brook, McCall.

1955-56

THIRD ROUND

Leeds 1 (Brook); Cardiff City 2. Att: 40,000
Wood, Dunn, Hair, Gibson, Charlton, Kerfoot, Williams, Brook, Charles, Vickers, Overfield.

1956-57

THIRD ROUND

Leeds 1 (Charles); Cardiff City 2. Att: 34,237
Wood, Dunn, Hair, Gibson, Charlton, Kerfoot, Meek, Charles, Brook, Forrest, Overfield.

1957-58

THIRD ROUND

Leeds 1 (Forrest); Cardiff City 2. Att: 30,374.
Wood, Dunn, Hair, Gibson, Charlton, Kerfoot, Meek, Cush, Forrest, Crowe, Overfield.

1958-59

THIRD ROUND

Luton Town 5, Leeds 1 (Shackleton)
Wood, Ashall, Hair, Cush, Charlton, Gibson, Humphries, Crowe, Shackleton, Revie, Overfield.

1959-60

THIRD ROUND

Aston Villa 2, Leeds 1 (McCole)
Wood, Ashall, Hair, Cush, Charlton, Gibson, Crowe, Cameron, McCole, Peyton, Meek.

1960-61

THIRD ROUND

Sheffield Wednesday 2, Leeds 0
Humphreys, Jones, Hair, Smith, Charlton, Goodwin, Francis, Cameron, McCole, Bremner, Grainger.

1961-62

THIRD ROUND

Leeds 2 (Peyton, Charlton); Derby County 2. Att: 27,089
Younger, Hair, Bell, Smith, Goodwin, McConnell, Bremner, McAdams, Charlton, Peyton, Mayers.

Replay

Derby County 3, Leeds 1 (McAdams)
Younger, Hair, Bell, Smith, Goodwin, McConnell, Bremner, McAdams, Charlton, Peyton, Mayers.

1962-63

THIRD ROUND

Leeds 3 (Charlton, Reaney, Hair); Stoke City 1. Att: 36,873
Sprake, Reaney, Hair, Bell, Charlton, Hunter, Henderson, Weston, Storrie, Giles, Johanneson.

FOURTH ROUND

Middlesbrough 0, Leeds 2 (Storrie, Johanneson)
Sprake, Reaney, Hair, Bell, Charlton, Hunter, Henderson, Weston, Storrie, Giles, Johanneson.

FIFTH ROUND

Nottingham Forest 3, Leeds 0
Sprake, Reaney, Hair, Bell, Charlton, Hunter, Henderson, Weston, Storrie, Giles, Johanneson

1963-64

THIRD ROUND

Cardiff City 0, Leeds 1 (Bremner)
Sprake, Reaney, Bell, Bremner, Goodwin, Hunter, Henderson, Weston, Lawson, Giles, Johanneson.

FOURTH ROUND

Leeds 1 (Lawson); Everton 1. Att: 48,286
Sprake, Reaney, Bell, Bremner, Madeley, Hunter, Henderson, Giles, Lawson, Collins, Johanneson.

Replay

Everton 2, Leeds 0
Sprake, Reaney, Bell, Bremner, Madeley, Hunter, Henderson, Giles, Lawson, Collins, Hawksby.

1964-65

THIRD ROUND

Leeds 3 (Greenhoff, Johanneson, Johnson); Southport 0. Att: 31,297
Sprake, Reaney, Cooper, Bremner, Charlton, Hunter, Greenhoff, Storrie, Johnson, Collins, Johanneson.

FOURTH ROUND

Leeds 1 (Storrie); Everton. Att: 50,051
Sprake, Reaney, Bell, Bremner, Charlton, Hunter, Giles, Weston, Storrie, Collins, Johanneson.

Replay

Everton 1, United 2 (Charlton, Weston)
Sprake, Reaney, Bell, Bremner, Charlton, Hunter, Giles, Weston, Storrie, Collins, Cooper.

FIFTH ROUND

Leeds 2 (Giles, Johanneson); Shrewsbury Town 0. Att: 47,740
Sprake, Reavey, Bell, Bremner, Charlton, Hunter, Giles, Weston, Storrie, Collins, Johanneson.

QUARTER FINAL

Crystal Palace 0, Leeds 3 (Peacock 2, Storrie)
Sprake, Reaney, Bell, Bremner, Charlton, Hunter, Giles, Storrie, Peacock, Collins, Cooper.

SEMI-FINAL
at Hillsborough

Leeds 0, Manchester United 0. Att: 65,000
Sprake, Reaney, Bell, Bremner, Charlton, Hunter, Giles, Storrie, Peacock, Collins, Johanneson.

Replay at Nottingham Forest

Leeds 1 (Bremner); Manchester United 0. Att: 46,300
Sprake, Reaney, Bell, Bremner, Charlton, Hunter, Giles, Storrie, Peacock, Collins, Cooper.

FINAL
at Wembley

Leeds 1 (Bremner); Liverpool 2 (after extra time)
Sprake, Reaney, Bell, Bremner, Charlton, Hunter, Giles, Storrie, Peacock, Collins, Johanneson.

1965-66

THIRD ROUND

Leeds 6 (Lorimer 3, Reaney, Greenhoff, Giles); Bury 0. Att: 30,384
Williamson, Reaney, Bell, Bremner, Charlton, Hunter, Greenhoff, Lorimer, Peacock, Giles, Johanneson.

FOURTH ROUND

Chelsea 1, Leeds 0
Sprake, Reaney, Bell, Bremner, Charlton, Hunter, Storrie, Lorimer, Madeley, Giles, O'Grady.

1966-67

THIRD ROUND

Leeds 3 (O'Grady, Bell, Johanneson); Crystal Palace 0. Att: 37,768
Sprake, Reaney, Bell, Bremner, Charlton, Hunter, O'Grady, Giles, Greenhoff, Madeley, E. Gray, Johanneson.

FOURTH ROUND

Leeds 5 (Lorimer 2, Madeley, Belfitt 2); West Bromwich Albion 0. Att 41,329
Sprake, Reaney, Bell, Madeley, Charlton, Hunter, Giles, Lorimer, Belfitt, E. Gray, O'Grady (Bates).

FIFTH ROUND

Sunderland 1, Leeds 1 (Charlton)
Sprake, Reaney, Bell, Bremner, Charlton, Hunter, Madeley, Belfitt, Greenhoff, Giles, Lorimer.

Replay

Leeds 1 (Giles); Sunderland 1. Att: 57,892
Sprake, Reaney, Bell, Bremner, Charlton, Hunter, Lorimer, Belfitt, Greenhoff, Giles, Johanneson (Cooper).

Second replay at Boothferry Park, Hull

Leeds 2 (Belfitt, Giles); Sunderland 1
Sprake, Reaney, Bell, Bremner, Charlton, Hunter, Lorimer, Belfitt, Greenhoff, Giles, Cooper.

QUARTER FINAL

Leeds 1 (Charlton); Manchester City 0. Att: 48,887
Sprake, Reaney, Bell, Bremner, Charlton, Hunter, Lorimer, Madeley, Peacock (Greenhoff), Giles, E. Gray.

SEMI-FINAL
at Villa Park

Leeds 0, Chelsea 1
Sprake, Reaney, Bell, Bremner, Madeley, Hunter, Giles, Belfitt (Lorimer), Greenhoff, E. Gray, Cooper.

1967-68

THIRD ROUND

Leeds 2 (Charlton, Lorimer); Derby County 0. Att: 39,753
Sprake, Reaney, Cooper, Bremner, Charlton (Madeley), Hunter, Greenhoff, Lorimer, Jones, Giles, E. Gray.

FOURTH ROUND

Leeds 2 (Jones, Giles); Nottingham Forest 1. Att: 51,739
Sprake, Reaney, Cooper, Bremner, Madeley, Hunter, Greenhoff, Lorimer, Jones, Giles, E. Gray.

FIFTH ROUND

Leeds 2 (Jones, Lorimer); Bristol City 0. Att: 45,227
Sprake, Reaney, Cooper, Bremner, Charlton, Hunter, Greenhoff, Lorimer, Jones, Giles (Madeley), Hibbitt.

QUARTER FINAL

Leeds 1 (Madeley); Sheffield United 0. Att: 48,322
Sprake, Reaney, Cooper, Bremner, Charlton, Hunter, Lorimer Madeley, Jones, Giles, O'Grady.

SEMI-FINAL
at Old Trafford

Leeds 0, Everton 1
Sprake, Reaney, Cooper, Bremner, Charlton, Hunter, Lorimer, Madeley, Jones, Giles, E. Gray.

1968-69

THIRD ROUND

Sheffield Wednesday 1, Leeds 1 (Lorimer)
Sprake, Reaney, Madeley, Bremner, Charlton, Hunter, O'Grady, Lorimer, Jones, Bates, E. Gray.

Replay

Leeds 1 (Johanneson); Sheffield Wednesday 3. Att. 48,234
Sprake, Reaney, Madeley, Bremner (Belfitt), Charlton, Hunter, E. Gray, Lorimer, Jones, Bates, Johanneson.

1969-70

THIRD ROUND

Leeds 2 (Giles, Jones); Swansea Town 1. Att: 30,246
Sprake, Reaney, Cooper, Bremner, Charlton, Hunter, Lorimer, Clarke, Jones, Giles, Madeley.

FOURTH ROUND

Sutton United 0, Leeds 6 (Clarke 4, Lorimer 2)
Harvey, Reaney, Cooper, Bremner, Charlton, Hunter, Lorimer, Clarke, Jones, Giles, Madeley.

FIFTH ROUND

Leeds 2 (Giles, Clarke); Mansfield Town 0. Att: 48,093
Sprake, Reaney, Cooper, Bremner, Charlton, Hunter, Lorimer, Clarke, Jones, Giles, E. gray.

QUARTER FINAL

Swindon Town 0, Leeds 2 (Clarke 2)
Sprake, Reaney, Cooper, Bremner, Charlton, Hunter, Madeley, Clarke, Jones, Giles, E. Gray.

SEMI-FINAL
at Hillsborough

Manchester United 0, Leeds 0
Sprake, Reaney, Cooper, Bremner, Charlton, Hunter, Lorimer (E. Gray), Clarke, Jones, Giles, Madeley.

Replay at Villa Park

Leeds 0, Manchester United 0
Sprake, Reaney, Cooper (Bates), Bremner, Charlton, Madeley, Lorimer, Clarke, Jones, Giles, E. Gray.

Second replay at Burden Park, Bolton

Manchester United 0, Leeds 1 (Bremner)
Sprake, Reaney, Cooper, Bremner, Charlton, Madeley, Lorimer, Clarke, Jones, Giles, E. Gray.

FINAL
at Wembley

Chelsea 2, Leeds 2 (Charlton, Jones) - After extra time
Sprake, Madeley, Cooper, Bremner, Charlton, Hunter, Lorimer, Clarke, Jones, Giles, E. Gray.

Replay at Old Trafford

Chelsea 2, Leeds 1 (Jones) - After extra time
Harvey, Madeley, Cooper, Bremner, Charlton, Hunter Lorimer, Clarke, Jones, Giles, E. Gray.

1970-71

THIRD ROUND

Rotherham 0, Leeds 0
Sprake, Reaney, Cooper, Bremner, Charlton, Hunter, Lorimer, Clarke, Jones, Giles, Madeley.

Replay

Leeds 3 (Lorimer 2, Giles); Rotherham 2. Att: 36,890
Sprake, Reaney, Cooper (Bates), Bremner, Charlton, Hunter, Lorimer, Clarke, Belfitt, Giles, Madeley.

FOURTH ROUND

Leeds 4 (Jones 3, Clarke); Swindon Town 0. Att: 36,985
Sprake, Reaney, Davey, Bates, Charlton, Hunter, Lorimer (Galvin), Clarke, Jones, Giles, Madeley.

FIFTH ROUND

Colchester United 3, Leeds 2 (Hunter, Giles)
Sprake, Reaney, Cooper, Bates, Charlton, Hunter, Lorimer, Clarke, Jones, Giles, Madeley.

1971-72

THIRD ROUND

Leeds 4 (Giles 2, Lorimer 2); Bristol Rovers 1. Att: 33,565
Sprake, Reaney, Cooper, Bremner, Madeley, Hunter, Lorimer, Bates, Jordon, Giles, E. Gray.

FOURTH ROUND

Liverpool 0, Leeds 0
Sprake, Reaney, Cooper, Bremner, Madeley, Hunter, Lorimer, Clarke, Jones, Giles, Bates.

Replay

Leeds 2 (Clarke); Liverpool 0. Att: 45,821
Sprake, Reaney, Cooper, Bremner, Charlton, Hunter, Lorimer, Clarke, Madeley, Giles, E. Gray.

FIFTH ROUND

Cardiff City 0, Leeds 2 (Giles 2)
Sprake, Madeley, Cooper, Bremner, Charlton, Hunter, Lorimer, Clarke, Jones, Giles, E. Gray.

QUARTER FINAL

Leeds 2 (Clarke, Charlton); Tottenham 1. Att: 43,937
Sprake, Madeley, Cooper, Bremner, Charlton, Hunter, Lorimer, Clarke, Jones, Giles, E. Gray.

SEMI-FINAL
at Hillsborough

Leeds 3 (Jones 2, Lorimer); Birmingham City 0
Harvey, Reaney, Madeley, Bremner, Charlton, Hunter, Lorimer, Clarke, Jones, Giles, E. Gray.

FINAL
at Wembley

Leeds 1 (Clarke); Arsenal 0
Harvey, Reaney, Madeley, Bremner, Charlton, Hunter, Lorimer, Clarke, Jones, Giles, E. Gray.

1972-73

THIRD ROUND

Norwich City 1, Leeds 1 (Lorimer)
Harvey, Reaney, Cherry, Bremner, Madeley, Hunter, Lorimer, Clarke, Jones, Giles, Bates.

Replay

Leeds 1 (Giles); Norwich City 1. Att: 36,087
Harvey, Reaney, Cherry. Bremner, Madeley, Hunter, Lorimer, Clarke, Jones, Giles, Bates.

Second Replay at Villa Park

Norwich City 0, Leeds 5 (Clarke 3, Jones, Lorimer)
Harvey, Reaney, Cherry, Bremner, Madeley, Hunter, Lorimer, Clarke (Yorath), Jones, Giles, Bates.

FOURTH ROUND

Leeds 2 (Clarke, Bates); Plymouth 1. Att: 38,374
Harvey, Reaney, Cherry, Yorath, Madeley, Hunter, Lorimer, Clarke, Jones, Giles, Bates.

FIFTH ROUND

Leeds 2 (Clarke 2); West Bromwich Albion 0. Att: 39,229
Harvey, Reaney, Cherry, Bremner, Madeley, Hunter, Lorimer, Clarke, Jones, Giles, E. Gray.

QUARTER FINAL

Derby County 0, Leeds 1 (Lorimer)
Harvey, Reaney, Cherry, Bremner, Madeley, Hunter, Lorimer, Clarke, Jones, Giles, E. Gray.

SEMI-FINAL
at Main Road

Leeds 1 (Bremner); Wolverhampton Wanderers 0
Harvey, Reaney, Cherry, Bremner, Charlton (Jordan), Yorath, Lorimer, Clarke, Jones, Giles, Madeley.

FINAL
at Wembley

Leeds 0, Sunderland 1 (Porterfield)
Harvey, Reaney, Cherry, Bremner, Madeley, Hunter, Lorimer, Clarke, Jones, Giles, E. Gray (Yorath).

1973-74

THIRD ROUND

Wolverhampton Wanderers 1, Leeds 1 (Lorimer)
Harvey, Reaney Cherry, Bremner, McQueen, Hunter, Lorimer, Jordan, Jones, Yorath, Madeley.

Replay

Leeds 1 (Jones); Wolves 0. Att: 42,747
Stewart, Reaney, Cherry, Bremner, McQueen (Yorath), Hunter, Lorimer, Jordan, Jones, Clarke, Madeley.

FOURTH ROUND

Peterborough United 1, Leeds 4 (Lorimer, Jordan 2, Yorath)
Harvey, Reaney, Cooper, Bremner, Ellam, Hunter, Lorimer, Yorath, Jordan, Cherry, Madeley.

FIFTH ROUND

Bristol City 1, Leeds 1 (Bremner)
Harvey, Yorath, Cherry, Bremner, McQueen, Hunter, Lorimer, Jordan, Jones, Giles, Madeley.

Replay

Leeds 0, Bristol City 1. Att: 47,128
Harvey, Cherry, Cooper, Bremner, Ellam, Hunter, Lorimer, Clarke, Jones, Giles (Jordan), Madeley.

1974-75

THIRD ROUND

Leeds 4 (E. Gray, Clarke 2, McKenzie); Cardiff City 1. Att: 31,572
Harvey, Reaney (Cherry), F. Gray, Bremner, McQueen, Madeley, McKenzie, Clarke, Lorimer, Giles, E. Gray.

FOURTH ROUND

Leeds 0, Wimbledon 0. Att: 46,230
Harvey, Reaney, F. Gray, Bremner, McQueen, Madeley, McKenzie, Yorath, Lorimer, Giles, E. Gray.

Replay

Wimbledon 0, Leeds 1 (Giles)
Harvey, Reaney, F. Gray, Bremner, Yorath, Madeley, McKenzie, Clarke, Jordan, Giles, E. Gray.

FIFTH ROUND

Derby County 0, Leeds 1 (Nish o.g.)
Stewart, Reaney, F. Gray, Bremner, McQueen, Madeley, McKenzie, Clarke, Jordan, Yorath, E. Gray.

QUARTER FINAL

Ipswich Town 0, Leeds 0
Stewart, Madeley, F. Gray, Bremner, McQueen, Hunter, Yorath, Clarke, Jones, Giles, E. Gray.

Replay

Leeds 1 (McKenzie); Ipswich Town 1. Att: 50,074
Stewart, Reaney (McKenzie), F. Gray, Bremner, Madeley, Hunter, Lorimer, Clarke, Jordan, Giles, Yorath.

Second replay at Leicester

Leeds 0, Ipswich Town 0
Stewart, Reaney, F. Gray, Bremner, Madeley, Hunter, Lorimer (McKenzie), Clarke, Jordan, Giles, Yorath.

Third replay at Leicester

Leeds 2 (Clarke, Giles); Ipswich Town 3
Stewart, Reaney, F. Gray, Bremner, Madeley, Hunter, E. Gray, Clarke, Jordan, Giles, Yorath (McKenzie)

1975-76

THIRD ROUND

Notts County 0, Leeds 1 (Clarke)
Harvey, Reaney, F. Gray, Bremner, Madeley, Cherry, Lorimer, Clarke, McKenzie, Hunter, Yorath.

FOURTH ROUND

Leeds 0, Crystal Palace 1. Att: 43,116
Harvey, Reaney, F. Gray, Bremner (Hunter), Madeley, Cherry, Lorimer, Clarke, McKenzie, Yorath, E. Gray.

1976-77

THIRD ROUND

Leeds 5 (Clarke, Reaney, Jordan, McQueen, Hampton); Norwich City 2. Att: 28,130
Harvey, Reaney, Hampton, F. Gray, McQueen, Madeley, Lorimer, Clarke, Jordan, Currie, E. Gray.

FOURTH ROUND

Birmingham City 1, Leeds 2 (Jordan, Clarke)
Harvey, Reaney, Hampton, Cherry McQueen, Madeley, F. Gray, Clarke, Jordan, Currie, E. Gray.

FIFTH ROUND

Leeds 1 (Cherry); Manchester City 0. Att: 47,731
Harvey, Reaney, Hampton, Cherry, McQueen, Madeley, F. Gray, Clarke, Jordan, Currie, E. Gray.

QUARTER FINAL

Wolverhampton Wanderers 0, Leeds 1 (E. Gray)
Stewart, Reaney, Hampton, Cherry, McQueen, Madeley, F. Gray, Clarke, Jordan, Currie, E. Gray.

SEMI-FINAL

at Hillsborough

Leeds 1 (Clarke); Manchester United 2
Stewart, Reaney, Hampton, Cherry, McQueen, Madeley, F. Gray (Lorimer), Clarke, Jordan, Currie, E. Gray.

1977-78

THIRD ROUND

Leeds 1 (F. Gray); Manchester City 2. Att: 38,000
Harvey, Reaney (Clarke), F. Gray, Cherry, McQueen, Madeley, Harris, Hankin, Currie, Flynn, Graham.

1978-79

THIRD ROUND

Hartlepool United 2, Leeds 6 (Hart, Graham, E. Gray 2, Harris, F. Gray)
Harvey, Cherry, F. Gray, Flynn, Hart, Madeley, E. Gray, Graham, Hawley, Currie, Harris.

FOURTH ROUND

Leeds 3 (F. Gray, Graham, Harris); West Bromwich Albion 3
(Game played at Albion because of FA ban on home cup ties at Ellan Road following pitch invasion previous season).
Harvey, Cherry, F. Gray, Flynn, Hart, Madeley, Harris, Stevenson, Hawley, Currie, Graham.

Replay also at Albion's ground

West Bromwich Albion 2, Leeds 0
Harvey, Cherry, F. Gray, Flynn, Parkinson, Madeley, Harris, Stevenson (Thomas), Hawley, Currie, Graham.

LEAGUE CUP

1964-65

SECOND ROUND

Leeds 3 (Hunter, Storrie, Belfitt); Huddersfield Town 2. Att: 9,837
Williamson, Wright, Bell, Bremner, Charlton, Hunter, Henderson, Storrie, Belfitt, Johnson, Cooper.

THIRD ROUND

Leeds 2 (Johanneson, Collins); Aston Villa 3. Att: 10,656
Williamson, Bell, Madeley, Charlton, Hunter, Greenhoff, Henderson, Belfitt, Collins, Johanneson.

1965-66

SECOND ROUND

Leeds 4 (Cooper, Johnson, Belfitt, Storrie); Hartlepool 2. Att: 11,081
Sprake, Reaney, Madeley, Johnson, Charlton, Hunter, Giles, Storrie, Belfitt, Bates, Cooper

THIRD ROUND

Leeds 2 (Madeley, Belfitt); West Bromwich Albion 4. Att: 13,455
Harvey, Davey, Bell, Storrie, Madeley, Wright, Weston, Belfitt, Hawkins, Johnson, Cooper.

1966-67

SECOND ROUND

Leeds 1 (Peacock); Newcastle United 0. Att: 18,131
Harvey, Reaney, Bell, Bremner, Charlton, Hunter, Lorimer, Madeley, Peacock, Giles, Johanneson.

THIRD ROUND

Preston 1, Leeds 1 (Storrie)
Sprake, Reaney, Bell, Bremner, Charlton, Madeley, Storrie, E. Gray, Peacock, Giles, Greenhoff.

Replay

Leeds 3 (Lorimer 2, Greenhoff); Preston 0. Att: 17,221
Sprake, Reaney, Bell, Bremner, Charlton, Hunter, O'Grady, Lorimer, Greenhoff, Madeley, Johanneson.

FOURTH ROUND

West Ham United 7, Leeds 0
Harvey, Reaney, Bell, Bremner, Charlton, Hunter, Madeley, Belfitt, Greenhoff (Bates), Giles, O'Grady.

1967-68

SECOND ROUND

Leeds 3 (Lorimer 3); Luton Town 1. Att: 11,473
Sprake, Reaney, Bell, Bremner, Charlton, Hunter, Lorimer, Belfitt (Johnson), Greenhoff, E. Gray, Cooper.

THIRD ROUND

Leeds 3 (Charlton, Johanneson, Greenhoff); Bury 0. Att: 20,927
Sprake, Reaney, Madeley, E. Gray, Charlton, Hunter, Greenhoff, Lorimer, Belfitt, Johnson, Johanneson.

FOURTH ROUND

Sunderland 0, Leeds 2 (Greenhoff 2)
Sprake, Reaney, Cooper, Bremner, Madeley, Hunter, Greenhoff, Belfitt, Hawkins (Bates), E. Gray, Hibbitt.

QUARTER FINAL

Leeds 2 (Bremner, Lorimer); Stoke City 0. Att: 24,558
Sprake, Reaney, Cooper, Bremner, Charlton, Hunter, Lorimer, Belfitt, Greenhoff, E. Gray (Bates), Hibbitt.

SEMI-FINAL

FIRST LEG

Derby County 0, Leeds 1 (Giles)
Sprake, Reaney, Cooper, Bremner, Charlton, Hunter, Greenhoff, Lorimer, Madeley, Giles, E. Gray.

SECOND LEG

Leeds 3 (Belfitt 2, E. Gray); Derby County 2. Att: 29,367

FINAL

at Wembley

Arsenal 0, Leeds 1 (Cooper)
Sprake, Reaney, Cooper, Bremner, Charlton, Hunter, Greenhoff, Lorimer, Madeley, Giles, E. Gray.

1968-69

SECOND ROUND

Leeds 1 (Jones); Charlton 0. Att: 18,860
Sprake, Reaney, Cooper, Bremner, Charlton, Hunter, Lorimer, Belfitt (Bates), Jones, Hibbitt, O'Grady.

THIRD ROUND

Leeds 2 (Johanneson, Jones); Bristol City 1. Att: 16,359
Sprake, Reaney, Cooper, Bremner, Madeley, E. Gray, O'Grady, Lorimer, Jones, Giles, Johanneson.

FOURTH ROUND

Crystal Palace 2, Leeds 1 (Madeley)
Sprake, Reaney, Cooper, E. Gray, Charlton, Hunter, O'Grady, Giles, Jones, Madeley, Lorimer.

1969-70

SECOND ROUND

Fulham 0, Leeds 1 (Charlton)
Harvey, Reaney, Cooper, Madeley, Charlton, E. Gray, Lorimer, Bates, Jones, Belfitt, Hibbitt.

THIRD ROUND

United 1 (Madeley); Chelsea 1. Att: 21,933
Sprake, Reaney, Cooper, Bremner, Madeley, Hunter, Lorimer, Belfitt, Jones, Giles, Hibbitt (Bates).

Replay

Chelsea 2, Leeds 0
Harvey, Reaney, Cooper, Bremner, Charlton, Hunter, Lorimer, Belfitt, Jones, Madeley, E. Gray.

1970-71

SECOND ROUND

Sheffield United 1, Leeds 0
Sprake, Madeley, Cooper, Bremner, Charlton (Belfitt), Hunter, Lorimer, Clarke, Jones, Bates, E. Gray.

1971-72

SECOND ROUND

Derby County 0, Leeds 0
Harvey, Reaney, Yorath, Bremner, Charlton, Hunter, Lorimer, Clarke, Belfitt, Giles, Madeley.

Replay

Leeds 2 (Lorimer 2); Derby County 0. Att: 29,132
Sprake, Reaney, Cooper, Bremner (Mann), Charlton, Hunter, Lorimer, Yorath, Belfitt, Giles, Madeley.

THIRD ROUND

West Ham United 0, Leeds 0
Sprake, Davey, Cooper, Bremner, Charlton, Hunter, Lorimer, Yorath, Belfitt, Giles, Madeley.

Replay

Leeds 0, West Ham 1 (after extra time). Att: 26,504
Harvey, Reaney, Cooper, Bremner, Charlton, Hunter, Lorimer, Clarke, Jones (E. Gray), Giles, Madeley.

1972-73

SECOND ROUND

Leeds 4 (Lorimer 2, Jones, Cherry); Burnley 0. Att: 20,857
Harvey, Reaney, Cherry, Bremner, Charlton, Hunter, Lorimer, Bates, Jordan, E. Gray, Galvin (Jones).

THIRD ROUND

Aston Villa 1, Leeds 1 (Charlton)
Harvey, Madeley, Cherry, Bremner, Charlton, Hunter, Lorimer, Clarke, Jones, Bates, Yorath.

Replay

Leeds 2 (Nicholl o.g., Jones); Aston Villa 0. Att: 28,894
Harvey, Madeley, Cherry, Bremner, Charlton (Yorath), Hunter, Lorimer, Clarke, Jones, Bates, E. Gray.

FOURTH ROUND

Liverpool 2, Leeds 2 (Jones, Lorimer)
Harvey, Madeley, Cherry, Bremner, Ellam, Hunter, Lorimer, Clarke, Jones, Bates, E. Gray.

Replay

Leeds 0, Liverpool 1. Att: 34,856
Harvey, Reaney, Cherry, Bremner, Charlton, Hunter, Lorimer, Clarke, Jones, Giles (Jordan), Madeley.

1973-74

SECOND ROUND

Ipswich Town 2, Leeds 0
Harvey, Reaney (O'Neill), Cherry, Bremner, Ellam, Hunter, Liddell, Yorath, Jones, Madeley, F. Gray.

1974-75

SECOND ROUND

Huddersfield Town 1, Leeds 1 (Lorimer)
Harvey, Reaney, Cherry, Bates, McQueen, Hunter, Lorimer, Clarke, Jordan, Giles, Madeley.

Relay

Leeds 1 (Clarke); Huddersfield Town 1. Att: 18,496
Harvey, Reaney, Cherry, Yorath, Madeley, Hunter, Lorimer, Clarke, Jordan, Giles (Bates), McKenzie.

Second replay at Elland road

Leeds 2 (Bates, Lorimer); Huddersfield Town 1. Att: 14,599
Harvey, Reaney, Cherry, Yorath, McQueen, Hunter, Lorimer, McKenzie, O'Hare, Bates (F. Gray), Madeley.

THIRD ROUND

Bury 1, Leeds 2 (Lorimer, Cherry)
Stewart, Reaney, Cherry, Bremner (Madeley), McQueen, Hunter, Lorimer, Cooper, Jordan, Yorath, McKenzie.

FOURTH ROUND

Chester 3, Leeds 0
Harvey, Reaney, Cooper, Yorath, McQueen, Cherry, Lorimer, Clarke, Jordan, Bremner (Bates), Madeley.

1975-76

SECOND ROUND

Leeds 3 (McKenzie, Lorimer, Clarke); Ipswich Town 2. Att: 15,318
Harvey, Cherry, F. Gray, Bremner, Madeley, Hunter, Lorimer, Clarke, McKenzie, Yorath, E. Gray.

THIRD ROUND

Leeds 0, Notts County 1. Att: 19,122
Harvey, Reaney, Cherry, Bremner, Madeley, Hunter, Lorimer, McNiven (Harris), McKenzie, F. Gray, E. Gray.

1976-77

SECOND ROUND

Stoke City 2, Leeds 1 (Currie)
Stewart, Reaney, F. Gray, Bremner, Madeley, Hunter, Cherry, Clarke, Jordan, Currie, Harris.

1977-78

SECOND ROUND

Rochdale 0, Leeds 3 (Jordan, Harris, Cherry)
Stewart, Reaney, F. Gray, Madeley, McQueen, Cherry, Lorimer, Hankin, Jordan, Currie, Graham (Harris).

THIRD ROUND

Leeds 4 (Jordan, Graham, Lorimer, Hankin); Colchester 0. Att: 17,713
Harvey, Cherry, F. Gray, Lorimer, Parkinson, Madeley, Graham, Hankin, Jordan, E. Gray, Harris.

FOURTH ROUND

Bolton Wanderers 1, Leeds 3 (Graham, Jordan, F. Gray)
Harvey, Reaney, F. Gray, Currie, Parkinson, Madeley, Harris, Hankin (Hampton), Jordan, Cherry, Graham.

QUARTER FINAL

Leeds 4 (Currie, Lorimer 2, E. Gray); Everton 1. Att: 35,020
Harvey, Reaney, F. Gray, Lorimer, Parkinson, Madeley, Cherry, Hankin, Currie, E. Gray, Graham.

SEMI-FINAL

FIRST LEG

Leeds 1 (E. Gray); Nottingham Forest 3. Att: 43,222
Harvey, Reaney, F. Gray, Lorimer (Harris), Parkinson, Madeley, Cherry, Hankin, Currie, E. Gray, Graham.

SECOND LEG

Nottingham Forest 4, Leeds 2 (F. Gray, Graham)
Stewart, Reaney, Hampton, Cherry, F. Gray, Madeley, E. Gray, Hankin, Currie, Clarke, Graham.

1978-79

SECOND ROUND

West Bromwich Albion 0, Leeds 0
Stewart, Madeley, F. Gray, Flynn, Hart, Stevenson, Hampton, Hankin, Hawley, Currie, Graham.

Replay

Leeds 0, West Bromwich Albion 0. Att: 29,316
Stewart, Stevenson, F. Gray, Flynn, Hart, Madeley, Cherry, Hankin, Hawley, Currie (E. Gray), Graham.

Second replay at Main Road

Leeds 1 (Hart); West Bromwich Albion 0
Harvey, Stevenson, Cherry, Flynn, Hart, Madeley, Thomas (Lorimer), Hinkin, E. Gray, F. Gray, Graham.

THIRD ROUND

Sheffield United 1, Leeds 4 (Currie, F. Gray, E. Gray 2)
Harvey, Stevenson, Cherry, Flynn, Hart, Hampton, E. Gray, Hankin, F. Gray, Currie, Graham.

FOURTH ROUND

Queens Park Rangers 0, Leeds 2 (Hawley, Hankin)
Harvey, Cherry, F. Gray, Flynn, Hart, Madeley, E. Gray, Hankin, Hawley, Currie, Graham.

QUARTER FINAL

Leeds 4 (Cherry, Currie, E. Gray, F. Gray); Luton Town 1. Att: 28,177
Harvey, Cherry, F. Gray, Flynn, Hart, Madeley E. Gray, Hankin, Hawley, Currie, Harris.

SEMI-FINAL

FIRST LEG

Leeds 2 (Currie, Hankin); Southampton 2. Att: 33,415
Harvey, Cherry, F. Gray, Flynn, Hart, Madeley, E. Gray, Hankin, Hawley, Currie, Graham.

SECOND LEG

Southampton 1, Leeds 0
Harvey, Cherry, F. Gray, Flynn, Hart, Madeley, E. Gray, Hankin, Hawley (Harris), Currie, Graham.

1978/79 DIVISION 1

	P	W	D	L	F	A	Pts
Liverpool	42	30	8	4	85	16	68
Nottingham F.	42	21	18	3	61	26	60
West Bromwich A.	42	24	11	7	72	35	59
Everton	42	17	17	8	52	40	51
Leeds Utd	42	18	14	10	70	52	50
Ipswich	42	20	9	13	63	49	49
Arsenal	42	17	4	11	61	48	48
Aston Villa	42	15	16	11	59	49	46
Manchester Utd	42	15	15	12	60	63	45
Coventry	42	14	16	12	58	68	44
Tottenham H.	42	13	15	14	48	61	41
Middlesbrough	42	15	10	17	57	50	40
Bristol City	42	15	10	17	47	51	40
Southampton	42	12	16	14	47	53	40
Manchester City	42	13	13	16	58	56	39
Norwich City	42	7	23	12	51	57	37
Bolton W.	42	12	11	19	54	75	35
Wolverhampton W.	42	13	8	21	44	68	34
Derby County	42	10	11	21	44	71	31
Q.P.R.	42	6	13	23	45	73	25
Birmingham City	42	6	10	26	37	64	22
Chelsea	42	5	10	27	44	92	20

1977/78 DIVISION 1

	P	W	D	L	F	A	Pts
Nottingham F.	42	25	14	3	69	24	64
Liverpool	42	24	9	9	65	34	57
Everton	42	22	11	9	76	45	55
Manchester City	42	20	12	10	74	51	52
Arsenal	42	21	10	11	60	37	52
West Bromwich A.	42	18	14	10	62	53	50
Coventry	42	18	12	12	75	62	48
Aston Villa	42	18	10	14	57	42	46
Leeds United	42	18	10	14	63	53	46
Manchester United	42	16	10	16	67	63	42
Birmingham City	42	16	9	17	55	60	41
Derby County	42	14	13	15	54	59	41
Norwich City	42	11	18	13	52	66	40
Middlesbrough	42	12	15	15	42	54	39
Wolverhampton W.	42	12	12	18	51	64	36
Chelsea	42	11	14	17	46	69	36
Bristol City	42	11	13	18	49	53	35
Ipswich Town	42	11	13	18	47	61	35
Q.P.R.	42	9	15	18	47	64	33
West Ham United	42	12	8	22	52	69	32
Newcastle United	42	6	10	26	42	78	22
Leicester City	42	5	12	25	26	70	22

1976/77 DIVISION 1

	P	W	D	L	F	A	Pts
Liverpool	42	23	11	8	62	33	57
Manchester City	42	21	14	7	60	34	56
Ipswich T	42	22	8	12	66	39	52
Aston Villa	42	22	7	13	76	50	51
Newcastle United	42	18	13	11	64	49	49
Manchester United	42	18	11	13	71	62	47
West Bromwich A.	42	16	13	13	62	56	45
Arsenal	42	16	11	15	64	59	43
Everton	42	14	14	14	62	64	42
Leeds United	42	15	12	15	48	51	42
Leicester C.	42	12	18	12	47	60	42
Middlesboro	42	14	13	15	40	44	41
Birmingham C.	42	13	12	17	63	61	38
Q.P.R.	42	13	12	17	47	52	38
Derby C.	42	9	19	14	50	55	37
Norwich C.	42	14	9	19	47	64	37
West Ham United	42	11	14	17	46	65	36
Bristol City	42	11	13	18	38	48	35
Coventry City	42	10	15	17	48	59	35
Sunderland	42	11	12	19	46	54	34
Stoke City	42	10	14	18	28	51	34
Tottenham H.	42	12	9	21	48	72	33

1975/76 DIVISION 1

	P	W	D	L	F	A	Pts
Liverpool	42	23	5	14	66	31	60
Queens Park R.	42	24	7	11	67	33	59
Manchester U.	42	23	9	10	68	42	56
Derby Co.	42	21	10	11	75	58	53
Leeds United	42	21	12	9	65	46	51
Ipswich T.	42	16	12	14	54	48	46
Leicester C.	42	13	10	19	48	51	45
Manchester C.	42	16	15	11	64	46	43
Tottenham H.	42	14	13	15	63	63	43
Norwich C.	42	16	16	10	58	58	42
Everton	42	15	15	12	60	66	42
Stoke C.	42	15	16	11	48	50	41
Middlesbrough	42	15	17	10	46	45	40
Coventry C.	42	13	15	14	47	57	40
Newcastle U.	42	15	18	9	71	62	39
Aston Villa	42	11	14	17	51	59	39
Arsenal	42	13	19	10	47	53	36
West Ham U.	42	13	19	10	48	71	36
Birmingham C.	42	13	22	7	57	75	33
Wolverhampton W.	42	10	22	10	51	68	30
Burnley	42	9	23	10	43	66	28
Sheffield U.	42	6	26	10	33	82	22

1974/75 DIVISION 1

	P	W	D	L	F	A	Pts.
Derby Co.	42	21	11	10	67	49	53
Liverpool	42	20	11	11	60	39	51
Ipswich T.	42	23	5	14	66	44	51
Everton	42	16	18	8	56	42	50
Stoke C.	42	17	15	10	64	48	49
Sheffield U.	42	18	13	11	58	51	49
Middlesbrough	42	18	12	12	54	40	48
Manchester C.	42	18	10	14	54	54	46
Leeds U.	42	16	13	13	57	49	45
Burnley	42	17	11	14	68	67	45
Q.P.R.	42	16	10	16	54	54	42
Wolverhampton W.	42	14	11	17	57	54	39
West Ham U.	42	13	13	16	58	59	39
Coventry C.	42	12	15	15	51	62	39
Newcastle U.	42	15	9	18	59	72	39
Arsenal	42	13	11	18	47	49	37
Birmingham C.	42	14	9	19	53	61	37
Leicester C.	42	12	12	18	46	60	36
Tottenham H.	42	13	8	21	52	63	34
Luton T.	42	11	11	20	47	65	33
Chelsea	42	9	15	18	42	72	33
Carlisle U.	42	12	5	25	43	59	29

1973/74 DIVISION 1

	P	W	D	L	F	A	Pts.
Leeds U.	42	24	14	4	66	31	62
Liverpool	42	22	13	7	52	31	57
Derby Co.	42	17	14	11	52	42	48
Ipswich T.	42	18	11	13	67	58	47
Stoke C.	42	15	16	11	54	42	46
Burnley	42	16	14	12	56	53	46
Everton	42	16	12	14	50	48	44
Q.P.R.	42	13	17	12	56	52	43
Leicester C.	42	13	16	13	51	41	42
Arsenal	42	14	14	14	49	51	42
Tottenham H.	42	14	14	14	45	50	42
Wolverhampton W.	42	13	15	14	49	49	41
Sheffield U.	42	14	12	16	44	49	40
Manchester C.	42	14	12	16	39	46	40
Newcastle U.	42	13	12	17	49	48	38
Coventry C.	42	14	10	18	43	54	38
Chelsea	42	12	13	17	56	60	37
West Ham U.	42	11	15	16	55	60	37
Birmingham C.	42	12	13	17	52	64	37
Southampton	42	11	14	17	47	68	36
Manchester U.	42	10	12	20	38	48	32
Norwich C.	42	7	15	20	37	62	29

1972/73 DIVISION 1

	P	W	D	L	F	A	Pts.
Liverpool	42	25	10	7	72	42	60
Arsenal	42	23	11	8	57	43	57
Leeds U.	42	21	11	10	71	45	53
Ipswich T.	42	17	14	11	55	45	48
Wolverhampton W.	42	18	11	13	66	54	47
West Ham U.	42	17	12	13	67	53	46
Derby Co.	42	19	8	15	56	54	46
Tottenham H.	42	16	13	13	58	48	45
Newcastle U.	42	16	13	13	60	51	45
Birmingham C.	42	15	12	15	53	54	42
Manchester C.	42	15	11	16	57	60	41
Chelsea	42	13	14	15	49	51	40
Southampton	42	11	18	13	47	52	40
Sheffield U.	42	15	10	17	51	59	40
Stoke C.	42	14	10	18	61	56	38
Leicester C.	42	10	17	15	40	46	37
Everton	42	13	11	18	41	49	37
Manchester U.	42	12	13	17	44	60	37
Coventry C.	42	13	9	20	40	55	35
Norwich C.	42	11	10	21	36	63	32
Crystal Palace	42	9	12	21	41	58	30
W.B.A.	42	9	10	23	38	62	28

1971/72 DIVISION 1

	P	W	D	L	F	A	Pts.
Derby Co.	42	24	10	8	69	33	58
Leeds U.	42	24	9	9	73	31	57
Liverpool	42	24	9	9	64	30	57
Manchester C.	42	23	11	8	77	45	57
Arsenal	42	22	8	12	58	40	52
Tottenham H.	42	19	13	10	63	42	51
Chelsea	42	18	12	12	58	49	48
Manchester U.	42	19	10	13	69	61	48
Wolverhampton W.	42	18	11	13	65	57	47
Sheffield U.	42	17	12	13	61	60	46
Newcastle U.	42	15	11	16	49	52	41
Leicester C.	42	13	13	16	41	46	39
Ipswich T.	42	11	16	15	39	53	38
West Ham U.	42	12	12	18	47	51	36
Everton	42	9	18	15	37	48	36
W.B.A.	42	12	11	19	42	54	35
Stoke C.	42	10	15	17	39	56	35
Coventry C.	42	9	15	18	44	67	33
Southampton	42	12	7	23	52	80	31
Crystal Palace	42	8	13	21	39	65	29
Nottingham F.	42	8	9	25	47	81	25
Huddersfield T.	42	6	13	23	27	59	25

1970/71 DIVISION 1

	P	W	D	L	F	A	Pts.
Arsenal	42	29	7	6	71	29	65
Leeds U.	42	27	10	5	72	30	64
Tottenham H.	42	19	14	9	54	33	52
Wolverhampton W.	42	22	8	12	64	54	52
Liverpool	42	17	17	8	42	24	51
Chelsea	42	18	15	9	52	42	51
Southampton	42	17	12	13	56	44	46
Manchester U.	42	16	11	15	65	66	43
Derby Co.	42	16	10	16	56	54	42
Coventry C.	42	16	10	16	37	38	42
Manchester C.	42	12	17	13	47	42	41
Newcastle U.	42	14	13	15	44	46	41
Stoke C.	42	12	13	17	44	48	37
Everton	42	12	13	17	54	60	37
Huddersfield T.	42	11	14	17	40	49	36
Nottingham F.	42	14	8	20	42	61	36
W.B.A.	42	10	15	17	58	75	35
C. Palace	42	12	11	19	39	57	35
Ipswich T.	42	12	10	20	42	48	34
West Ham U.	42	10	14	18	47	60	34
Burnley	42	7	13	22	29	63	27
Blackpool	42	4	15	23	34	66	23

1969/70 DIVISION 1

	P	W	D	L	F	A	Pts.
Everton	42	29	8	5	72	34	66
Leeds U.	42	21	15	6	84	49	57
Chelsea	42	21	13	8	70	50	55
Derby Co.	42	22	9	11	64	37	53
Liverpool	42	20	11	11	65	42	51
Coventry	42	19	11	12	58	48	49
Newcastle U.	42	17	13	12	57	35	47
Manchester U.	42	14	17	11	66	61	45
Stoke C.	42	15	15	12	56	52	45
Manchester C.	42	16	11	15	55	48	43
Tottenham H.	42	17	9	16	54	55	43
Arsenal	42	12	18	12	51	49	42
Wolverhampton W.	42	12	16	14	55	57	40
Burnley	42	12	15	15	56	61	39
Nottingham F.	42	10	18	14	50	71	38
W.B.A.	42	14	9	19	58	66	37
West Ham U.	42	12	12	18	51	60	36
Ipswich T.	42	10	11	21	40	63	31
Southampton	42	6	17	19	46	67	29
C. Palace	42	6	15	21	34	68	27
Sunderland	42	6	14	22	30	68	26
Sheffield W.	42	8	9	25	40	71	25

1968/69 DIVISION 1

	P	W	D	L	F	A	Pts.
Leeds U.	42	27	13	2	66	26	67
Liverpool	42	25	11	6	63	24	61
Everton	42	21	15	6	77	36	57
Arsenal	42	22	12	8	56	27	56
Chelsea	42	20	10	12	73	53	50
Tottenham H.	42	14	17	11	61	51	45
Southampton	42	16	13	13	57	48	45
West Ham U.	42	13	18	11	66	50	44
Newcastle U.	42	15	14	13	61	55	44
W.B.A.	42	16	11	15	64	67	43
Manchester U.	42	15	12	15	57	53	42
Ipswich T.	42	15	11	16	59	60	41
Manchester C.	42	15	10	17	64	55	40
Burnley	42	15	9	18	55	82	39
Sheffield W.	42	10	16	16	41	54	36
Wolverhampton W.	42	10	15	17	41	58	35
Sunderland	42	11	12	19	43	67	34
Nottingham F.	42	10	13	19	45	57	33
Stoke C.	42	9	15	18	40	63	33
Coventry C.	42	10	11	21	46	64	31
Leicester C.	42	9	12	21	39	68	30
Q.P.R.	42	4	10	28	39	95	18

1967/68 DIVISION 1

	P	W	D	L	F	A	Pts.
Manchester C.	42	26	6	10	86	43	58
Manchester U.	42	24	8	10	89	55	56
Liverpool	42	22	11	9	71	40	55
Leeds U.	42	22	9	11	71	41	53
Everton	42	23	6	13	67	40	52
Chelsea	42	18	12	12	62	68	48
Tottenham H.	42	19	9	14	70	59	47
W.B.A.	42	17	12	13	75	62	46
Arsenal	42	17	10	15	60	56	44
Newcastle U.	42	13	15	14	54	67	41
Nottingham F.	42	14	11	17	52	64	39
West Ham U.	42	14	10	18	73	69	38
Leicester C.	42	13	12	17	64	69	38
Burnley	42	14	10	18	64	71	38
Sunderland	42	13	11	18	51	61	37
Southampton	42	13	11	18	66	83	37
Wolverhampton W.	42	14	8	20	66	75	36
Stoke C.	42	14	7	21	50	73	35
Sheffield W.	42	11	12	19	51	63	34
Coventry C.	42	9	15	18	51	71	33
Sheffield U.	42	11	10	21	49	70	32
Fulham	42	10	7	25	56	98	27

1966/67 DIVISION 1

	P	W	D	L	F	A	Pts.
Manchester U.	42	24	12	6	84	45	60
Nottingham F.	42	23	10	9	64	41	56
Tottenham H.	42	24	8	10	71	48	56
Leeds U.	42	22	11	9	62	42	55
Liverpool	42	19	13	10	64	47	51
Everton	42	19	10	13	65	46	48
Arsenal	42	16	14	12	58	47	46
Leicester C.	42	18	8	16	78	71	44
Chelsea	42	15	14	13	67	62	44
Sheffield U.	42	16	10	16	52	59	42
Sheffield W.	42	14	13	15	56	47	41
Stoke C.	42	17	7	18	63	58	41
W.B.A.	42	16	7	19	77	73	39
Burnley	42	15	9	18	66	76	39
Manchester C.	42	12	15	15	43	52	39
West Ham U.	42	14	8	20	80	84	36
Sunderland	42	14	8	20	58	72	36
Fulham	42	11	12	19	71	83	34
Southampton	42	14	6	22	74	92	34
Newcastle U.	42	12	9	21	39	81	33
Aston Villa	42	11	7	24	54	85	29
Blackpool	42	6	9	27	41	76	21

1965/66 DIVISION 1

	P	W	D	L	F	A	Pts.
Liverpool	42	26	9	7	79	34	61
Leeds U.	42	23	9	10	79	38	55
Burnley	42	24	7	11	79	47	55
Manchester U.	42	18	15	9	84	59	51
Chelsea	42	22	7	13	65	53	51
W.B.A.	42	19	12	11	91	69	50
Leicester C.	42	21	7	14	80	65	49
Tottenham H.	42	16	12	14	75	66	44
Sheffield U.	42	16	11	15	56	59	43
Stoke C.	42	15	12	15	65	64	42
Everton	42	15	11	16	56	62	41
West Ham U.	42	15	9	18	70	83	39
Blackpool	42	14	9	19	55	65	37
Arsenal	42	12	13	17	62	75	37
Newcastle U.	42	14	9	19	50	63	37
Aston Villa	42	15	6	21	69	80	36
Sheffield W.	42	14	8	20	56	66	36
Nottingham F.	42	14	8	20	56	72	36
Sunderland	42	14	8	20	51	72	36
Fulham	42	14	7	21	67	85	35
Northampton T.	42	10	13	19	55	92	33
Blackburn R.	42	8	4	30	57	88	20

1964/65 DIVISION 1

	P	W	D	L	F	A	Pts.
Manchester U.	42	26	9	7	89	39	61
Leeds U.	42	26	9	7	83	52	61
Chelsea	42	24	8	10	89	54	56
Everton	42	17	15	10	69	60	49
Nottingham F.	42	17	13	12	71	67	47
Tottenham H.	42	19	7	16	87	71	45
Liverpool	42	17	10	15	67	73	44
Sheffield W.	42	16	11	15	57	55	43
West Ham U.	42	19	4	19	82	71	42
Blackburn R.	42	16	10	16	83	79	42
Stoke C.	42	16	10	16	67	66	42
Burnley	42	16	10	16	70	70	42
Arsenal	42	17	7	18	69	75	41
W.B.A.	42	13	13	16	70	65	39
Sunderland	42	14	9	19	64	74	37
Aston Villa	42	16	5	21	57	82	37
Blackpool	42	12	11	19	67	78	35
Leicester C.	42	11	13	18	69	85	35
Sheffield U.	42	12	11	19	50	64	35
Fulham	42	11	12	19	60	78	34
Wolverhampton W.	42	13	4	25	59	89	30
Birmingham C.	42	8	11	23	64	96	27

1963/64 DIVISION 2

	P	W	D	L	F	A	Pts.
Leeds U.	42	24	15	3	71	34	63
Sunderland	42	25	11	6	81	37	61
Preston N.E.	42	23	10	9	79	54	56
Charlton Ath.	42	19	10	13	76	70	48
Southampton	42	19	9	14	100	73	47
Manchester C.	42	18	10	14	84	66	46
Rotherham U.	42	19	7	16	90	78	45
Newcastle U.	42	20	5	17	74	69	45
Portsmouth	42	16	11	15	79	70	43
Middlesbrough	42	15	11	16	67	52	41
Northampton T.	42	16	9	17	58	60	41
Huddersfield T.	42	15	10	17	57	64	40
Derby Co.	42	14	11	17	56	67	39
Swindon T.	42	14	10	18	57	69	38
Cardiff C.	42	14	10	18	56	81	38
Leyton O.	42	13	10	19	54	72	36
Norwich C.	42	11	13	18	64	80	35
Bury	42	13	9	20	57	73	35
Swansea	42	12	9	21	63	74	33
Plymouth Arg.	42	8	16	18	45	67	32
Grimsby T.	42	9	14	19	47	75	32
Scunthorpe U	42	10	10	22	52	82	30

1962/63 DIVISION 2

	P	W	D	L	F	A	Pts.
Stoke C.	42	20	13	9	73	50	53
Chelsea	42	24	4	14	81	42	52
Sunderland	42	20	12	10	84	55	52
Middlesbrough	42	20	9	13	86	85	49
Leeds U.	42	19	10	13	79	53	48
Huddersfield T.	42	17	14	11	63	50	48
Newcastle U.	42	18	11	13	79	59	47
Bury	42	18	11	13	51	47	47
Scunthorpe U.	42	16	12	14	57	59	44
Cardiff C.	42	18	7	17	83	73	42
Southampton	42	17	8	17	72	67	42
Plymouth Arg.	42	15	12	15	76	73	42
Norwich C.	42	17	8	17	80	79	42
Rotherham U.	42	17	6	19	67	74	40
Swansea	42	15	9	18	51	72	39
Portsmouth	42	13	11	18	63	79	37
Preston N.E.	42	13	11	18	59	74	37
Derby Co.	42	12	12	18	61	72	36
Grimsby T.	42	11	13	18	55	66	35
Charlton Ath.	42	13	5	24	62	94	31
Walsall	42	11	9	22	53	89	31
Luton T.	42	11	7	24	61	84	29

1961/62 DIVISION 2

	P	W	D	L	F	A	Pts.
Liverpool	42	27	8	7	99	43	62
Leyton O.	42	22	10	10	69	40	54
Sunderland	42	22	9	11	85	50	53
Scunthorpe U.	42	21	7	14	86	71	49
Plymouth Arg.	42	19	8	15	75	75	46
Southampton	42	18	9	15	77	62	45
Huddersfield T.	42	16	12	14	67	59	44
Stoke C.	42	17	8	17	55	57	42
Rotherham U.	42	16	9	17	70	76	41
Preston N.E.	42	15	10	17	55	57	40
Newcastle U.	42	15	9	18	64	58	39
Middlesbrough	42	16	7	19	76	72	39
Luton T.	42	17	5	20	69	71	39
Walsall	42	14	11	17	70	75	39
Charlton Ath.	42	15	9	18	69	75	39
Derby Co.	42	14	11	17	68	75	39
Norwich C.	42	14	11	17	61	70	39
Bury	42	17	5	20	52	76	39
Leeds U.	42	12	12	18	50	61	36
Swansea T.	42	12	12	18	61	83	36
Bristol R.	42	13	7	22	53	81	33
Brighton	42	10	11	21	42	86	31

1960/61 DIVISION 2

	P	W	D	L	F	A	Pts.
Ipswich T.	42	26	7	9	100	55	59
Sheffield U.	42	26	6	10	81	51	58
Liverpool	42	21	10	11	87	58	52
Norwich C.	42	20	9	13	70	53	49
Middlesbrough	42	18	12	12	83	74	48
Sunderland	42	17	13	12	75	60	47
Swindon T.	42	18	11	13	77	73	47
Southampton	42	18	8	16	84	81	44
Scunthorpe U.	42	14	15	13	69	64	43
Charlton Ath.	42	16	11	15	97	91	43
Plymouth Arg.	42	17	8	17	81	82	42
Derby Co.	42	15	10	17	80	80	40
Luton T.	42	15	9	18	71	79	39
Leeds U.	42	14	10	18	75	83	38
Rotherham U.	42	12	13	17	65	64	37
Brighton	42	14	9	19	61	75	37
Bristol R.	42	15	7	20	73	92	37
Stoke C.	42	12	12	18	51	59	36
Leyton O.	42	14	8	20	55	78	36
Huddersfield T.	42	13	9	20	62	71	35
Portsmouth	42	11	11	20	64	91	33
Lincoln C.	42	8	8	26	48	95	24

DIVISION 1

	P	W	D	L	F	A	Pts.
Burnley	42	24	7	11	85	61	55
Wolverhampton W.	42	24	6	12	106	67	54
Tottenham H.	42	21	11	10	86	50	53
W.B.A.	42	19	11	12	83	57	49
Sheffield W.	42	19	11	12	80	59	49
Bolton W.	42	20	8	14	59	51	48
Manchester U.	42	19	7	16	102	80	45
Newcastle U.	42	18	8	16	82	78	44
Preston N.E.	42	16	12	14	79	76	44
Fulham	42	17	10	15	73	80	44
Blackpool	42	15	10	17	59	71	40
Leicester C.	42	13	13	16	66	75	39
Arsenal	42	15	9	18	68	80	39
West Ham U.	42	16	6	20	75	91	38
Manchester C.	42	17	3	22	78	84	37
Everton	42	13	11	18	73	78	37
Blackburn R.	42	16	5	21	60	70	37
Chelsea	42	14	9	19	76	91	37
Birmingham C.	42	13	10	19	63	80	36
Nottingham F.	42	13	9	20	50	74	35
Leeds U.	42	12	10	20	65	92	34
Luton T.	42	9	12	21	50	73	30

1958/59 DIVISION 1

	P	W	D	L	F	A	Pts.
Wolverhampton W.	42	28	5	9	110	49	61
Manchester U.	42	24	7	11	103	66	55
Arsenal	42	21	8	13	88	68	50
Bolton W.	42	20	10	12	79	66	50
W.B.A.	42	18	13	11	88	68	49
West Ham U.	42	21	6	15	85	70	48
Burnley	42	19	10	13	81	70	48
Blackpool	42	18	11	13	66	49	47
Birmingham C.	42	20	6	16	84	68	46
Blackburn R.	42	17	10	15	76	70	44
Newcastle U.	42	17	7	18	80	80	41
Preston N.E.	42	17	7	18	70	77	41
Nottingham F.	42	17	6	19	71	74	40
Chelsea	42	18	4	20	77	98	40
Leeds U.	42	15	9	18	57	74	39
Everton	42	17	4	21	71	87	38
Luton T.	42	12	13	17	68	71	37
Tottenham H.	42	13	10	19	85	95	36
Leicester C.	42	11	10	21	67	98	32
Manchester C.	42	11	9	22	64	95	31
Aston Villa	42	11	8	23	58	87	30
Portsmouth	42	6	9	27	64	112	21

1957/58 DIVISION 1

	P	W	D	L	F	A	Pts.
Wolverhampton W.	42	28	8	6	103	47	64
Preston N.E.	42	26	7	9	100	51	59
Tottenham H.	42	21	9	12	93	77	51
W.B.A.	42	18	14	10	92	70	50
Manchester C.	42	22	5	15	104	100	49
Burnley	42	21	5	16	80	74	47
Blackpool	42	19	6	17	80	67	44
Luton T.	42	19	6	17	69	63	44
Manchester U.	42	16	11	15	85	75	43
Nottingham F.	42	16	10	16	69	63	42
Chelsea	42	15	12	15	83	79	42
Arsenal	42	16	7	19	73	85	39
Birmingham C.	42	14	11	17	76	89	39
Aston Villa	42	16	7	19	73	86	39
Bolton W.	42	14	10	18	65	87	38
Everton	42	13	11	18	65	75	37
Leeds U.	42	14	9	19	51	63	37
Leicester C.	42	14	5	23	91	112	33
Newcastle U.	42	12	8	22	73	81	32
Portsmouth	42	12	8	22	73	88	32
Sunderland	42	10	12	20	54	97	32
Sheffield W.	42	12	7	23	69	92	31

1956/57 DIVISION 1

	P	W	D	L	F	A	Pts.
Manchester U.	42	28	8	6	103	54	64
Tottenham H.	42	22	12	8	104	56	56
Preston N.E.	42	23	10	9	84	56	56
Blackpool	42	22	9	11	93	65	53
Arsenal	42	21	8	13	85	69	50
Wolverhampton W.	42	20	8	14	94	70	48
Burnley	42	18	10	14	56	50	46
Leeds U.	42	15	14	13	72	63	44
Bolton W.	42	16	12	14	65	65	44
Aston Villa	42	14	15	13	65	55	43
W.B.A.	42	14	14	14	59	61	42
Birmingham C.*	42	15	9	18	69	69	39
Chelsea*	42	13	13	16	73	73	39
Sheffield W.	42	16	6	20	82	88	38
Everton	42	14	10	18	61	79	38
Luton T.	42	14	9	19	58	76	37
Newcastle U.	42	14	8	20	67	87	36
Manchester C.	42	13	9	20	78	88	35
Portsmouth	42	10	13	19	62	92	33
Sunderland	42	12	8	22	67	88	32
Cardiff C.	42	10	9	23	53	88	29
Charlton Ath.	42	9	4	29	62	120	22

1955/56 DIVISION 2

	P	W	D	L	F	A	Pts.
Sheffield W.	42	21	13	8	101	62	55
Leeds U.	42	23	6	13	80	60	52
Liverpool	42	21	6	15	85	63	48
Blackburn R.	42	21	6	15	84	65	48
Leicester C.	42	21	6	15	94	78	48
Bristol R.	42	21	6	15	84	70	48
Nottingham F.	42	19	9	14	68	63	47
Lincoln C.	42	18	10	14	79	65	46
Fulham	42	20	6	16	89	79	46
Swansea T.	42	20	6	16	83	81	46
Bristol C.	42	19	7	16	80	64	45
Port Vale	42	16	13	13	60	58	45
Stoke C.	42	20	4	18	71	62	44
Middlesbrough	42	16	8	18	76	78	40
Bury	42	16	8	18	86	90	40
West Ham U.	42	14	11	17	74	69	39
Doncaster R.	42	12	11	19	69	96	35
Barnsley	42	11	12	19	47	84	34
Rotherham U.	42	12	9	21	56	75	33
Notts. Co.	42	11	9	22	55	82	31
Plymouth Arg.	42	10	8	24	54	87	28
Hull C.	42	10	6	26	53	97	26

1954/55 DIVISION 2

	P	W	D	L	F	A	Pts.
Birmingham C.	42	22	10	10	92	47	54
Luton T.	42	23	8	11	88	53	54
Rotherham U.	42	25	4	13	94	64	54
Leeds U.	42	23	7	12	70	53	53
Stoke C.	42	21	10	11	69	46	52
Blackburn R.	42	22	6	14	114	79	50
Notts. Co.	42	21	6	15	74	71	48
West Ham U.	42	18	10	14	74	70	46
Bristol R.	42	19	7	16	75	70	45
Swansea T.	42	17	9	16	86	83	43
Liverpool	42	16	10	16	92	96	42
Middlesbrough	42	18	6	18	73	82	42
Bury	42	15	11	16	77	72	41
Fulham	42	14	11	17	76	79	39
Nottingham F.	42	16	7	19	58	62	39
Lincoln C.	42	13	10	19	68	79	36
Port Vale	42	12	11	19	48	71	35
Doncaster R.	42	14	7	21	58	95	35
Hull C.	42	12	10	20	44	69	34
Plymouth Arg.	42	12	7	23	57	82	31
Ipswich T.	42	11	6	25	57	92	28
Derby Co.	42	7	9	26	53	82	23

1953/54 DIVISION 2

	P	W	D	L	F	A	Pts.
Leicester C.	42	23	10	9	97	60	56
Everton	42	20	16	6	92	58	56
Blackburn R.	42	23	9	10	86	50	55
Nottingham F.	42	20	12	10	86	59	52
Rotherham U.	42	21	7	14	80	67	49
Luton T.	42	18	12	12	64	59	48
Birmingham C.	42	18	11	13	78	58	47
Fulham	42	17	10	15	98	85	44
Bristol R.	42	14	16	12	64	58	44
Leeds U.	42	15	13	14	89	81	43
Stoke C.	42	12	17	13	71	60	41
Doncaster R.	42	16	9	17	59	63	41
West Ham U.	42	15	9	18	67	69	39
Notts. Co.	42	13	13	16	54	74	39
Hull C.	42	16	6	20	64	66	38
Lincoln C.	42	14	9	19	65	83	37
Bury	42	11	14	17	54	72	36
Derby Co.	42	12	11	19	64	82	35
Plymouth Arg.	42	9	16	17	65	82	34
Swansea T.	42	13	8	21	58	82	34
Brentford	42	10	11	21	40	78	31
Oldham Ath.	42	8	9	25	40	89	25

1952/53 DIVISION 2

	P	W	D	L	F	A	Pts.
Sheffield U.	42	25	10	7	97	55	60
Huddersfield	42	24	10	8	84	33	58
Luton T.	42	22	8	12	84	49	52
Plymouth Arg.	42	20	9	13	65	60	49
Leicester C.	42	18	12	12	89	74	48
Birmingham C.	42	19	10	13	71	66	48
Nottingham F.	42	18	8	16	77	67	44
Fulham	42	17	10	15	81	71	44
Blackburn R.	42	18	8	16	68	65	44
Leeds U.	42	14	15	13	71	63	43
Swansea T.	42	15	12	15	78	81	42
Rotherham U.	42	16	9	17	75	74	41
Doncaster R.	42	12	16	14	58	64	40
West Ham U.	42	13	13	16	58	60	39
Lincoln C.	42	11	17	14	64	71	39
Everton	42	12	14	16	71	75	38
Brentford	42	13	11	18	59	76	37
Hull C.	42	14	8	20	57	69	36
Notts. Co.	42	14	8	20	60	88	36
Bury	42	13	9	20	53	81	35
Southampton	42	10	13	19	68	85	33
Barnsley	42	5	8	29	47	108	18

1951/52 **DIVISION 2**

	P	W	D	L	F	A	Pts.
Sheffield W.	42	21	11	10	100	66	53
Cardiff C.	42	20	11	11	72	54	51
Birmingham C.	42	21	9	12	67	56	51
Nottingham F.	42	18	13	11	77	62	49
Leicester C.	42	19	9	14	78	64	47
Leeds U.	42	18	11	13	59	57	47
Everton	42	17	10	15	64	58	44
Luton T.	42	16	12	14	77	78	44
Rotherham U.	42	17	8	17	73	71	42
Brentford	42	15	12	15	54	55	42
Sheffield U.	42	18	5	19	90	76	41
West Ham U.	42	15	11	16	67	77	41
Southampton	42	15	11	16	61	73	41
Blackburn R.	42	17	6	19	54	63	40
Notts. Co.	42	16	7	19	71	68	39
Doncaster R.	42	13	12	17	55	60	38
Bury	42	15	7	20	67	69	37
Hull C.	42	13	11	18	60	70	37
Swansea T.	42	12	12	18	72	76	36
Barnsley	42	11	14	17	59	72	36
Coventry C.	42	14	6	22	59	82	34
Q.P.R.	42	11	12	19	52	81	34

1950/51 **DIVISION 2**

	P	W	D	L	F	A	Pts.
Preston N.E.	42	26	5	11	91	49	57
Manchester C.	42	19	14	9	89	61	52
Cardiff C.	42	17	16	9	53	45	50
Birmingham C.	42	20	9	13	64	53	49
Leeds U.	42	20	8	14	63	55	48
Blackburn R.	42	19	8	15	65	66	46
Coventry C.	42	19	7	16	75	59	45
Sheffield U.	42	16	12	14	72	62	44
Brentford	42	18	8	16	75	74	44
Hull C.	42	16	11	15	74	70	43
Doncaster R.	42	15	13	14	64	68	43
Southampton	42	15	13	14	66	73	43
West Ham U.	42	16	10	16	68	69	42
Leicester C.	42	15	11	16	68	58	41
Barnsley	42	15	10	17	74	68	50
Q.P.R.	42	15	10	17	71	82	40
Notts. Co.	42	13	13	16	61	60	39
Swansea T.	42	16	4	22	54	77	36
Luton T.	42	9	14	19	57	70	32
Bury	42	12	8	22	60	86	32
Chesterfield	42	9	12	21	44	69	30
Grimsby T.	42	8	12	22	61	95	28

1949/50 **DIVISION 2**

	P	W	D	L	F	A	Pts.
Tottenham H.	42	27	7	8	81	35	61
Sheffield W.	42	18	16	8	67	48	52
Sheffield U.	42	19	14	9	68	49	52
Southampton	42	19	14	9	64	48	52
Leeds U.	42	17	13	12	54	45	47
Preston N.E.	42	18	9	15	60	49	45
Hull C.	42	17	11	14	64	72	45
Swansea T.	42	17	9	16	53	49	43
Brentford	42	15	13	14	44	49	43
Cardiff C.	42	16	10	16	41	44	42
Grimsby T.	42	16	8	18	74	73	40
Coventry C.	42	13	13	16	55	55	39
Barnsley	42	13	13	16	64	67	39
Chesterfield	42	15	9	18	43	47	39
Leicester C.	42	12	15	15	55	65	39
Blackburn R.	42	14	10	18	55	60	38
Luton T.	42	10	18	14	41	51	38
Bury	42	14	9	19	60	65	37
West Ham U.	42	12	12	18	53	61	36
Q.P.R.	42	11	12	19	40	57	34
Plymouth Arg.	42	8	16	18	44	65	32
Bradford P.A.	42	10	11	21	51	77	31

1948/49 **DIVISION 2**

	P	W	D	L	F	A	Pts.
Fulham	42	24	9	9	77	37	57
W.B.A.	42	24	8	10	69	39	56
Southampton	42	23	9	10	69	36	55
Cardiff C.	42	19	13	10	62	47	51
Tottenham H.	42	17	16	9	72	44	50
Chesterfield	42	15	17	10	51	45	47
West Ham U.	42	18	10	14	56	58	46
Sheffield W.	42	15	13	14	63	56	43
Barnsley	42	14	12	16	62	61	40
Luton T.	42	14	12	16	55	57	40
Grimsby T.	42	15	10	17	72	76	40
Bury	42	17	6	19	67	76	40
Q.P.R.	42	14	11	17	44	62	39
Blackburn R.	42	15	8	19	53	63	38
Leeds U.	42	12	13	17	55	63	37
Coventry C.	42	15	7	20	55	64	37
Bradford P.A.	42	13	11	18	65	78	37
Brentford	42	11	14	17	42	53	36
Leicester C.	42	10	16	16	62	79	36
Plymouth Arg.	42	12	12	18	49	64	36
Nottingham F.	42	14	7	21	50	54	35
Lincoln C.	42	8	12	22	53	91	28

1947/48 **DIVISION 2**

	P	W	D	L	F	A	Pts.
Birmingham C.	42	22	15	5	55	24	59
Newcastle U.	42	24	8	10	72	41	56
Southampton	42	21	10	11	71	53	52
Sheffield W.	42	20	11	11	66	53	51
Cardiff C.	42	18	11	13	61	58	47
West Ham U.	42	16	14	12	55	53	46
W.B.A.	42	18	9	15	63	58	45
Tottenham H.	42	15	14	13	56	43	44
Leicester C.	42	16	11	15	60	57	43
Coventry C.	42	14	13	15	59	52	41
Fulham	42	15	10	17	47	46	40
Barnsley	42	15	10	17	62	64	40
Luton T.	42	14	12	16	56	59	40
Bradford P.A.	42	16	8	18	68	72	40
Brentford	42	13	14	15	44	61	40
Chesterfield	42	16	7	19	54	55	39
Plymouth Arg.	42	9	20	13	40	58	38
Leeds U.	42	14	8	20	62	72	36
Nottingham F.	42	12	11	19	54	60	35
Bury	42	9	16	17	58	68	34
Doncaster R.	42	9	11	22	40	66	29
Millwall	42	9	11	22	44	74	29

1946/47 **DIVISION 1**

	P	W	D	L	F	A	Pts.
Liverpool	42	25	7	10	84	52	57
Manchester U.	42	22	12	8	95	54	46
Wolverhampton W.	42	25	6	11	98	56	56
Stoke C.	42	24	7	11	90	53	55
Blackpool	42	22	6	14	71	70	50
Sheffield U.	42	21	7	14	89	75	49
Preston N.E.	42	18	11	13	76	74	47
Aston Villa	42	18	9	15	67	53	45
Sunderland	42	18	8	16	65	66	44
Everton	42	17	9	16	62	67	43
Middlesbrough	42	17	8	17	73	68	42
Portsmouth	42	16	9	17	66	60	41
Arsenal	42	16	9	17	72	70	41
Derby Co.	42	18	5	19	73	79	41
Chelsea	42	16	7	19	69	84	39
Grimsby T.	42	13	12	17	61	82	38
Blackburn R.	42	14	8	20	45	53	36
Bolton W.	42	13	8	21	57	69	34
Charlton Ath.	42	11	12	19	57	71	34
Huddersfield	42	13	7	22	53	79	33
Brentford	42	9	7	26	45	88	25
Leeds U.	42	6	6	30	45	90	18

1938/39 **DIVISION 1**

	P	W	D	L	F	A	Pts.
Everton	42	27	5	10	88	52	59
Wolverhampton W.	42	22	11	9	88	39	55
Charlton Ath.	42	22	6	14	75	59	50
Middlesbrough	42	20	9	13	93	74	49
Arsenal	42	19	9	14	55	41	47
Derby Co.	42	19	8	15	66	55	46
Stoke C.	42	17	12	13	71	68	46
Bolton W.	42	15	15	12	67	58	45
Preston N.E.	42	16	12	14	63	69	44
Grimsby T.	42	16	11	15	61	69	43
Liverpool	42	14	14	14	62	63	42
Aston Villa	42	15	11	16	71	60	41
Leeds U.	42	16	9	17	59	67	41
Manchester U.	42	11	16	15	57	65	38
Blackpool	42	12	14	16	58	68	38
Sunderland	42	13	12	17	54	67	38
Portsmouth	42	12	13	17	47	70	37
Brentford	42	14	8	20	53	74	36
Huddersfield	42	12	11	19	58	64	35
Chelsea	42	12	9	21	64	80	33
Birmingham	42	12	8	22	62	84	32
Leicester C.	42	9	11	22	48	82	29

1937/38 **DIVISION 1**

	P	W	D	L	F	A	Pts.
Arsenal	42	21	10	11	77	44	52
Wolverhampton W.	42	20	11	11	72	49	51
Preston N.E.	42	16	17	9	64	44	49
Charlton Ath.	42	16	14	12	65	51	46
Middlesbrough	42	19	8	15	72	65	46
Brentford	42	18	9	15	69	59	45
Bolton W.	42	15	15	12	64	60	45
Sunderland	42	14	16	12	55	57	44
Leeds U.	42	14	15	13	64	69	43
Chelsea	42	14	13	15	65	65	41
Liverpool	42	15	11	16	65	71	41
Blackpool	42	16	8	18	61	66	40
Derby Co.	42	15	10	17	66	87	40
Everton	42	16	7	19	79	75	39
Huddersfield	42	17	5	20	55	68	39
Leicester C.	42	14	11	17	54	75	39
Stoke C.	42	13	12	17	58	59	38
Birmingham	42	10	18	14	58	62	38
Portsmouth	42	13	12	17	62	68	38
Grimsby T.	42	13	12	17	51	68	38
Manchester C.	42	14	8	20	80	77	36
W.B.A.	42	14	8	20	74	91	36

1936/37 **DIVISION 1**

	P	W	D	L	F	A	Pts.
Manchester C.	42	22	13	7	107	61	57
Charlton Ath.	42	21	12	9	58	49	54
Arsenal	42	18	16	8	80	49	52
Derby Co.	42	21	7	14	96	90	49
Wolverhampton W.	42	21	5	16	84	67	47
Brentford	42	18	10	14	82	78	46
Middlesbrough	42	19	8	15	74	71	46
Sunderland	42	19	6	17	89	87	44
Portsmouth	42	17	10	15	62	66	44
Stoke C.	42	15	12	15	72	57	42
Birmingham	42	13	15	14	64	60	41
Grimsby T.	42	17	7	18	86	81	41
Chelsea	42	14	13	15	52	55	41
Preston N.E.	42	14	13	15	56	67	41
Huddersfield	42	12	15	15	62	64	39
W.B.A.	42	16	6	20	77	98	38
Everton	42	14	9	19	81	78	37
Liverpool	42	12	11	19	62	84	35
Leeds U.	42	15	4	23	60	80	34
Bolton W.	42	10	14	18	43	66	34
Manchester U.	42	10	12	20	55	78	32
Sheffield W.	42	9	12	21	53	69	30

1935/36 DIVISION 1

	P	W	D	L	F	A	Pts.
Sunderland	42	25	6	11	109	74	56
Derby Co.	42	18	12	12	61	52	48
Huddersfield	42	18	12	12	59	56	48
Stoke C.	42	20	7	15	57	57	47
Brentford	42	17	12	13	81	60	46
Arsenal	42	15	15	12	78	48	45
Preston N.E.	42	18	8	16	67	64	44
Chelsea	42	15	13	14	65	72	43
Manchester C.	42	17	8	17	68	60	42
Portsmouth	42	17	8	17	54	67	42
Leeds U.	42	15	11	16	66	64	41
Birmingham	42	15	11	16	61	63	41
Bolton W.	42	14	13	15	67	76	41
Middlesbrough	42	15	10	17	84	70	40
Wolverhampton W.	42	15	10	17	77	76	40
Everton	42	13	13	16	89	89	39
Grimsby T.	42	17	5	20	65	73	39
W.B.A.	42	16	6	20	89	88	38
Liverpool	42	13	12	17	60	64	38
Sheffield W.	42	13	12	17	63	77	38
Aston Villa	42	13	9	20	81	110	35
Blackburn R.	42	12	9	21	55	96	33

1934/35 DIVISION 1

	P	W	D	L	F	A	Pts.
Arsenal	42	23	12	7	115	46	58
Sunderland	42	19	16	7	90	51	54
Sheffield W.	42	18	13	11	70	64	49
Manchester C.	42	20	8	14	82	67	48
Grimsby T.	42	17	11	14	78	60	45
Derby Co.	42	18	9	15	81	66	45
Liverpool	42	19	7	16	85	88	45
Everton	42	16	12	14	89	88	44
W.B.A.	42	17	10	15	83	83	44
Stoke C.	42	18	6	18	71	70	42
Preston N.E.	42	15	12	15	62	67	42
Chelsea	42	16	9	17	73	82	41
Aston Villa	42	14	13	15	74	88	41
Portsmouth	42	15	10	17	71	72	40
Blackburn R.	42	14	11	17	66	78	39
Huddersfield	42	14	10	18	76	71	38
Wolverhampton W.	42	15	8	19	88	94	38
Leeds U.	42	13	12	17	75	92	38
Birmingham	42	13	10	19	63	81	36
Middlesbrough	42	10	14	18	70	91	34
Leicester C.	42	12	9	21	61	86	33
Tottenham H.	42	10	10	22	54	93	30

1933/34 DIVISION 1

	P	W	D	L	F	A	Pts.
Arsenal	42	25	9	8	75	47	59
Huddersfield	42	23	10	9	90	61	56
Tottenham H.	42	27	7	14	79	56	49
Derby Co.	42	17	11	14	68	54	45
Manchester C.	42	17	11	14	65	72	45
Sunderland	42	16	12	14	81	56	44
W.B.A.	42	17	10	15	78	70	44
Blackburn R.	42	18	7	17	74	81	43
Leeds U.	42	17	8	17	75	66	42
Portsmouth	42	15	12	15	52	55	42
Sheffield W.	42	16	9	17	62	67	41
Stoke C.	42	15	11	16	58	71	41
Aston Villa	42	14	12	16	78	75	40
Everton	42	12	16	14	62	63	40
Wolverhampton W.	42	14	12	16	74	86	40
Middlesbrough	42	16	7	19	68	80	39
Leicester C.	42	14	11	17	59	74	39
Liverpool	42	14	10	18	79	87	38
Chelsea	42	14	8	20	67	69	36
Birmingham	42	12	12	18	54	56	36
Newcastle U.	42	10	14	18	68	77	34
Sheffield U.	42	12	7	23	58	101	31

1932/33 DIVISION 1

	P	W	D	L	F	A	Pts.
Arsenal	42	25	8	9	118	61	58
Aston Villa	42	23	8	11	92	67	54
Sheffield W.	42	21	9	12	80	68	51
W.B.A.	42	20	9	13	83	70	49
Newcastle U.	42	22	5	15	71	63	49
Huddersfield	42	18	11	13	66	53	47
Derby Co.	42	15	14	13	76	69	44
Leeds U.	42	15	14	13	59	62	44
Portsmouth	42	18	7	17	74	76	43
Sheffield U.	42	17	9	16	74	80	43
Everton	42	16	9	17	81	74	41
Sunderland	42	15	10	17	63	80	40
Birmingham	42	14	11	17	57	57	39
Liverpool	42	14	11	17	79	84	39
Blackburn R.	42	14	10	18	76	102	38
Manchester C.	42	16	5	21	68	71	37
Middlesbrough	42	14	9	19	63	73	37
Chelsea	42	14	7	21	63	73	35
Leicester C.	42	11	13	18	75	89	35
Wolverhampton W.	42	13	9	20	80	96	35
Bolton W.	42	12	9	21	78	92	33
Blackpool	42	14	5	23	69	85	33

1931/32 DIVISION 2

	P	W	D	L	F	A	Pts.
Wolverhampton W.	42	24	8	10	115	49	56
Leeds U.	42	22	10	10	78	54	54
Stoke C.	42	19	14	9	69	48	52
Plymouth Arg.	42	20	9	13	100	66	49
Bury	42	21	7	14	70	58	49
Bradford P.A.	42	21	7	14	72	63	49
Bradford C.	42	16	13	13	80	61	45
Tottenham H.	42	16	11	15	87	78	43
Millwall	42	17	9	16	61	61	43
Charlton Ath.	42	17	9	16	61	66	43
Nottingham F.	42	16	10	16	77	72	42
Manchester U.	42	17	8	17	71	72	42
Preston N.E.	42	16	10	16	75	77	42
Southampton	42	17	7	18	66	77	41
Swansea T.	42	16	7	19	73	75	39
Notts. Co.	42	13	12	17	75	75	38
Chesterfield	42	13	11	18	64	86	37
Oldham Ath.	42	13	10	19	62	84	36
Burnley	42	13	9	20	59	87	35
Port Vale	42	13	7	22	58	89	33
Barnsley	42	12	9	21	55	91	33
Bristol C.	42	6	11	25	39	78	23

1930/31 DIVISION 1

	P	W	D	L	F	A	Pts.
Arsenal	42	28	10	4	127	59	66
Aston Villa	42	25	9	8	128	78	59
Sheffield W.	42	22	8	12	102	75	52
Portsmouth	42	18	13	11	84	67	49
Huddersfield	42	18	12	12	81	65	48
Derby Co.	42	18	10	14	94	79	46
Middlesbrough	42	19	8	15	98	90	46
Manchester C.	42	18	10	14	75	70	46
Liverpool	42	15	12	15	86	85	42
Blackburn R.	42	17	8	17	83	84	42
Sunderland	42	16	9	17	89	85	41
Chelsea	42	15	10	17	64	67	40
Grimsby T.	42	17	5	20	82	87	39
Bolton W.	42	15	9	18	68	81	39
Sheffield U.	42	14	10	18	78	84	38
Leicester C.	42	16	6	20	80	95	38
Newcastle U.	42	15	6	21	78	87	36
West Ham U.	42	14	8	20	79	94	36
Birmingham	42	13	10	19	55	70	36
Blackpool	42	11	10	21	71	125	32
Leeds U.	42	12	7	23	68	81	31
Manchester U.	42	7	8	27	53	115	22

1929/30 DIVISION 1

	P	W	D	L	F	A	Pts.
Sheffield W.	42	26	8	8	105	57	60
Derby Co.	42	21	8	13	90	82	50
Manchester C.	42	19	9	14	91	81	47
Aston Villa	42	21	5	16	92	83	47
Leeds U.	42	20	6	16	79	63	46
Blackburn R.	42	19	7	16	99	93	45
West Ham U.	42	19	5	18	86	79	43
Leicester C.	42	17	9	16	86	90	43
Sunderland	42	18	7	17	76	80	43
Huddersfield	42	17	9	16	63	69	43
Birmingham	42	16	9	17	67	62	41
Liverpool	42	16	9	17	63	79	41
Portsmouth	42	15	10	17	66	62	40
Arsenal	42	14	11	17	78	66	39
Bolton W.	42	15	9	18	74	74	39
Middlesbrough	42	16	6	20	82	84	38
Manchester U.	42	15	8	19	67	88	38
Grimsby T.	42	15	7	20	73	89	37
Newcastle U.	42	15	7	20	71	92	37
Sheffield U.	42	15	6	21	91	96	36
Burnley	42	14	8	20	79	97	36
Everton	42	12	11	19	80	92	35

1928/29 DIVISION 1

	P	W	D	L	F	A	Pts.
Sheffield W.	42	21	10	11	86	62	52
Leicester C.	42	21	9	12	96	67	51
Aston Villa	42	23	4	15	98	81	50
Sunderland	42	20	7	15	93	75	47
Liverpool	42	17	12	13	90	64	46
Derby Co.	42	18	10	14	86	71	46
Blackburn R.	42	17	11	14	72	63	45
Manchester C.	42	18	9	15	95	86	45
Arsenal	42	16	13	13	77	72	45
Newcastle U.	42	19	6	17	70	72	44
Sheffield U.	42	15	11	16	86	85	41
Manchester U.	42	14	13	15	66	76	41
Leeds U.	42	16	9	17	71	84	41
Bolton W.	42	14	12	16	73	80	40
Birmingham	42	15	10	17	68	77	40
Huddersfield	42	14	11	17	70	61	39
West Ham U.	42	15	9	18	86	96	39
Everton	42	17	4	21	63	75	38
Burnley	42	15	8	19	81	103	38
Portsmouth	42	15	6	21	56	80	36
Bury	42	12	7	23	62	99	31
Cardiff C.	42	8	13	21	43	59	29

1927/28 DIVISION 2

	P	W	D	L	F	A	Pts.
Manchester C.	42	25	9	8	100	59	59
Leeds U.	42	25	7	10	98	49	57
Chelsea	42	23	8	11	75	45	54
Preston N.E.	42	22	9	11	100	66	53
Stoke C.	42	22	8	12	78	59	52
Swansea T.	42	18	12	12	75	63	48
Oldham Ath.	42	19	8	15	75	51	46
W.B.A.	42	17	12	13	90	70	46
Port Vale	42	18	8	16	68	57	44
Nottingham F.	42	15	10	17	83	84	40
Grimsby T.	42	14	12	16	69	83	40
Bristol C.	42	15	9	18	76	79	39
Hull C.	42	12	15	15	41	54	39
Barnsley	42	14	11	17	65	85	39
Notts Co.	42	13	12	17	68	74	38
Wolverhampton W.	42	13	10	19	63	91	36
Southampton	42	14	7	21	68	77	35
Reading	42	11	13	18	53	75	35
Blackpool	42	13	8	21	83	101	34
Clapton O	42	11	12	19	55	85	34
Fulham	42	13	7	22	68	89	33
South Shields	42	7	9	26	56	111	23

1926/27 DIVISION 1

	P	W	D	L	F	A	Pts.
Newcastle U.	42	25	6	11	96	58	56
Huddersfield	42	17	17	8	76	60	51
Sunderland	42	21	7	14	98	70	49
Bolton W.	42	19	10	13	84	62	48
Burnley	42	19	9	14	91	80	47
West Ham U.	42	19	8	15	86	70	46
Leicester C.	42	17	12	13	85	70	46
Sheffield U.	42	17	10	15	74	86	44
Liverpool	42	18	7	17	69	61	43
Aston Villa	42	18	7	17	81	83	43
Arsenal	42	17	9	16	77	86	43
Derby Co.	42	17	7	18	86	73	41
Tottenham H.	42	16	9	17	76	78	41
Cardiff C.	42	16	9	17	55	65	41
Manchester U.	42	13	14	15	52	64	40
Sheffield W.	42	15	9	18	75	92	39
Birmingham	42	17	4	21	64	73	38
Blackburn R.	42	15	8	19	77	96	38
Bury	42	12	12	18	68	77	36
Everton	42	12	10	20	64	90	34
Leeds U.	42	11	8	23	69	88	30
W.B.A.	42	11	8	23	65	86	30

1925/26 DIVISION 1

	P	W	D	L	F	A	Pts.
Huddersfield	42	23	11	8	92	60	57
Arsenal	42	22	8	12	87	63	52
Sunderland	42	21	6	15	96	80	48
Bury	42	20	7	15	85	77	47
Sheffield U.	42	19	8	15	102	82	46
Aston Villa	42	16	12	14	86	76	44
Liverpool	42	14	16	12	70	63	44
Bolton W.	42	17	10	15	75	76	44
Manchester U.	42	19	6	17	66	73	44
Newcastle U.	42	16	10	16	84	75	42
Everton	42	12	18	12	72	70	42
Blackburn R.	42	15	11	16	91	80	41
W.B.A.	42	16	8	18	79	78	40
Birmingham	42	16	8	18	66	81	40
Tottenham H.	42	15	9	18	66	79	39
Cardiff C.	42	16	7	19	61	76	39
Leicester C.	42	14	10	18	70	80	38
West Ham U.	42	15	7	20	63	76	37
Leeds U.	42	14	8	20	64	76	36
Burnley	42	13	10	19	85	108	36
Manchester C.	42	12	11	19	89	100	35
Notts. Co.	42	13	7	22	54	74	33

1924/25 DIVISION 1

	P	W	D	L	F	A	Pts.
Huddersfield	42	21	16	5	69	28	58
W.B.A.	42	23	10	9	58	34	56
Bolton W.	42	22	11	9	76	34	55
Liverpool	42	20	10	12	63	55	50
Bury	42	17	15	10	54	51	49
Newcastle U.	42	16	16	10	61	42	48
Sunderland	42	19	10	13	64	51	48
Birmingham	42	17	12	13	49	53	46
Notts. Co.	42	16	13	13	42	31	45
Cardiff C.	42	16	11	15	56	51	43
Manchester C.	42	17	9	16	76	68	43
Tottenham H.	42	15	12	15	52	43	42
West Ham U.	42	15	12	15	62	60	42
Sheffield U.	42	13	13	16	55	63	39
Aston Villa	42	13	13	16	58	71	39
Blackburn R.	42	11	13	18	53	66	35
Everton	42	12	11	19	40	60	35
Leeds U.	42	11	12	19	46	59	34
Burnley	42	11	12	19	46	75	34
Arsenal	42	14	5	23	46	58	33
Preston N.E.	42	10	6	26	37	74	26
Nottingham F.	42	6	12	24	29	65	24

1923/24 DIVISION 2

	P	W	D	L	F	A	Pts
Leeds United	42	21	12	9	61	35	54
Bury	42	21	9	12	63	35	51
Derby County	42	21	9	12	75	42	51
Blackpool	42	18	13	11	72	47	49
Southampton	42	17	14	11	52	31	48
Stoke	42	14	18	10	44	42	46
Oldham Ath.	42	14	17	11	45	52	45
Sheffield W.	42	16	12	14	54	51	44
South Shields	42	17	10	15	49	50	44
Clapton O.	42	14	15	13	40	36	43
Barnsley	42	16	11	15	57	61	43
Leicester City	42	17	8	17	64	54	42
Stockport County	42	13	16	13	44	52	42
Manchester Utd	42	13	14	15	52	44	40
C. Palace	42	13	13	16	53	65	39
Port Vale	42	13	12	17	50	66	38
Hull City	42	10	17	15	46	51	37
Bradford City	42	11	15	16	35	48	37
Coventry City	42	11	13	18	52	68	35
Fulham	42	42	10	14	18	45	56
Nelson	42	10	13	19	40	74	33
Bristol City	42	7	15	20	32	65	29

1922/23 DIVISION 2

	P	W	D	L	F	A	Pts
Notts County	42	23	7	12	46	34	53
West Ham United	42	20	11	11	63	38	51
Leicester City	42	21	9	12	65	44	51
Manchester United	42	17	14	11	51	36	48
Blackpool	42	18	11	13	60	43	47
Bury	42	18	11	13	55	46	47
Leeds United	42	18	11	13	43	36	47
Sheffield W.	42	17	12	13	54	47	46
Barnsley	42	17	11	14	62	51	45
Fulham	42	16	12	14	43	32	44
Southampton	42	14	14	14	40	40	42
Hull City	42	14	14	14	43	45	42
South Shields	42	15	10	17	35	44	40
Derby County	42	14	11	17	46	50	39
Bradford City	42	12	13	17	41	45	37
Port Vale	42	14	9	19	39	51	37
Coventry City	42	15	7	20	46	63	37
Clapton O.	42	12	12	18	40	50	36
Stockport Co.	42	14	8	20	43	58	36
Rotherham Co.	42	13	9	20	44	63	35
Wolverhampton W.	42	9	9	24	42	77	27

1921/22 DIVISION 2

	P	W	D	L	F	A	Pts
Nottingham F.	42	22	12	8	51	30	56
Stoke City	42	18	16	8	60	44	52
Barnsley	42	22	8	12	67	52	52
West Ham United	42	20	8	14	52	39	48
Hull City	42	19	10	13	51	41	48
Gateshead	42	17	12	13	43	38	46
Fulham	42	18	9	15	57	38	45
Leeds United	42	16	13	13	48	38	45
Leicester City	42	14	17	11	39	34	45
Sheffield Wednesday	42	15	14	13	47	50	44
Bury	42	15	10	17	54	55	40
Derby County	42	15	9	18	60	64	39
Notts County	42	12	15	15	47	51	39
Crystal Palace	42	13	13	16	45	51	39
Leyton Orient	42	15	9	18	43	50	39
Rotherham United	42	14	11	17	32	43	39
Wolverhampton W.	42	13	11	18	44	49	37
Port Vale	42	14	8	20	43	57	36
Blackpool	42	15	5	22	44	57	35
Coventry City	42	12	10	20	51	60	34
Bradford	42	12	9	21	46	62	33
Bristol City	42	12	9	21	37	58	33

1920/21 DIVISION 2

	P	W	D	L	F	A	Pts
Birmingham City	42	24	10	8	79	38	58
Cardiff City	42	24	10	8	59	32	58
Bristol City	42	19	13	10	49	29	51
Blackpool	42	20	10	12	54	42	50
West Ham United	42	19	10	13	51	30	48
Notts County	42	18	11	13	55	40	47
Leyton Orient	42	16	13	13	43	42	45
Gateshead	42	17	10	15	61	46	44
Fulham	42	16	10	16	43	47	42
Sheffield Wednesday	42	15	11	16	48	48	41
Bury	42	15	10	17	45	49	40
Leicester City	42	12	16	14	39	46	40
Hull City	42	10	20	12	43	53	40
Leeds United	42	14	10	18	40	45	38
Wolverhampton W.	42	16	6	20	49	66	38
Barnsley	42	10	16	16	48	50	36
Port Vale	42	11	14	17	43	49	36
Nottingham F.	42	12	12	18	48	55	36
Rotherham United	42	12	12	18	37	53	36
Stoke City	42	12	11	19	46	56	35
Coventry City	42	12	11	19	39	70	35
Stockport County	42	9	12	21	42	75	30

1919/20 DIVISION 2

	P	W	D	L	F	A	Pts
Tottenham H.	42	32	6	4	102	32	70
Huddersfield Town	42	28	8	6	97	38	64
Birmingham City	42	24	8	10	85	34	56
Blackpool	42	21	10	11	65	47	52
Bury	42	20	8	14	60	44	48
Fulham	42	19	9	14	61	50	47
West Ham United	42	19	9	14	47	40	47
Bristol City	42	13	17	12	46	43	43
Gateshead	42	15	12	15	58	48	42
Stoke City	42	18	6	18	60	54	42
Hull City	42	18	6	18	78	72	42
Barnsley	42	15	10	17	61	55	40
Leeds Utd/Port Vale*	42	16	8	18	59	62	40
Leicester City	42	15	10	17	41	61	40
Leyton Orient	42	16	6	20	51	59	38
Stockport County	42	14	9	19	52	61	37
Rotherham United	42	13	8	21	51	83	34
Nottingham F.	42	11	9	22	43	73	31
Wolverhampton W.	42	10	10	22	55	80	30
Coventry City	42	9	11	22	35	73	29
Lincoln City	42	9	9	24	44	101	27
Grimsby Town	42	10	5	27	34	75	25

* Port Vale took over fixtures in October after Leeds club had temporarily resigned.

Acknowledgements

When I was asked to write this history of Leeds United my first reaction was to turn down the invitation because I feared I may be unable to give sufficient time to do this interesting subject the justice it undoubtedly deserves.

However, having accepted the challenge I spent many hours engrossed in dusty decaying files researching a subject which became more and more intriguing to me, despite the fact that my efforts were hampered by the loss of most of the Club's early records in the disastrous stand fire.

As a result of this, I am indebted greatly to the *Evening Post*, at Leeds, for their willingness to allow me the freedom to use their sporting records and photographs. Without this assistance from my employers I would have been unable to write in depth about the Club's vital early years.

It would be remiss of me not to mention the help given, whenever possible, by Leeds United General Manager and Secretary Keith Archer and former player Tom Holley. I also wish to place on record my sincere thanks to my understanding wife Margaret and to our children Helen and Michael, who may well have thought they had lost their father during the months it took me to put this book together.

Finally my thanks are due to you, the reader. I only hope you derived as much pleasure from reading my book as I did writing it.

DON WARTERS

LOS

LOS

ROMAN

TOM NAEGELS

MEULENHOFF | MANTEAU

Voor
Jef Gastmans
(1913-2002)
en
Rik Naegels
(1920-2002),
mijn bompa's.

For S.,
who will make it.

1

Bompa is zelfmoord aan het plegen. Hij is negenentachtig. Hij heeft overwogen om uit het raam te springen, zijn polsen door te snijden of een overdosis medicijnen te nemen, maar heeft besloten om te stoppen met eten. Een langzame dood, die blijk geeft van discipline, moed en wilskracht. Een dood die bij bompa past.

Het duurt lang voor je zo sterft. Hij is al een week bezig. Voorlopig met weinig resultaat.

Bompa ligt in het ziekenhuis. Hij heeft een luier aan, en in zijn penis zit een buisje dat zijn aanhoudend druppelende urine opvangt in een doorschijnend plastic zakje dat met een haakje aan het ziekenhuisbed hangt. Als hij beweegt in zijn slaap, dan trekt het buisje aan zijn piemel. Dat doet zo'n pijn dat hij wakker schiet. 'Dan loopt mijn wekker af.' Tien, vijftien keer per nacht. Overdag dommelt hij in, en dan gebeurt hetzelfde.

Een week eerder is hij opgenomen om bestraald te worden. De poliepen in zijn blaas waren groter geworden. Ze verhinderden hem het plassen. Bij elke beweging maakten ze hun aanwezigheid kenbaar met pikhouwelen, drilboren en ultrafijne scalpels; toen al sliep hij nauwelijks.

'Meneer Lorreyne, we zullen moeten bestralen.'

'Een mens moet ergens aan sterven.'

'Een paar weken, en u bent weer de oude. U kunt nog tien jaar leven.'

'Ik wil geen tien jaar meer leven.'

'Ha ha ha, meneer Lorreyne.'

Na de bestraling was bompa incontinent. Voor en ach-

ter. De achterkant zou misschien genezen. De voorkant niet. Hij kon nog steeds tien jaar leven, zij het in een stoel, in een rusthuis, met een luier aan.
Toen besloot bompa om te sterven.

2

Op een dag, meer dan vijftien jaar geleden, verloor bompa zijn rechternetvlies. Hoe het precies gebeurd is, dat weet hij zelf niet, maar plots was het weg. Als hij zijn linkeroog toekneep, dan zag hij niks.
Op een dag, meer dan tien jaar geleden, sprong een adertje in zijn linkernetvlies. Een bloeddruppel stolde pal in het midden ervan. Hij had het gehoord, vertelde hij. Hij had het horen springen, voor het raam wazig werd en de wereld veranderde in een halo rond een donkere kern. In het midden van zijn gezichtsveld zweefde een vaag oplichtende, roodbruine, op sommige plaatsen bijna zwarte bal. Hij leefde in een permanente zonsverduistering.
Hij negeerde het. Fietste naar het park, en reed bijna onder een auto. Ging vissen, en kwam huilend thuis omdat zijn lijn in de knoop was geraakt. Bleef kaarten, en werd bedrogen. Biljartte, en kreeg ruzie omdat hij het laken stukmaakte. Las kranten met een enorm vergrootglas, en werd steeds bozer over de staat van de wereld.
Dit was het ergste wat een mens kon overkomen, vond hij. Dit was wat men bedoelde als men het had over mensonwaardig. Een man zonder ogen, wat was die nog? Niet in staat tot het kleinste. Zelfs om zijn onderbroek aan te trekken, had hij hulp nodig.

Toen werd hij doof.
Nee, niet doof. Net zomin als hij echt blind was, was hij volledig doof. Hij hoorde nog net genoeg om te beseffen dat hij niet hoorde. Een echte dove en een echte

blinde weten niet beter. Voor hen kon het zijn alsof er gewoon geen geluid en geen beeld bestond. Maar hij... hij hoorde geluiden, maar verstond ze niet. Hij zag beelden, maar kreeg ze nooit scherp. Stel het je maar eens voor... Permanent proberen om toch iets te zien, iets te begrijpen... Voortdurend turen, de oren spitsen, zoeken naar de juiste hoek. En dan de paranoia: wie lopen er om me heen, wat doen ze, praten ze over mij, draaien ze me een loer? En de eenzaamheid. Hij, die zo graag discussieerde... Het simpelste gesprek kon hij niet meer volgen. Als hij iets zei, was het op het verkeerde moment of ging het over het verkeerde onderwerp. Dachten we dat hij dat niet merkte?
Dit was het niet. Zo'n leven wilde hij niet. Als er ook maar iets bij kwam dat hem nog meer zou beperken, dan hoefde het voor hem niet meer.

3

Ik ben aan het scheiden van mijn eerste vrouw.
Aansteller. Saskia en ik gaan gewoon uit elkaar. Gebeurt elke dag. Zeven jaar bij elkaar geweest, waarvan drie samengewoond. Klassiek verhaal.
Dingen die je niet mag doen in zo'n situatie:

1. In de auto Eminem draaien.

Bijna twee voetgangers doodgereden.

Bitch I'm-a kill you! You don't wanna fuck with me!
Girls neither, you ain't nuttin' but a slut to me!
Bitch I'm-a kill you! You ain't got the balls to beef
We ain't gon' never stop beefin' I don't squash the beef
You better kill me! I'm-a be another rapper dead
For poppin' off at the mouth with shit I shouldn't-a said

Afgelopen nacht was de eerste die Sas in haar nieuwe woning doorgebracht heeft. Het deed me niks. Ik ben uit geweest en pas rond drie uur thuisgekomen. Ik was kalm. Ik dacht niet aan haar.
Oké, ik kon niet slapen. Gebeurt meer. Tijd doorgebracht met namen zoeken die beginnen met de laatste letter van de naam die je voordien genoemd hebt. Carla Aaron Nero Otje Evert Tonnus Sam Mandinka Abel Layla Atrejoe Ep Pebbles.
Weekend Knack gelezen (seksleven van Dirk Draulans).
Haar spiegelbal van het plafond geschroefd (op een wankele keukenstoel in het donker met een schroeven-

draaier boven mijn hoofd – godverdrek wat een gezeik! De schroeven vielen op de grond, rolden in de spleten tussen de planken. Ze liggen er nog.)
En nu zit ik in de auto, op weg naar de zot van de dag waar ik een reportage over moet maken voor de krant waar ik al vier jaar voor werk. Ik ben de chef zotten-van-de-dag van de redactie. Alle weirdo's met een Project mag ik opbellen, interviewen, doen geloven dat we het echt belangwekkend vinden wat ze doen, en nee, dat we hen niet belachelijk zullen maken. Vandaag: de man die een eenzame strijd voert tegen een speelstraat. Een eenmansbuurtcomité. Perfect.

Wooooooo!
Dat was een vrachtwagen.
Ik dacht dat ik niet moe was maar in de auto slaag ik er niet in mijn ogen open te houden. Alle ramen staan open, de radio speelt op volle kracht, ik zing mee, ik sla de maat met mijn hoofd, maar niettemin vallen mijn ogen dicht en zwalk ik van het ene rijvak naar het andere. Fuck you, klootzak in kut-BMW!
En –
Het moest er van komen.
Ik kan echt niet langer dan twee seconden in slaap gesukkeld zijn. Lang genoeg om tegen die boomcar voor me op te botsen.
Gelukkig nogal traag. Ik was aan het afremmen voor het rode licht. Eigenlijk stond ik al bijna stil. Het is in die laatste meters dat mijn ogen gewonnen hebben van Eminem.
O shit, ik ga sterven. De kerel die uit die auto komt – betatoeëerd, leren broek, piercings in de neus, dat ze er zo nog maken. Hij gaat me mollen!

Nee, het is zijn moeder die me gaat mollen. Een dikke, zonnebankbruine vrouw, pas gepermanent, wolk van haarlak, overal ringen en een luipaardblouse met diep decolleté, stapt uit en begint me in plat Antwerps uit te schelden.
'Kunde gij nie uit uw doppen zien, loempe kloefkapper!'
In een reflex antwoord ik met mijn zachtste, diepste stem in mijn allerbeschaafdste Nederlands. De presentator van het late-night jazzprogramma. Dat maakt haar nog razender.
'Och hoort hem! "Uw wagen heeft geen schrammetje." Stukske voddevent! Prulmanneke!'
Ondertussen probeert tattoo-zoon duidelijk te maken dat de auto inderdaad niet beschadigd is en dat ze beter instapt. Het verkeerslicht is op groen gesprongen. Overal proberen auto's langs ons heen te komen. Ze rijden over het trottoir, een botst bijna tegen het verkeerslicht. Overreden worden terwijl je uitgescholden wordt door een razende Antwerpse del met gecraqueleerde borsten – is dat geen einde voor een schrijver?

4

Een halfuur te laat kom ik aan in café Terminus, een van die tavernes op de Rooseveltplaats die zich hun glorietijd zelf al niet meer herinneren. Mijn zot van de dag is er nog, een kleine ronde man van rond de vijftig met een te grote bril. Hij veert op als ik me voorstel. Erg vindt hij het niet dat ik te laat ben, druk, files, hij kent er alles van. Hij behandelt me met gedecideerde onderdanigheid, zoals hij denkt dat een man van de wereld met de pers omgaat. Mijn fotograaf Jonas is geïrriteerd: hij heeft een halfuur alleen met de man moeten doorbrengen.

Onze man is accountant. Hij nuttigt de lunch met een collega, een karikatuur van de willoze eenzame: dikke brillenglazen, vet sluik haar, visogen, beate glimlach en een bewonderende houding tegenover om het even wie er in een omtrek van vijf meter in zijn buurt staat. De zot van de dag vraagt of hij zijn maaltijd mag beëindigen. Dat sta ik toe.

Ze eten in stilte, die ze af en toe doorbreken met een 'Lekker hè?' Kalfskoteletjes met aardappeltjes en prinsessenboontjes, en lichte huiswijn. Het dessert is een profiterole. De collega vergeet de slagroom van zijn bovenlip te vegen.

Na de profiterole komt de accountant tot de kern van de zaak. De kern van de zaak is zijn straat. Zijn straat is gelegen in Borgerhout, zoals ik weet sowieso niet de aangenaamste buurt om te wonen. Nu hebben zijn buren, zonder hem te consulteren, beslist om die buurt nog onaangenamer te maken, ironisch – of tragisch, zo ik

wil – genoeg in een allicht goedbedoelde poging om de sfeer er net te verbeteren.
Een week lang zal zijn straat elke middag tussen een en acht afgesloten worden voor het verkeer. Ze wordt dan een zogenaamde 'speelstraat' – onze man maakt zelf de aanhalingstekens met gebogen vingers in de lucht – wat inhoudt dat de kinderen vrij spel krijgen, met krijtjes op de grond mogen tekenen, op een springkasteel springen, met fietsjes rondrijden...
'Een ramp voor het verkeer. En onnodig. Om de hoek is er een groot plein, waar iedereen die wil kan gaan spelen...'
Een overweldigende meerderheid van de straatbewoners is tegen de speelstraat. Hij is slechts hun woordvoerder. Ze hebben hem naar voren geschoven omdat hij het nogal goed kan uitleggen. Zegt men over hem. Hoort hij zeggen. Relatief natuurlijk. Maar het is wel zijn werk, dingen kunnen uitleggen. Als accountant moet je dat kunnen.
Vijf brieven heeft hij al naar het stadsbestuur geschreven. Denk ik dat hij al antwoord heeft gekregen? Hij heeft de steun van het Vlaams Blok en de VLD, maar die hebben niets in de pap te brokkelen. Nu heeft hij ingezien dat het zo niet werkt. Wat hij nodig heeft – wat *ze* nodig hebben, die overweldigende meerderheid van straatbewoners van wie hij de woordvoerder is – is een ludieke actie, om de aandacht van de media te trekken. De media hebben de macht. Als het in de media komt, dan zwichten de politici.
Dus hebben ze aan hun protest een wedstrijd gekoppeld. Een quiz. Voor alle inwoners van de straat. Op een zelfgetypt en -gestencild blad, dat hij in alle brievenbussen van de straat heeft gestoken, staan zes vragen

over de speelstraat. De persoon met de meeste juiste antwoorden wint een reis voor twee naar Spanje. Anderen krijgen reiskoffers of flessen kwaliteitswijn. 'De prijzen komen van sponsors. Ze doen allemaal mee. Alle grote zaken en bekende firma's uit de buurt. Ze zijn er allemaal tegen. Een overweldigende meerderheid.'

VERBROEDERINGSWEDSTRIJD

1. Hoeveel autobestuurders die tussen 13 en 20 uur door onze straat wensen te rijden, maar die er tengevolge van de versperring door de 'speelstraat' niet door konden, hebben gevloekt?
2. Hoeveel liters benzine en/of diesel zullen er verkwist worden, dus milieubelastend zijn, tengevolge van voormelde speelstraat, als men zou kunnen veronderstellen dat de versperring gemiddeld 1,5 kilometer omweg vergt, hetgeen een gemiddeld meerverbruik per wagen inhoudt van 1,5 deciliter en bv. over gans deze periode 1000 wagens deze zinloze hinder dienen te ondergaan?
3. Wat is de kostprijs van de uren economisch tijdverlies die deze 1.000 wagens tezamen lijden, ervan uitgaande dat het tijdverlies 10 minuten per auto is en 1 uur 38 euro bedraagt?
4. Hoeveel kinderen tussen 2 en 12 jaar wonen er in onze straat te Antwerpen-Borgerhoud?
5. Hoeveel mensen wonen en/of werken er in onze straat?
6. Hoeveel ingevulde formulieren 'VERBROEDERINGSWEDSTRIJD' zullen wij voor het eind van deze week ontvangen hebben?

Ik kan het zien, het is ludiek. Al heeft niet iedereen evenveel gevoel voor humor, blijkbaar. 'Ik heb al dreigbrieven ontvangen. Briefjes met van die grote, agressieve letters: STOP HIER NU EENS MEE. Sommigen van mijn achterban durven de straat niet meer op, uit angst voor de eigen buurtbewoners. Bij Pim Fortuyn is het ook zo begonnen.'

Heeft hij al gezegd dat hij de steun heeft van de VLD en het Vlaams Blok? Denk ik dat het geholpen heeft?

Terwijl hij voortratelt, duikt de man eindeloos kopieën op van officiële brieven, wetteksten en telefoonnummers van andere mensen die ik zéker moet bellen, die kunnen het nog veel straffer zeggen dan hij, want hij is nog een gematigd man. En wat vind ik er zelf van? Hij stelt mijn mening erg op prijs. Per slot van rekening ben ik een verstandig iemand die beroepshalve met veel mensen spreekt. Heeft hij geen gelijk?

'Mmm', zeg ik.

Dat doe ik te aanmoedigend. Of net niet, wie zal het zeggen? In ieder geval zet het hem aan om een vrouw op te bellen, een buur van hem, die het nog beter kan zeggen. Waarom denken mensen altijd dat journalisten drie pagina's aan hun zaak zullen wijden? Beseft hij dan niet dat het mij niet om die speelstraat gaat, maar om *hem*? Dat ik dit stuk alleen maak omdat hij zo'n freak is, en omdat mijn krant graag freaks opvoert?

'Mevrouw' – wie spreekt er zijn buren aan met mevrouw? Zeg toch Mia, of Sandra, of hoe heet het mens? – 'U spreekt hier met uw buurman.' – Ook dat nog, uw buurman. Je ziet het zo voor je, hoe ze elkaar 's ochtends groeten: dag mevrouw, dag buurman, al jarenlang, en nog nooit bij elkaar binnen geweest voor thee met ge-

bak – 'Ik heb een journalist bij me. Jaaaa, een journalist. Het loopt, mevrouw. Ze zijn erin geïnteresseerd. U weet, ik kan het zo'n beetje uitleggen hè. Ha-ha. Het is per slot van rekening mijn beroep. Ik dacht, mevrouw, dat hij misschien met u kon praten. Zegt u het hem maar eens allemaal zoals het is. Wat u allemaal meegemaakt hebt.'
Waarna ik, of ik nu wil of niet, de gsm tegen mijn oor gedrukt krijg. En een tirade onderga van een hysterische vrouw die met zo'n schelle stem spreekt dat ik haar nauwelijks versta. Wat is dit, een parodie? Er was tegen haar schenen geschopt, haar deur was beklad, die rotkinderen met hun krijtjes waren met opzet voor háár deur komen kriebelen, en wie mag het afwassen?
'Mmm', zeg ik. Ik noteer niets. De vermoeidheid klopt in mijn slapen, de stem van de buurvrouw galmt door mijn hoofd en ik onderga twee emoties tegelijkertijd: een intense afkeer van deze zielepoten die mijn tijd verdoen en hun wijk verpesten met hun een leven lang gefnuikte pogingen om de mensen te worden die ze nooit zullen zijn, en een diep mededogen met deze ongelukkige zielen, stadsgenoten van mij, die menen dat hun ongeluk hun door anderen wordt aangedaan.
'Lach ik een beetje commercieel?' vraagt de man aan Jonas, die hem op zijn restaurantstoel fotografeert, met de halfopgegeten profiterole op de voorgrond. 'Zal ik een glas wijn vasthouden, om bourgondisch te lijken?'

5

Jonas en ik rijden naar de straat waar de man woont, om de speelstraters aan het woord te laten. Woord en wederwoord, een groot journalistiek principe zoals gewoonlijk toegepast op een banale zaak.
We rijden over de Turnhoutsebaan Borgerhout binnen. Ons hart gaat sneller kloppen. Borgerhout! Tot in Nederland weten ze wat dat betekent: somberheid, tastbare angst, vuil, dagelijkse relletjes tussen oude, verbitterde Vlamingen die hun gezellige gemeente hebben zien verkrotten en de gespierde, jonge, balorige Maghrebijnen die in die krotten wonen. De wieg van het Vlaams Blok! En daar rijden wij nu binnen!
(Ik laat even ruimte voor verschrikte blikken.)
Ik zal zelfs meer zeggen: hier kom ik vandaan. Mijn hele jeugd heb ik in de gemeente gewoond.
(Nog verschriktere blikken.)
Ik geniet van het prestige dat die eenvoudige mededeling met zich brengt. Als ik merk dat mijn Borgerhout-aura echt scoort, dan gooi ik er de Borgerhoutmythe tegenaan. Jazeker, het is een dagelijks gevecht om te overleven. Je moet de taal van de straat kennen. Respect afdwingen. Maar zodra je hun respect hebt, dan ben je een van hen. Een makak uit het getto. De Vlaamse Eminem.
Eigenlijk kom ik uit een deel van Borgerhout waar alleen blanke Vlamingen wonen, een rustige voorstad die meer wegheeft van Wilrijk dan van om het even welk grootsteeds getto. Eigenlijk ben ik, voor ik voor de krant werkte, nooit in dat andere, mediagenieke Borgerhout

geweest. Eigenlijk heb ik sindsdien gemerkt dat veel van de verhalen die met Borgerhout geassocieerd worden, zich afspelen in aangrenzende wijken zoals de Seefhoek, Stuivenberg en de Dam, wijken die qua vuil en spanningen en balorigheid veel hoger scoren, maar namen hebben die minder tot de verbeelding spreken. Maar laat dat de pret niet drukken: ik ben een kind van Borgerhout. En kinderen van Borgerhout, dat weet iedereen, die hebben een *street credibility* waar die van Ice-T bij verbleekt. Hoed u voor Tom Naegels en zijn posse.

We parkeren onze auto op de hoek van de speelstraat en wandelen de autovrije buurt in. Spontaan komt er een glimlach op onze lippen. Hoe kleurrijk is het! Kijk eens aan zeg. De levenslust spat ervan af. Over de hele lengte van de mooie, verzorgde, dure straat (Is dit Borgerhout? Kan niet!) prijken uitbundige krijttekeningen. Meisjes spelen met hoelahoeps, jongens met loopfietsjes en zelfgemaakte vliegtuigjes, en voor de deuren van de burgerhuizen met de blauwe of grasgroene deuren en kindertekeningen voor de ramen, staan de glunderende, gelukkige, mooie jonge mensen die de ouders zijn van deze blije spelende kinderen, en die de speelstraat georganiseerd hebben. Het weer is mooi en zij keuvelen voor hun deur, terwijl ze toezicht houden op de kinderen. Ze zijn architect, designer, kok, decorbouwer, illustrator van kinderboeken. Ze hebben pannenkoeken gebakken met de kinderen en een van de jonge vaders, de kok, heeft een workshop eiwitkloppen gegeven. Ik krijg een zelfgemaakte meringue aangeboden, die heerlijk smaakt.
Dat wordt een mooie reportage. De beelden zeggen alles:

de sombere oude kale man met zijn profiterole in de donkere taverne naast de blije jonge mensen met hun vele lachende kinderen in de zon. Oud – jong, donker – zon, boos – blij, boekhouder – designer, profiterole – meringue. Mijn tekst blijft neutraal, zij het *tongue-in-cheek*. De goede verstaander weet wie de winnaar is. Hoe simpel het leven in deze stad, waar een kindertekening alles zegt wat gezegd moet worden!

6

Mijn gsm gaat. Nadia. Ik ben te moe, ik heb een uur naar een nurkse boekhouder en een scheldende Antwerpse moeten luisteren en een uur naar positieve jonge ouders. Ik moet nog een stuk schrijven. Wil ze me één dag met rust laten?

Nadia is de vrouw voor wie ik Saskia verlaat. Ze is Pakistaanse, eenentwintig, en één jaar in België. Ze is hartveroverend in haar dramatiek, ophitsend in haar nukkigheid, en vreselijk moeilijk om te doorgronden. En ik die dacht dat je veertig moest zijn om daarvoor je zekerheden op te geven.

'Tom, ik móést je stem horen! Alleen jouw stem kan mijn dag maken.'

Ik weet niet wat ik op zo'n zin moet zeggen. Er valt een stilte. Door de telefoon gaat het nooit zo goed.

'Hoe was jouw dag?' vraagt ze met haar dubbele tong.

'Ik ben met een man gaan praten', zeg ik. Ik praat traag en duidelijk. 'Het was heel grappig. In zijn straat spelen kinderen. Ze tekenen op straat. Hij kan er niet rijden met zijn auto. Hij houdt daar niet van. Nu doet hij een wedstrijd. Je kunt flessen wijn winnen.'

Perfect uitgelegd. Heel knap.

'De kinderen winnen wijn?'

'Neenee. Hij is tégen de kinderen. Hij geeft wijn aan wie tegen de kinderen is. En een reis.'

'Ries?'

'Een reis. Holiday. To Pakistan. Als prijs van de wedstrijd.'

'Why Pakistan?'

'Neenee, niet naar Pakistan. Het zou ironisch zijn als ze... Laat maar zitten. Vergeet Pakistan. Was a joke. Gewoon, die man is zo freaky dat hij sponsors zoekt om spelende kinderen, die één week – één week maar! – in zijn straat buiten spelen...'

Soms vraag ik me af of ik haar onbewust het gevoel wil geven dat ze nooit zal begrijpen waar ik mee bezig ben. Waarom kan ik niet gewoon iets leuks vertellen? Iets kleins? Niet altijd die ingewikkelde dingen. Hoe leg je uit wat er grappig is aan een man die een quiz organiseert tegen een speelstraat? Waarom zou zij dat grappig vinden? Ze neemt het gewoon aan als een van de vele vreemde dingen die hier gebeuren. België is een land waar het altijd regent, waar vrienden een afspraak maken als ze bij elkaar op bezoek komen en waar mannen flessen wijn weggeven als ze niet willen dat er kinderen in hun straat spelen.

Nadia lacht toch. Om mij een plezier te doen.

'Die is echt grappig, die man!'

7

Bompa is wakker geworden in zijn eigen pis. De luier heeft de toevloed van een hele nacht niet kunnen houden. Zijn pyjamajasje heeft het opgezogen. Toen hij ontwaakte, kleefde het zuur tegen zijn knokige lijf. Het is al de derde keer dat dat gebeurt.

Hij huilt van vernedering, frustratie, razernij en machteloosheid.

Zijn neef Fons is langs geweest. Het heeft hem meer geergerd dan goed gedaan, zoals het meeste bezoek hem ergert. Alsof hij verwacht dat we hem persoonlijk het spuitje zullen geven; en als we dat niet doen, wat komen we hier dan zoeken?

'Hij staat hier dan maar wat, en frummelt wat aan mijn hand. En hij komt mij vertellen: "Bob, ge moet meer moed scheppen." Moed! Wat komt die schijtluis mij vertellen wat moed is? Om door te leven, daar hebt ge geen moed voor nodig. Te durven sterven, dát is moedig.'

'Fons zal ook niet goed geweten hebben wat te zeggen, hè bompa.'

Het is dan ook niet simpel om die depressieve bejaarde die al negen dagen zijn bed niet uit kan níét te ontstemmen. Wat zeg je tegen hem, als het minste hem razend maakt? Fons had er niets beters op gevonden dan staalhard te ontkennen dat bompa kanker had. Kwestie van de moed erin te houden. 'Ge moet meer moed pakken, Bob, gij hebt ommes geen kanker.' Had hij de kracht gehad, bompa had hem buitengekegeld. 'Wie denkt hij dat ik ben? Een uil? Waarvoor bestralen ze me dan? Voor een valling?'

Hij neemt zijn pillen voor zijn hart niet meer, in de hoop dat hij een hartaanval krijgt.
Ik heb net dezelfde drang om hem de doodsgedachte uit het hoofd te praten. Hij *gaat* nog niet dood. Alle dokters zeggen het: Bob Lorreyne is lang niet terminaal. Logisch dat hij zich nu even slecht voelt. Zo'n bestraling is een ingrijpende zaak. Maar als hij zich nog enkele weken herstel wil gunnen, dan zal in elk geval de pijn toch al verdwenen zijn. Het kan toch dat hij zich binnenkort weer beter voelt? Dat kan toch? De dokters weten het toch beter? Nog *tien jaar* hebben ze gezegd. Tien jaar! Wat is dan enkele weken ongemak?
Ik oogst een minachtende blik. Begin ik ook? Ben ik ook een leugenaar, een dienaar van de lepe dokters die een mens ten koste van alles in leven willen houden? Ik stel hem teleur.
Er zijn maar twee soorten mensen: mensen die hem gelijk geven, en achterbakse leugenaars.

Hij vraagt naar mijn andere bompa, Bert. Die is een paar maanden geleden gestorven. Ook kanker, de prostaat in zijn geval. Uitgezaaid in alle richtingen.
Of hij ook bestraald was?
Of hij ook zo afviel?
Of hij veel pijn had?
Bompa Bert woonde in een verzorgingstehuis. De laatste maand kon hij zijn bed niet meer uit. Hij dronk alleen nog cola uit een babybeker met een plastic teutje waar hij niettemin nog veel mee morste. Zijn pyjamakraag stond stijf van de suiker. Zijn nek plakte. Zijn tong was zwart en zo dik dat hij nauwelijks nog kon praten. Niemand begreep wat hij vertelde. Hij herhaalde het drie,

vier keer. 'Hee ha hoe he hoe.' 'Wat zeg je, bompa?' Hij zonk gefrustreerd in zijn kussen terug. Wij zaten gefrustreerd naast zijn bed. Later zei hij niks meer. Hij keek je gewoon aan, of sliep terwijl je naast hem zat en dacht: dit zijn de laatste gesprekken, ik moet iets belangrijks zeggen, wat kan ik zoal vertellen?

Toen bompa Bert nog niet zo ver heen was, werd hij 's nachts soms in paniek wakker, sprong uit bed maar haalde het toilet niet meer. Dan stroomde de diarree over de vloer van zijn kamer. Beschaamd probeerde hij het zelf schoon te maken, maar hij maakte het alleen erger. Als vader hem de volgende ochtend kwam bezoeken, was alles onder de stront gesmeerd. Bompa zat er op zijn knieën tussen, hoofdschuddend, niet begrijpend wat hem overkwam, waarom hij dit nog moest meemaken.

Toen hij nog wel kon praten, heeft hij meermaals gevraagd om te mogen sterven. Ook hem werd dat geweigerd. Als we bejaarden zouden euthanaseren omdat ze het in hun broek doen, dan zouden we er véél moeten doodmaken hoor...

Pas toen hij echt bijna dood was, hebben ze hem een spuitje gegeven. Zijn lijden is met een dag verkort. Wat maakt het dan uit, euthanasie?

Dat durf ik bompa niet te vertellen. Ik zeg dat bompa Bert veel verder heen was dan hij. Bij hem was de kanker al uitgezaaid voor ze hem ontdekten. Er was nog weinig aan te doen. Maar bij jou hebben ze het onder controle! De bestralingen hebben gewerkt! De kanker is weg! Nog tien jaar!

'Ik ben ertoe in staat hoor,' glimlacht hij, 'om uit het raam te springen. Gelooft ge me niet?'

8

Ik heb een vergissing begaan. Ik heb bompa verteld over een manuscript dat ik aan het redigeren ben. (Dat is een van mijn bijverdiensten.) Een boek over Palestina. Het was gewoon om iets te vertellen te hebben! Ik bedoelde er niks mee! Het gaat goed met mij, ja, veel werk, het weer is mooi, wil je nog altijd dood? en o ja, ik ben een boek over Palestina aan het redigeren.

Vergéét dat ik dat gezegd heb!

Helaas –

'Pa-le-stina.'

(Wat? Pale-? Neeeehehehe, ha-ha-ha bompa, je wéét toch hoe doof je bent?)

'Ik heb Israël nog weten stichten.'

(Staatsman uit Deurne, strijder naast Ben Goerion.)

'Die Palestijnen hadden NIKS.'

(Ooooh boy.)

'En de joden hebben daar ALLES gebracht.'

(Mijn boek zegt net het tegenovergestelde.)

'En nu dat de Palestijnen alles hebben, willen ze onafhankelijk zijn!'

(Ondergaan. Niet reageren.)

'En nu vechten ze daar om de heilige grond, maar ik zeg: heeeej mannekes, geen enkele grond is heilig hé, het is uw oorlog en vecht hem uit, maar niet op mijn grond want dit is mijn grond, en die is heilig voor mij...'

(Dit neemt een verkeerde wending.)

'...en ik heb die bewerkt voor mijn kinderen en nu komen ze naar hier en ze hebben NIKS en ineens willen ze ALLES...'

(Wat was het verband?)

‘...zonder dat ze er hier voor gevochten hebben en van die socialisten MAG dat allemaal, terwijl de socialisten zouden moeten weten dat ge moet VECHTEN voor uw rechten en dat ge rechten niet zomaar krijgt, dus ik zeg: JA, Eigen Volk Eerst is een goeie slogan en dan moogt gij zeggen wat ge wilt...’

(Ik zeg niks.

Ik bén hier niet eens.)

‘...maar die Bob Cools en die Janssens die doen méér voor de ommo’s dan voor ons, de ommo’s en de Palestijnen krijgen hier alles en zie mij hier zitten, ik vraag één ding, één simpel ding: baas te zijn over mijn eigen leven, maar in dit land zijn we zelfs over ons eigen leven niet meer baas.’

(Klaar?)

(Angstige blik naar de verpleegsters en de kamergenoten. Hebben ze iets gehoord? Ze geven geen krimp.)

Van racisme naar homofobie en terug, van Israel naar Deurne, van de internationale politiek naar zijn ziekenhuisbed – geen man die de wereld zo synthetisch overschouwt als bompa.

9

Laat er geen twijfel over bestaan. Zonder bompa was het Belgische socialisme nooit van de grond gekomen. Emile Vandervelde, Paul-Henri Spaak en Achille Van Acker mogen de hemel op hun blote knieën danken dat ze een beroep konden doen op Bob Lorreyne. Vanuit Deurne, onbekend voor de partijmogols die achter zijn rug de boel aan het versjacheren waren, was hij de speerpunt van de arbeidersstrijd. De man heeft langer gestaakt dan hij gewerkt heeft! *Als* hij al een dag gewerkt heeft! Elke patroon wist het nog voor hij zijn contract tekende: Bob Lorreyne pikte het niet. Hij was sneller weg dan ze hem in dienst konden nemen. Onrecht! Kuiperijen! Machtsmisbruik! Altijd stond Lorreyne te tieren, altijd klaar om zijn ontslag te geven of te krijgen. De enige reden dat hij overleefde, was dat hij de volgende dag alweer nieuw werk had. De beste brillandeur van Antwerpen, dat was hij. Voor de rijkste joden gewerkt. De grootste stenen geslepen. De diamanten die nu schitteren in kronen en halssnoeren van filmsterren en prinsessen, daar heeft hij zijn ogen op kapotgewerkt. Of je denkt toch niet dat die blindheid toevallig gekomen is?

Zo werd het mij verteld.

Wij kregen geen verhalen opgedist over Marx, Lenin of Castro. Het socialisme, dat was bompa. Het is nog maar recent dat ik besef dat hij de industriële revolutie niet meegemaakt heeft, dat hij altijd heeft mogen stemmen, dat de achturendag al ingevoerd was voor hij geboren werd, ja, dat de eerste grote sociale verworvenheden eigenlijk al verworven *waren*, toen hij begon te werken.

Bompa is opgegroeid tijdens de hoogtijdagen van het Antwerpse socialisme. Zijn held was Camille Huysmans. Bompa was vijf toen Huysmans in 1918 naar Antwerpen kwam en ervoor zorgde dat de plaatselijke federatie, een krabbenmand die ten onder ging aan interne twisten, de sterkste werd van de partij. Antwerpen werd een rood bolwerk. Dankzij Huysmans wonnen de socialisten in Antwerpen in 1919 verpletterend de verkiezingen. Een derde van de stad had op hen gestemd. Op straat telden de mensen koppen: een twee drie, een socialist! In 1921 traden ze toe tot het schepencollege. In 1933 werd Huysmans voor de eerste keer burgemeester.

Bompa spiegelde zich aan hem. Hij kleedde zich net zo verfijnd, op het dandyeske af. Hij probeerde net zo eloquent te praten. Hij imiteerde Huysmans' zegswijzen, zoals de repliek tegen iemand die net iets doms heeft gevraagd: 'Zeg eens, is het púmmel of pummèl?' Het lijdt geen twijfel dat bompa van zichzelf dacht dat ze veel gemeen hadden. Grootheidswaan, zoals steeds, al had hij ook niet helemaal ongelijk. Even koppig, even hard, even spotziek, even helder van geest, evenveel misprijzen voor wie minder intelligent was. Even idealistisch en rechtdoorzee ook, even overtuigd dat wat zij bedacht hadden het beste was voor iedereen. Camille Huysmans was zo verstandig dat hij twee jaar te vroeg naar school ging – bompa één. Ze waren allebei koleriek. Ze hielden er allebei van om hun vrouw zowel thuis als in het publiek te kleineren. ('Tettebet' noemde Huysmans zijn Martha.) Ze hadden dezelfde hobby: vissen. Ze waren allebei mager en pezig. En op het einde van zijn leven was Huysmans een ziekelijk koppige oude man die zijn

eigen aftakeling niet kon aanvaarden en iedereen tegen zich in het harnas joeg. Bompa net zo.
Bompa heeft Huysmans maar één keer persoonlijk ontmoet. Dat gebeurde in 1960. Moeder was zestien, en ze had een welsprekendheidswedstrijd gewonnen. (Later werd ze de ster van een socialistische amateurtoneelkring.) Haar prijs was een fotoboek over de Antwerpse havenarbeiders. Die werd haar overhandigd door Huysmans, bijna negentig maar pas getrouwd met een vrouw van achtendertig, nog steeds volksvertegenwoordiger en nog steeds razend populair.
Bompa had zich gekleed als zijn idool, afgeborsteld, met een strikje. Huysmans monsterde hem geamuseerd en zei, half tot moeder, half tot de zaal: 'Men zegt, altijd als ik er niet bij ben, dat er in Antwerpen een niet nader genoemd aantal onechte kinderen van Camille Huysmans rondlopen. Het is tot mijn schrik dat ik vaststel dat er in deze stad ook onechte Camille Huysmansen zelf zijn!'
De zaal schaterde.
'Meneer', ging Huysmans door. 'Als ik morgen er de kop bij neerleg, mag ik u dan vragen om mijn plaats in te nemen in het parlement? Ik verzeker u: als u uw dochter voor u laat spreken, zal niemand het verschil merken!'
Andermaal hilariteit.
'Enfin', besloot Huysmans, terwijl hij moeder het boek overhandigde. 'Ik begrijp in ieder geval hoe het komt dat deze jongedame de prijs krijgt. Hoe kan het anders voor mijn eigen dochter?'
Dat laatste schreef hij ook in het boek: 'Voor mijn lieve dochter bij mijn dubbelganger, Kamiel.'
Bompa ging het podium af met een rood hoofd, veroor-

zaakt door een mengeling van verlegenheid, schaamte en trots. Mijn tweede ik, had Huysmans hem genoemd. Mijn dubbelganger...

Niet veel later zou bompa teleurgesteld raken in de oude patron. Toen Huysmans zich in 1961 nogmaals verkiesbaar stelde, was het de eerste keer dat bompa niet meer op hem stemde. Hij vond Huysmans te oud, en geestelijk niet meer helder. En toen Huysmans op zijn vierennegentigste een eigen partij begon, liet bompa hem vallen. Dramatisch moment: tijdens de 1-meistoet van 1965 was er voor Huysmans geen plaats op de eretribune. Hij volgde de stoet als toeschouwer, op een stoeltje op het trottoir in de Kloosterstraat. Niemand van de partijmilitanten keurde hem een blik waardig. Bompa, er vast van overtuigd dat de oud-burgemeester zijn bastaard-ik zou herkennen, draaide in het voorbijgaan zijn hoofd demonstratief weg.

Nadien heeft bompa nooit meer een politieke held gehad. Hij werd steeds bitterder over de partij. Als hij erover sprak, was het somber, traag, en eindigde het in een vloek. De teloorgang van de Volkshuizen, het opdoeken van de coöperatieven, het faillissement van de *Volksgazet*... De partij verraadde alles waardoor ze groot geworden was.

De miljoenenput die burgemeester Craeybeckx naliet: hij had het altijd voorspeld, dat het met die dronkelap de verkeerde kant op zou gaan.

En dacht Bob Cools echt dat hij dat tij kon keren door Antwerpen Culturele Hoofdstad van Europa te maken? Welke volksmens had daar iets aan?

Na het Agustaschandaal sprak hij weken niet meer. En

als hij sprak, wensten wij dat hij zweeg. Zoveel bitterheid en haat die uit één man kwamen...
Ik betrapte hem terwijl hij aan het huilen was. Hij sloeg met zijn vuist op tafel, de tranen stroomden over zijn wangen en hij vloekte voor zich uit in een lege kamer. Wie huilt er nu om politiek?
Zelfs de vakbonden raakten uit de gratie. 'Ze staken voor alles. Niemand is nog content. Wij hadden *redenen* om te staken. De halve diamantsector is afgedankt en niemand van de vakbonden die daar een kik over gegeven heeft. Kapotgewerkt heb ik mijn ogen op die stenen en niemand bij de vakbonden die daar ooit iets aan gedaan heeft. Maar als ze nu langer dan vijf uur per dag moeten werken, als ze niet allemaal én op skiverlof én naar Benidorm én tussendoor een week naar New York kunnen: de blok erop!'
Ruzie dat ik in die tijd met hem gemaakt heb! Ik was een puber, mijn opvattingen waren zuiver en onbuigzaam. Ik was ervan overtuigd dat hij op het Vlaams Blok stemde, al heb ik dat eigenlijk nooit zeker geweten. We hebben een keer zo hard tegen mekaar geschreeuwd dat we aan het einde allebei huilden. Dat vond hij erg. Toen ik wegging, kwam hij me achterna en zei hij: 'Politiek mag nooit een familie kapotmaken.'
Ik was daar toen niet zo van overtuigd.
De laatste tien jaar breidde de bitterheid zich uit naar de hele wereld. Hij werd onuitstaanbaar, overdreven principieel, koppig tot het uiterste. Toen hij aan de kassa in de GB twintig frank te weinig terugkreeg, bleef hij een halve dag wachten tot de kassa's nageteld werden, zijn gelijk bewezen werd en hij zijn muntstuk in ontvangst mocht nemen.

Hij was beheerder van een biljartlokaal en alle biljartlokalen kregen een televisie van de gemeente. Hij is hem gaan terugbrengen. Had de stad geld te veel?
Toen het bestuur van de Goede Woning, de socialehuisvestingsmaatschappij waarvan hij zijn flatje huurde, besloot om de balustrades op de balkons van de flats blauw te schilderen, was hij razend omdat ze zijn mening daarover niet gevraagd hadden. Vijftig jaar woonde hij er al! Vijftig jaar gaf hij een deel van zijn loon af. Hij had een huis kunnen kopen met dat geld. Hij had de Goede Woning rijk gemaakt. Maar eventjes komen vragen of hij wel een blauwe balustrade op zijn balkon wou, dat was te veel. Hij vond blauwe balustrades lelijk. Zo. Wat waren ze van plan daarmee te doen?
Ze deden er niets mee.
Hij belde alle stadsdiensten op, de *Gazet van Antwerpen*, *De Morgen* – toch ooit een socialistische krant –, maar vond niemand die hem gelijk gaf. Daarna vroeg hij aan mij of ik er geen reportage over kon schrijven. Ik werkte toch ook voor een krant? Ik maakte hem wijs dat ik het met de redactie zou bespreken, deed dat niet, kreeg een week later dezelfde vraag en moest hem toen wel teleurstellen. Zijn eigen kleinzoon zag niet in wat het onrecht was van een blauwe balustrade.
'Het zijn zijn ogen', zei de familie. Zijn ogen, zijn oren, zijn gezondheid. We moesten dat begrijpen: zo'n fiere man, die fysiek aftakelde, deed soms nukkig.
Op een zaterdag, twee weken voor de verkiezingen van 1995, in volle Agustacrisis, ging hij kijken naar Marcel Colla. De baron van Deurne was zijn kiesvee komen toelachen. Hij had het niet over de crisis waar zijn partij zich in bevond, maar hij had het gezellig gemaakt. Hij

had voor iedereen koffiekoeken laten aanrukken, en gratis koffie en pils, en Colla deed een dansje met Maria van achter de bar. De tandeloze partijsoldaten grijnsden en joelden, porden Colla in zijn buik en vertelden hem dat ze zijn vader nog gekend hadden, en of hij zich hen nog herinnerde, van vroeger op het korfbal?
Colla herinnerde zich iedereen. Ja natuurlijk, Franske! En Joske! Hoe is het met Solange?!
Socialist zijn betekende veel namen kunnen onthouden.
Plots stond bompa op. Eerst hadden ze hem niet opgemerkt. Magere kleine oude man, je zou hem zo omverduwen. Moest hij naar het toilet? Nee, dat moest hij niet. Hij wou iets zeggen. Op zulke ogenblikken was zijn blindheid en doofheid een voordeel. Een: hij zag niet dat iedereen hem met opzet negeerde, dat een vrouw gebaarde dat hij weer moest gaan zitten, dat men hem probeerde in te sluiten. Twee: hij hoorde niet dat iedereen bleef doorpraten. Drie: hij praatte zo luid, om zichzelf te kunnen horen, dat de zaal uiteindelijk wel móést luisteren naar wat hij te zeggen had.
Hij slingerde Colla in zijn pafferige gezicht dat er koffiekoeken waren, en met welk geld die betaald waren, dat van de Fransen of dat van de Italianen? Colla zag er wel uit alsof er wat van dat geld aan zijn vingers was blijven plakken. In ieder geval had hij te veel van zijn eigen koffiekoeken gegeten, de vette aap! Had Colla ooit één dag gestaakt? Had Colla honger moeten lijden? Was het om papmannetjes als Colla aan de macht te brengen dat hij, Bob Lorreyne, zijn leven aan de partij had gegeven?
Ze hebben bompa naar buiten gebracht. De volgende dag leverde hij zijn partijkaart in.
Hij heeft nog een week gewacht op het telefoontje van

de partij. Een leven lang militant, ze moesten hem toch kennen? Ze zouden hem toch smeken om te blijven? Ze zouden hem toch niet laten gaan?
Ze lieten hem wel gaan.
Hij ging met opgeheven hoofd.

10

28 MEI 2002. – **Wet betreffende de euthanasie**

(met de belangrijke passages door mij becommentarieerd)

ALBERT II, Koning der Belgen,
Aan allen die nu zijn en hierna wezen zullen, Onze Groet.
De Kamers hebben aangenomen en Wij bekrachtigen hetgeen volgt:

Artikel 1. Deze wet regelt een aangelegenheid als bedoeld in artikel 78 van de Grondwet.

HOOFDSTUK I. – **Algemene bepalingen**

Art. 2. Voor de toepassing van deze wet wordt onder euthanasie verstaan het opzettelijk levensbeëindigend handelen door een andere dan de betrokkene, op diens verzoek.

('Diens' verwijst naar 'de betrokkene', neem ik aan, en niet naar 'een andere dan de betrokkene'?)

HOOFDSTUK II. – **Voorwaarden en procedure**

Art. 3. §1. De arts die euthanasie toepast, pleegt geen misdrijf wanneer hij er zich van verzekerd heeft dat:

– de patiënt een meerderjarige of een ontvoogde minderjarige is die handelingsbekwaam en bewust is op het ogenblik van zijn verzoek;

(Ja.)

– het verzoek vrijwillig, overwogen en herhaald is, en niet tot stand gekomen is als gevolg van enige externe druk;

(Hij heeft het nu al honderd keer gevraagd!)

– de patiënt zich in een medisch uitzichtloze toestand bevindt van aanhoudend en ondraaglijk fysiek of psychisch lijden dat niet gelenigd kan worden, en dat het gevolg is van een ernstige en ongeneeslijke, door ongeval of ziekte veroorzaakte aandoening; en hij de in deze wet voorgeschreven voorwaarden en procedures heeft nageleefd.

(Shit.)

§2. Onverminderd bijkomende voorwaarden die de arts aan zijn ingrijpen wenst te verbinden, moet hij vooraf en in alle gevallen:

1° de patiënt inlichten over zijn gezondheidstoestand en zijn levensverwachting, met de patiënt overleg plegen over zijn verzoek tot euthanasie en met hem de eventueel nog resterende therapeutische mogelijkheden, evenals die van de palliatieve zorg, en hun gevolgen bespreken. Hij moet met de patiënt tot de overtuiging komen dat er voor de situatie waarin deze zich bevindt geen redelijke andere oplossing is en dat het verzoek van de patiënt berust op volledige vrijwilligheid;

(En wie heeft het laatste woord over wat een redelijke andere oplossing is? De patiënt of de dokter?)

2° zich verzekeren van het aanhoudend fysiek of psychisch lijden van de patiënt en van het duurzaam karakter van zijn verzoek. Daartoe voert hij met de patiënt meerdere gesprekken die, rekening houdend met de ontwikkeling van de gezondheidstoestand van de patiënt, over een redelijke periode worden gespreid;

(Bompa: 'Hoe dikwijls MOET ik het nog herhalen? Snappen ze het niet na één keer? Zijn die dokters DOOF of zo?')

3° een andere arts raadplegen over de ernstige en ongeneeslijke aard van de aandoening en hem op de hoog-

te brengen van de redenen voor deze raadpleging. De geraadpleegde arts neemt inzage van het medisch dossier, onderzoekt de patiënt en moet zich vergewissen van het aanhoudend en ondraaglijk fysiek of psychisch lijden dat niet gelenigd kan worden. Hij stelt een verslag op van zijn bevindingen.
De geraadpleegde arts moet onafhankelijk zijn ten opzichte van zowel de patiënt als de behandelende arts en bevoegd om over de aandoening in kwestie te oordelen. De behandelende arts brengt de patiënt op de hoogte van de resultaten van deze raadpleging;
4° indien er een verplegend team is, dat in regelmatig contact staat met de patiënt, het verzoek van de patiënt bespreken met het team of leden van dat team;
5° indien de patiënt dat wenst, het verzoek van de patiënt bespreken met zijn naasten die hij aanwijst;
6° zich ervan verzekeren dat de patiënt de gelegenheid heeft gehad om over zijn verzoek te spreken met de personen die hij wenste te ontmoeten.
§3. Indien de arts van oordeel is dat de patiënt kennelijk niet binnen afzienbare tijd zal overlijden, moet hij bovendien :
1° een tweede arts raadplegen, die psychiater is of specialist in de aandoening in kwestie, en hem op de hoogte brengen van de redenen voor deze raadpleging. De geraadpleegde arts neemt inzage van het medisch dossier, onderzoekt de patiënt en moet zich vergewissen van het aanhoudend en ondraaglijk fysiek of psychisch lijden dat niet gelenigd kan worden *(Alweer. Hoeveel mensen moeten zich daarvan vergewissen?)*, en van het vrijwillig, overwogen en herhaald karakter van het verzoek. Hij stelt een verslag op van zijn bevindingen. De geraadpleegde

arts moet onafhankelijk zijn ten opzichte van zowel de patiënt als de behandelende arts en de eerste geraadpleegde arts. De behandelende arts brengt de patiënt op de hoogte van de resultaten van deze raadpleging;
2° minstens één maand laten verlopen tussen het schriftelijke verzoek van de patiënt en het toepassen van de euthanasie.

(Een volle MAAND? Bompa wordt zot als hij dat hoort!)

§4. Het verzoek van de patiënt moet op schrift zijn gesteld.

(Shit)

Het document wordt opgesteld, gedateerd en getekend door de patiënt zelf. Indien de patiënt daartoe niet in staat is, gebeurt het op schrift stellen door een meerderjarige persoon die gekozen is door de patiënt en geen materieel belang mag hebben bij de dood van de patiënt. Deze persoon maakt melding van het feit dat de patiënt niet in staat is om zijn verzoek op schrift te formuleren en geeft de redenen waarom. In dat geval gebeurt de opschriftstelling in bijzijn van de arts en noteert die persoon de naam van die arts op het document. Dit document dient bij het medisch dossier te worden gevoegd. De patiënt kan te allen tijde het verzoek herroepen, waarna het document uit het medisch dossier wordt gehaald en aan de patiënt wordt teruggegeven.

§5. Alle verzoeken geformuleerd door de patiënt, alsook de handelingen van de behandelende arts en hun resultaat, met inbegrip van het (de) verslag(en) van de geraadpleegde arts(en), worden regelmatig opgetekend in het medisch dossier van de patiënt.

En blablabla, de rest doet niet ter zake tot:

HOOFDSTUK VI. – Bijzondere bepalingen

Art. 14. Het verzoek en de wilsverklaring bedoeld in de artikelen 3 en 4 van deze wet hebben geen dwingende waarde.

Geen arts kan worden gedwongen euthanasie toe te passen.

Geen andere persoon kan worden gedwongen mee te werken aan het toepassen van euthanasie.

Weigert de geraadpleegde arts euthanasie toe te passen, dan moet hij dit de patiënt of de eventuele vertrouwenspersoon tijdig laten weten waarbij hij de redenen van zijn weigering toelicht. Berust zijn weigering op een medische grond dan wordt die in het medisch dossier van de patiënt opgetekend.

De arts die weigert in te gaan op een euthanasieverzoek moet, op verzoek van de patiënt of de vertrouwenspersoon, het medisch dossier van de patiënt meedelen aan de arts die is aangewezen door de patiënt of de vertrouwenspersoon.

> *(En waarom staat er nergens: 'De arts die weigert in te gaan op een euthanasieverzoek moet een arts zoeken die wél bereid is in te gaan op dat verzoek, en mag niet stoppen met zoeken tot hij die gevonden heeft'?)*

Art. 15. Een persoon die overlijdt ten gevolge van euthanasie toegepast met toepassing van de voorwaarden gesteld door deze wet, wordt geacht een natuurlijke dood te zijn gestorven wat betreft de uitvoering van de overeenkomsten waarbij hij partij was, en met name de verzekeringsovereenkomsten.

De bepalingen van artikel 909 van het Burgerlijk Wetboek zijn mede van toepassing op de in artikel 3 bedoelde leden van het verplegend team.

Art. 16. Deze wet treedt in werking ten laatste drie maanden nadat ze in het Belgisch Staatsblad is bekendgemaakt.
Kondigen deze wet af, bevelen dat zij met 's Lands zegel zal worden bekleed en door het Belgisch Staatsblad zal worden bekendgemaakt.
Brussel, 28 mei 2002.
ALBERT
Van Koningswege:
De Minister van Justitie,
M. VERWILGHEN
Met 's Lands zegel gezegeld:
De Minister van Justitie,
M. VERWILGHEN

Daar heb je het.
Bompa komt niet in aanmerking.

Blind en doof zijn en het in je broek doen is geen 'ondraaglijk fysiek lijden dat niet gelenigd kan worden'. Voor hém, ja, maar dokters hebben nu eenmaal een andere waardeschaal, als het over lijden gaat.
Wie niet ondraaglijk afziet, heeft een leven met voldoende kwaliteit. De wet zegt niets over levensmoe zijn, over verveling, over vernedering, over frustratie, over zelfrespect, over handicaps die je alles afnemen wat je leuk vindt. De wet zegt niets over luiers die losscheuren en pis die onderhemdjes doordrenkt, over explosieve diarree, over naakt naar een wasbak moeten lopen en je daar in de kou te staan scheren terwijl je huilt omdat je dat allemaal niet meer wil meemaken, over buisjes in je piemel die je wakker houden en het gevoel dat je te oud

bent geworden om al die ellende te doorstaan.
En psychisch lijden dan? Hoe kun je dat vaststellen? Een beetje depressie, een doodswens, het gevoel tot in je ziel gekrenkt te zijn, je eigen identiteit niet meer kunnen beleven – dat is toch geen ondraaglijke psychische pijn? Dat maakt ieder van ons mee, als het onze tijd is.

Wie gaat het bompa vertellen? Hij die zo rekent op de nieuwe wet? 'Sorry bompa, je lijdt niet genoeg. Dat heeft de wetgever voor jou beslist.'

11

Wij zijn thuis vrijzinnig. In plaats van mijn communie heb ik het Feest van de Vrijzinnige Jeugd gedaan. In plaats van een kruis hing bij ons een grote litho van de vrijzinnige fakkel. In opbouw, uiteraard, want een vrijzinnig Vlaanderen, ontworsteld aan de beknottende obscurantistische greep van welke godsdienst dan ook, is iets dat we met vereende krachten tot stand brengen.
De drie thema's die in mijn familie het meest de gemoederen verhitten zijn onderwijs, abortus en euthanasie. Onderwijs, daar zetten ze zelf hun beste krachten voor in. Allemaal geven ze les in het officieel onderwijs, bolwerk tegen het machtige katholieke net. Abortus, dat is eindelijk legaal, en aangezien er geen jonge vrouwen in de familie zijn, is het thema minder heet dan de twee andere. Euthanasie is het laatste strijdpunt. Er gaat geen maand voorbij of moeder leest een artikel voor uit het tijdschrift van het Humanistisch Verbond, waarin gepleit wordt voor het recht op waardig sterven. 'Waardig!' declameert moeder. 'Waardig is het sleutelwoord. Voor mij geen aftakeling in een karretje. Voor mij geen zever uit de mondhoeken en niet meer weten wie ik ben. Ik wil bij mijn volle verstand en nog in volle gezondheid kunnen zeggen: het is mooi geweest, nú is het gedaan.'
Zoals haar overtuiging dat eist, zet moeder zich in om bompa zijn euthanasie te gunnen. Er gaat geen dag voorbij of ze hangt met een of andere instantie aan de lijn om inlichtingen in te winnen en formulieren te bestellen om het ziekenhuis op zijn verantwoordelijkheid te

wijzen. Waarom zijn we naar een vrijzinnig ziekenhuis gegaan? Toch niet om dezelfde jezuïetenpraat te krijgen als in Sancta-Caritas! Ze heeft de dokters al tien keer duidelijk gemaakt dat het zijn liefste wens is, dat de hele familie erachter staat, dat het bijna een religieuze kwestie is voor ons.

Niettemin. Er is een verschil tussen vechten voor het recht op waardig sterven voor iedereen, en datzelfde recht voor je eigen vader. Ik loop bij haar aan en ze zit suf op de grond. Voor haar ligt een fotoalbum uit haar jeugd. Zij als driejarig meisje met bompa in het park. Zij met bompa op een picknick in Sint-Job. Ernaast liggen de artikelen van het Humanistisch Verbond die ze in de loop der jaren gespaard heeft, de tientallen eendere pleidooien voor waardig sterven. Ze huilt.

'Ik weet niet meer of ik juist zit. Ik ben hem *dood* aan het laten gaan. Mijn eigen vader. Ik *wil* niet dat hij doodgaat! Al die dokters doen hun uiterste best om hem te genezen en wat doe ik? Ik wil hen dat beletten.'

Ik zeg haar dat ze daar goed aan doet. Dat de wil van de persoon zelf de doorslag geeft. Dat je baas bent over je eigen leven. Wie wil sterven, moet dat kunnen.

De dokters spreken ons geduldig tegen. Vriendelijk maar kordaat. Euthanasie *is* niet zomaar zeggen: nu is het voor mij genoeg geweest, ik stop ermee. Dat is zelfmoord. Euthanasie heeft niets te maken met de vernedering van het aftakelen, het ongemak van in een rolstoel zitten, de tragiek van je eigen kinderen niet meer herkennen. Het gaat om pijn. En bovenal om een akkoord tussen patiënt en dokter, een consensus, zoals altijd in de medische ethiek.

Ze begrijpt het, en ze wil het niet begrijpen. Euthanasie

is *simpel*. Voor: iedereen met een beetje verstand in zijn kop en een hart in zijn lijf. Tegen: de katholieken. Maar deze dokters zijn niet katholiek!

12

De Strangers hebben tweeënvijftig jaar bestaan. En nu houden ze ermee op. Met een afscheidsconcert in de Elisabethzaal.

De Strangers zijn een komisch gezelschap van vier zangers, die covers brengen van internationale hits met een eigen tekst in het Antwerps dialect. Ze zijn de laatste overlevenden van de ooit zo rijke Antwerpse volkscultuur, die in heel Vlaanderen populair was. In de jaren zeventig en tachtig stonden ze ettelijke keren in de hitparade. Ze hadden eigen programma's op de televisie.

Ik ben een fan van De Strangers. Ik ken meer dan tien van hun teksten zo van buiten. Hoewel ik normaal geen Antwerps spreek, vloeit bij het meezingen dat boerse, besmette, onweerstaanbare dialect uit mij. Op mijn elfde heb ik tijdens een schoolfeest *Chop-soy Fighting* gezongen, terwijl ik met mijn vingers spleetogen trok.

(Op de melodie van Kung Fu Fighting*)*

Gist're zennekik goe gewete
bij de chinees gon ete
mor ik had m'n cens vergete
en toen heeget er op gezete
't was ambras mè de garçon
omda'k ni betale kon
en toen goot diê vuile smous
me kostuum vol currysaus
dus ge zie da zo van hier
dakkik toen koleirig wier

daarom gooide-n-ik van den toog
recht ne loempia in z'n oog

Ik heb op de redactie gevochten om het concert te mogen verslaan. Niet dat iemand anders kandidaat was. Niemand van mijn collega's begrijpt mijn voorliefde voor Antwerpse volkskunst. Ze vinden ze flauw, boertig, op het randje van racistisch (en vaak erover). Vooroorlogs vermaak dat enkel nog leeft bij marginalen en oude liberalen.

Ik weet ook niet precies waarom ik ervan hou. Gewoon, omdat het volks is? En omdat ik opgegroeid ben met het idee dat wat volks is goed is? Wat betekent het anders, uit een rode familie te komen? Economisch: niets meer. Sociaal: weinig. Cultureel: alles. Links zijn is: een zijn met de gewone man. Toch? Zelfs al heb ik zelf gestudeerd, zelfs al ben ik schrijver en journalist, het maakt me geen haar beter dan wie de universiteit van het leven doorlopen heeft. Zelfs al spreek ik zelf redelijk algemeen Nederlands, het dialect is een pure, echtere taal, de taal van ruwe waarheid en spontane humor waarin je gedachten en emoties kunt uitdrukken die ik niet eens kan denken of voelen. Zelfs al draag ik zelf sobere kleren, zelfs al hou ik mijn lichaamshaar binnen de perken: ik hou van snorren en tapijtjes in de nek en dikke pensen en gouden kettingen en trainingsbroeken en geblondeerde permanents. Dat is hoe het volk zich kleedt en wie daarmee spot, is alle voeling met de wereld kwijt. De volksmens is een ideaal: recht voor z'n raap, het hart op de tong, als-we-dat-al-niet-meer-mogen-zeggen, ieder-zijn-gedacht-maar-mij-maakt-ge-niks-wijs.

In november 1992 was het afgelopen met De Strangers. De groep bestond toen veertig jaar en was al die tijd geliefd om haar grappige, soms scherpe teksten die de mening van de straat vertolkten. Maar nu was het Vlaams Blok doorgebroken. Zijn bolwerk was Antwerpen, zijn kernpubliek bestond uit volksmensen, fans van De Strangers. Het was een tijd waarin mensen die niet op het Blok gestemd hadden, zich voorbereidden op de oorlog en de deportaties die komen zouden. Het was een tijd waarin reportages op televisie werden uitgezonden over kiezers van het Vlaams Blok die in hun platste Antwerps vertelden dat ze een geweer hadden gekocht, en dat ze hun Marokkaanse buren gerust omver zouden durven knallen.

In dat klimaat besloten De Strangers om in te gaan op het verzoek van het Vlaams Blok om op zijn partijfeest op te treden. Ze zongen *De Ziekenkas,* het verhaal van een Marokkaan die al jaren leeft van het geld dat hij krijgt van het ziekenfonds, hoewel hij eigenlijk niet ziek is.

Hij was ne Marokkaan en hij kwam uit Marokko
daar liet 'm dertien kind'ren achter en 'n geit
hier at 'm pistolees mè heps en kees en choco
en kreeg het wreed on z'ne lever na nen tijd
hier waarkten-hem 'n maand of acht in e fabrikske
mor mè diê lever wier 'm waarkonbekwaam
a ging in ziekekas en doet al jare nikske
na krijge z'hem nog mè giên stokken hier vandaan
ikke in ziekekas, ik hemme e goe leve
in ziekeka, ziekaka, ziekakas
ikke niks waarke, en toch mij centjes geve

de ziekeka, ziekaka, ziekakas
allah is groot, mor ziekekas is groter
alleen nog hebbe ene grote wens
hier nog wa blijf, en nog wa centjes poter
dan ikke terug en in Marokko rijke mens.

De Strangers hadden pech dat er een televisieploeg aanwezig was. Van de ene dag op de andere waren ze ongewenst. Geplande optredens werden afgezegd. Op de radio werden hun platen geweerd. Op televisie waren ze niet meer welkom. Ze kregen dreigtelefoons. Hun platenfirma gooide hen eruit. Alleen bejaarden kwamen nog naar hun optredens. Een van de populairste Vlaamse groepen, een groep die meer dan twintig nummeréén hits had gescoord, een groep die ontvangen was door ministers en de koning, werd zo het symbool van verbitterd, marginaal, racistisch Antwerpen.

Tot nu. Bij hun afscheid staan de kranten vol met reportages over de groep, die het langer heeft uitgehouden dan de Rolling Stones. Alex, John, Bob en Nest mogen in tientallen interviews komen uitleggen dat zij geen racisten zijn, maar gezellige volksjongens, die met iedereén goedmoedig de spot drijven.

Ik heb meegedaan aan de rehabilitatie van de groep. Omdat ik zelf een fan ben. Omdat ik niet geloof dat ze echt racistisch zijn. Omdat de heksenjacht op De Strangers een jacht op de hele Antwerpse volkscultuur was. De elite spuwde het volk uit – ha nee, daar deed ik niet aan mee! Ik heb een lang interview gepubliceerd met de vier, waarin ze uitgebreid mochten bewijzen hoe sympathiek ze wel waren en hoe unfair ze behandeld werden.

Ik ben nog geen vijf minuten binnen of ik word aangeklampt door Nest, de joviaalste van de vier. 'Tommeke! Tommeke van de Gazet! Fantástisch dat ge zijt gekomen. Mannen!'

Hij roept er de anderen bij.

'Hier zie, Tom Naegels. Da's ne straffe gast. Amai da's ne straffe gast.'

Hij bokst me tegen de schouder, hij geeft me zijn typische Nest-lach. Hij trekt andere voorbijgangers aan hun jasje, stelt ze aan me voor en herhaalt wat voor straffe gast ik ben. Nest is het typevoorbeeld van de Antwerpse pocher. Als hij ergens binnenkomt, mept hij iedereen op de rug en buldert: 'Gij zijt ne straffe gast! Gij zijt de man!' Hartelijk. (Oppervlakkig.) Warm. (Brallerig.) Open. (Windbuil.) Zo is de volksmens.

John, de grapjas van de groep, doet alsof hij me een hand wil geven, trekt ze op het laatste ogenblik weg en zet me een neus. Iedereen schatert. Dan maakt hij een grap over zijn schoonmoeder. Nee, hij maakt niet eens een grap, hij zegt gewoon iets van 'Amai gij ziet zuur, precies mijn schoonmoeder'. Het slaat nergens op, en toch lacht iedereen, omdat het over een schoonmoeder gaat. Schoonmoeder is een signaal om te lachen.

Dat is volkse humor. Schoonmoeders kijven, Hollanders zijn gierig, getrouwde mannen zitten onder de plak, postbodes en agenten drinken graag een pintje en Marokkanen hebben tien kinderen en profiteren van den dop. Het herkenningseffect, niet de verrassing, maakt het grappig. Dat is wat wij, gestudeerden, vergeten zijn.

De Elisabethzaal stroomt vol. Meer dan duizend permanents, snorren, gouden kettinkjes en pensen waggelen naar binnen. Ik mag hen staande houden en vragen

waarom ze naar het concert komen. Waarom ze na al die tijd nog van De Strangers houden. De antwoorden zijn duidelijk. Omdat het plezante mannen zijn. Altijd opgewekt. Omdat ze nog echt iets kunnen. Omdat het gewone volksmensen zijn, die de taal van de straat spreken. En omdat het erg is wat ze met hen gedaan hebben.
Het concert begint en het moet gezegd, De Strangers zijn knappe zangers. Zelfs op hun zeventigste klinkt hun meerstemmige zang foutloos, zelfs in de a-capellapassages. Het optreden verloopt in de stijl van de oude revues, die voor de Tweede Wereldoorlog populair waren. Er komen bevriende artiesten liedjes zingen, het geheel wordt in uiterst beschaafd Nederlands aan elkaar gepraat door een andere veterane, Conny Neefs.
Tussen de liedjes door worden er moppen getapt. Zo vertelt John dat hij op zoek is geweest naar een nonnenkostuum, maar dat hij er nergens nog een vond omdat alle kerken weg waren. 'Dus ben ik maar naar Borgerhout gegaan en heb ik dit gevonden!'
Met een ingenieuze beweging trekt John de rok die hij draagt in één ruk over zijn hoofd en hop, hij heeft een boerka aan.
'Zo lopen ze er daar allemaal bij!' schatert hij.
De zaal ontploft. Als John op zijn knieën valt om in de richting van Mekka te bidden, onderwijl met een scherpe neusstem 'Allaaaaaaaah!' zingend, doen tranen rouge en make-up over wangen uitlopen. Pensen schudden, snorren ritselen, gouden kettingen klingelen. Terwijl het toch niet zo grappig is. Ten eerste is het niet waar, er loopt bijna niemand in boerka in Borgerhout, ten tweede is er niet eens een grap verteld. Hij heeft gewoon een boerka aangedaan en 'Allah' gezegd!
Volkshumor, Tom. Schoonmoeders kijven, stadsambte-

naren zijn lui en moslims dragen boerka's. Het volk houdt van tradities. Jij houdt van het volk.
De grap wordt uitgewerkt. John is gestopt met bidden en doet alsof hij Arabisch praat: 'Achamchamcham, ai ai ai achamacham. Mech mech mech banana patata ai ai chamcham!' Het publiek gaat nu helemaal uit zijn dak. Een laaiend applaus steekt op. Een vrouw zoekt in haar tas naar een zakdoek, maar laat de tas vallen omdat ze zo schokt. 'Banana patata!' giert ze. Ze stoot haar buurvrouw aan: 'Banana patata!'
De Ziekenkas spelen De Strangers niet meer. Ze durven niet. Toch zingen ze heel even, echt heel even maar, één zinnetje. Een sample. Door een ander liedje heen. 'Ikke in ziekekas, ik hemme een goe leven' – dat is alles. En opnieuw davert de zaal van het applaus, het voetgestamp, het gejuich.
(Ze lachen veel harder dan om de grappen over Hollanders of Spanjaarden.)
En toch zijn het geen racisten!
(Weet ik.)
(Vind ik.)
(Denk ik.)
(Geloof ik.)
Ik heb met deze mensen gesproken! Het zijn gezellige, joviale, hartelijke mensen, eenvoudige warme mensen die drinken uit de authentieke bron van volkse kennis. Arbeiders, zoals bompa vroeger. Ze hebben plezier en houden van het leven. Wie ben ik om mijn smaak van humor aan hen op te dringen? Mag er dan niet om alles gelachen worden?
De andere journalisten slaan hun handen voor hun gezicht of kijken naar hun schoenen. 'Dit is Antwerpen', zucht een collega. 'Dit kan alleen hier.'

13

Na het concert ga ik naar Nadia. Het is vreemd om, na die overdosis Vlaamse volksmensen met hun banana-patata-geschater, door Borgerhout en de Seefhoek te lopen en niets anders te zien dan Arabieren, Afrikanen en Oost-Europeanen. Zouden ze weten dat vlakbij een zaal propvol Vlamingen zich net een breuk heeft gelachen om een karikaturale voorstelling van hun kledij en hun taal? Hoe zouden ze reageren als ik nu luidkeels 'Chamchamcham ai ai banana patata' begin te roepen? Zouden ze aanvaarden dat dat Vlaamse humor is?
Ik vecht tegen het onbehaaglijke gevoel de enige blanke in de wijk te zijn. Er is niets bedreigends aan deze mensen. Ze trekken zich niets aan van mij. (Maar ze zijn met zovelen!) Ze staan gewoon in grote groepen geanimeerd op straat te praten. (Waarom doen ze alles in groep?) Mijn hart gaat naar hen uit. Zij zijn de echte verworpenen der aarde, die nog lang niet ontwaakt zijn. Maarrrrr! Laten we niet de fouten maken van het verleden, om ofwel sympathie te hebben voor de gewone blanke Antwerpenaar die het niet zo breed heeft, ofwel voor de zwarte medemens. Ze zijn allebei het volk. Ik hou van hen allebei.
Ik ga Nadia's huis binnen. Ik schud mijn hoofd als de klink in mijn hand achterblijft en zet ze er zo goed als ik kan weer aan. De trap is wankel, het behang in de gang bladdert van de muren. Maar haar flatje is gezellig en netjes, ze staat me in het deurgat glunderend op te wachten en ik kus haar vol overgave.
Na de kus slaat ze haar handen voor mijn ogen. Ze gie-

chelt en leidt me door haar flat, langs het immense bed dat het midden van de ruimte inneemt en de doorgang naar de keuken bijna blokkeert. Daar haalt ze haar handen weg en juicht: 'Ta-daa!'
Ik zie haar keuken, verlicht door een flikkerende tl-lamp, de kale, kleine kamer met de kastjes die altijd openvallen (ik vermoed dat haar hele flat scheef staat, want zowel de deuren van de kleerkast als die van de keukenkast vallen wijd open), de stoelen met de metalen poten en het namaakleren zitvlak, en de enige tafel van de flat. Op die tafel staan twee borden en daarvoor twee lange rode brandende kaarsen. Kerstkaarsen. In groene plastic houdertjes in de vorm van een hulstblad.
'Ta-daa', zegt Nadia opnieuw, onzekerder nu.
Juist, sorry, vergeten.
'Maar dat is prachtig!'
Te laat, niet overtuigend genoeg, maar ze besluit het te negeren. 'Nee?' glundert ze. 'Is niet zo romantic maar beetje ja?'
Waarom zie ik dat dat kerstkaarsen zijn? Waarom kan ik niet gewoon denken: Goh, kaarsen, lekker romantisch? Vanwaar die mentale glimlach (een spottende! Geef maar toe!) om die plastic hulstbladeren? Voel ik me te goed voor hulstbladeren misschien? Voel ik me beter dan haar omdat ik weet welke kaarsen bij welke gelegenheid horen? Kijk ik neer op haar koekjesdozenromantiek? En waarom dan? Omdat die niet echt is? Voor haar is ze echt! Voor haar zijn die kerstkaarsen een authentieke manier om te tonen dat ze van me houdt en dat ze gezellig met mij de avond wil doorbrengen. En wat doe ik, monsieur superieur? Ik zie ons in een Franse tragikomedie, het blije meisje en de slome jon-

gen, genietend van kerstkaarsen in de late zomer in hun troosteloze keukentje.

Nadia heeft me een heel nieuwe soort liefde leren kennen: die zonder woorden. Voor veel mensen is dat de allerhoogste vorm maar voor een schrijver is het aanpassen. Ik verlang er vreselijk naar om bij haar te zijn, alleen weet ik nooit wat tegen haar te zeggen. Het is niet dat er een taalprobleem is. We spreken allebei goed Engels en haar Nederlands wordt steeds beter. We hebben een onderwerpenprobleem. Waarover praat je met iemand die tot vorig jaar in Pakistan woonde?
'Hoe was concert?' vraagt ze.
'Goed', zeg ik.
(Nu moet ik vertellen over het concert. We kunnen die eeuwige stiltes alleen doorbreken als we tegen elkaar praten.)
'Het was een groep Antwerpenaars.'
'Ze waren van Antwerpen?'
'Ja. Zangers. Van Antwerpen. Vier. En ze zijn grappig.'
'Op welke manier?'
(Goeie vraag. Hoe kan ik de geestigheid van het platte Antwerpse dialect duidelijk maken aan iemand die niet eens gewoon Nederlands spreekt?)
'Ze zingen in het dialect van Antwerpen. Ze nemen een bekend liedje, en ze spelen het zelf, maar met een andere tekst. Een grappige tekst. Ken je *Bambolero* van The Gipsy Kings?'
'Nee.'
Hier gaan we. Eerst zing ik *Bambolero*, en dan op die melodie 'De paella van Manuela', en dan vertaal ik de tekst van dat liedje in het Engels, ik leg uit wat paella is,

en wat flamenco is, en dat flamencozangers kreunen – ik kreun als een flamencozanger – en dat het grappig is als De Strangers op dezelfde manier kreunen – ik zing flamenco-kreunend 'Ik moet die paella ni hemmen!' –, ik stamp met mijn voeten, leg uit dat het grappig is om vier oude Antwerpenaars op dezelfde manier met hun voeten te zien rakketakken, ik leg de woordspeling uit in 'heure garnot was zo plat as ne pladijs' en uiteindelijk heeft ze een redelijke theoretische kennis van de relatie tussen Spanje, flamenco, paella, The Gipsy Kings, oude mannen, het Antwerps en waarom ik die combinatie grappig vind.
'Belgen verkleden zich graag', lacht ze. 'Dat is wat Belgen leuk vinden.'
Is dat wat ik net heb uitgelegd?

De bel gaat. Het is Nadia's buurvrouw, een Soedanese die zich voorstelt als Didi. Nadia kijkt verstoord.
'Dag Didi', zeg ik. 'Ik ben Tom.'
Ik glimlach warm en open, om te tonen dat ik een warme en open man ben, voor wie ze niet bang hoeft te zijn.
'Me Didi', herhaalt ze. Ze lacht ook.
'Ik Tom', herhaal ik. We staan naar elkaar te lachen.
Ze vraagt hoe het met me gaat. 'Goed', zeg ik. Verlegen verschuilt ze zich achter het gordijn dat de slaapkamer van de woonkamer scheidt en zegt, nu in het Nederlands: 'Ik ben Didi.'
'Hallo Didi', zeg ik. Ik spreek traag en articuleer duidelijk.
'Hoe gaat het?'
'Goed', zeg ik opnieuw.
Didi kijkt smekend naar Nadia, die hatelijk terugstaart.

'Didi wil een aanvraag indienen om Belg te worden', zucht ze. Didi knikt enthousiast. Blijkt dat ze op haar aanvraag drie referenties nodig heeft van echte, autochtone Belgen die verklaren dat Didi het verdient om Belg te zijn. En of ik een van die drie wil zijn.
Maar ik ken haar helemaal niet!
De twee andere Belgen ook niet, zo maakt ze me duidelijk. Dat is dus geen probleem.
Kent ze dan geen enkele Belg? vraag ik. Een die met kennis van zaken iets positiefs over haar kan schrijven?
Nee, geen enkele.
En weer dat onbehaaglijke gevoel. Wat is er mis met mij? Ik hou van deze mensen! Ze zijn het volk, de verworpenen der etc. Als ze Belg wil zijn, dan moet dat worden toegejuicht.
Ik blijk plots veel meer belang te hechten aan mijn nationaliteit dan ik altijd heb beweerd. Hoe kan ze Belg worden als ze geen enkele Belg kent? Dat betekent toch dat ze niet geïntegreerd is?
(Wat kan het jou schelen? Ze wil gewoon je handtekening.)
(Ze wil Belg zijn omdat ze dan meer geld krijgt van de sociale zekerheid.)
(Leugenaar! Racist!)
(Wat gebeurt er als men ontdekt dat ik een valse getuigenis heb afgelegd? Wat als ze Belg wordt en dat misbruikt om weet ik wat te doen? Vijfde colonne, terrorisme, gezinshereniging... Waarom komt die verantwoordelijkheid naar mij?)
(Een handtekening! Je helpt haar ermee. Lief meisje, vast allerlei ergs meegemaakt, eindelijk in het veilige België. En jij vermoedt enkel kwaads!)

Ik lees de papieren. De eerste getuigenis beweert dat Didi zeer goed Nederlands spreekt. Ik probeer een gesprek met haar – dat valt tegen. De andere benadrukt vooral hoe vriendelijk ze is. Dat lijkt wel zo te zijn.
Didi kijkt vragend naar Nadia: wat is er mis met jouw vriend? De vorige twee Belgen tekenden gewoon.
(Misschien heeft ze ze gewoon op straat aangesproken.)
Ik schrijf: 'Ik ken Didi als vriendin van vrienden, en elke keer dat ik haar ontmoette, was ze vriendelijk. Ze wil graag Belg worden. Tom Naegels.'
Niemand kan zeggen dat het niet waar is.

Als Didi weg is, begint Nadia een tirade tegen Afrikanen die al jaren hier zijn, geen woord Nederlands kennen, geen enkele Belg kennen, geen werk zoeken en toch Belg willen worden. Onverbeterlijke roddelaars, die dagenlang met elkaar lullen – maar iets van hun leven maken? Ho maar!
Ik sla haar verbaasd gade en zeg: 'Ik was vergeten dat je niet van gekleurde mensen houdt.'
Dat had ik beter niet gezegd. Ze houdt onmiddellijk op.
'Ik hou wel van zwarte mensen, Tom.'
O jee.
'Ik weet dat je van zwarte mensen houdt.'
'Als je dat weet, waarom zeg je dat dan?'
'Het was een grap. Ironie.'
'Niemand zegt zoiets als grap!'
'Maar je was zo boos aan het afgeven op Didi. Dus dacht ik, het zou ironisch zijn als jij, als donkere vrouw...'
'Ik probeer alle mensen te respecteren, Tom. Ik respecteer wat ze zijn in mijn hart.'
Ik kan er niets aan doen: ik vecht om een glimlach te

onderdrukken. Dat maakt het alleen erger.
'Je lacht me uit! Je vindt me belachelijk!'
Welnee, natuurlijk niet. Maar 'Ik respecteer iedereen in mijn hart' – sorry, mijn ironiefilter kan dat niet aan. Hatelijke ironie! Nadia respecteert iedereen in haar hart: dat is mooi, dat is bewonderenswaardig, dat is niet iets om mee te lachen. Ze is goed, ze is puur, ze is oprecht – ik ben alleen sarcastisch en cynisch en ik voel me er nog superieur om ook.
Is dit een cultuurverschil? Misschien komt ze uit een land waar ironie niet bestaat. Ach, kom nou! Cultuur gaat over de scheiding van Kerk en Staat, over de positie van de vrouw en de erkenning van democratische basiswaarden. Niet over de toon waarop je iets zegt, toch?

Nadia en ik liggen in bed. We hebben ruzie. Ze is nog steeds boos omdat ik de indruk gewekt heb dat ze niet iedereen, blank en zwart, respecteert in haar hart. Ik heb geen zin meer in de discussie en ga met mijn rug naar haar toe liggen.
Zij: 'Jij voelt je bwaaf?'
Ik: (zwijg).
Zij: 'Ik weet dat je niet slaapt. Voel je je bwaaf?'
Ik (schokschouderend): 'Misschien.'
Zij (draait zich pathetisch om): 'Ik vergeef het mezelf nooit!'
Ik (draai me verbaasd om): 'Nadia, ik ben niet kwaad, oké?'
'Maar je zei dat je je bwaaf voelde!'
'Bwaaf, ja, not angry!'
'Bwaaf is angry! O is much worse!'
'Niet waar!'

'O, Tom zeg niet dat bwaaf niet bwaaf is! Ik weet wat bwaaf is!'
'Ja maar ik wist niet dat bwaaf voor jou betekende: heel kwaad. Voor mij betekent bwaaf: een beetje gefrustreerd.'
'Frustreet?'
'Geïrriteerd, verveeld, prikkelbaar.'
'Gebruik makkelijke woorden.'
'Dit zijn makkelijke woorden!'
'Je zei dat je bwaaf was! Ik vergeef het mezelf nooit!'

14

Of hij dan geen honger heeft, vraag ik.
Elke vraag stuit op minachting. Elk gespreksonderwerp is banaal, een lichtzinnigheid van de levenden, iets ondraaglijk frivools dat verbleekt bij zijn strijd van de doden. Wie denkt er aan honger als er enkel aan sterven gedacht wordt?
Het is een karwei om hem te bezoeken. Zo somber, zo geïrriteerd als hij is. De verpleegsters klagen steen en been, dat meneer Lorreyne zo'n lastige man is.
Hij krijgt antidepressiva. Hij verstopt ze onder zijn matras.
Ik heb mijn walkman voor hem bij me. Als hij dan geen tv kan kijken, als hij niet kan lezen en zich verveelt, misschien kan hij naar muziek luisteren?
Hij legt de walkman in zijn la.
Naast zijn bed staat een grote plastic zak met volgescheten en volgepiste kleren. Die neemt moeder straks mee om thuis te wassen. De lakens zijn van zijn benen gegleden. Ik zou zijn dij met één hand kunnen omvatten. En wit dat die dij is. En slap. Twee weken liggen en alle spieren zijn afgestorven. Hij kan niet meer lopen, zelfs al zou hij willen.
Ik heb al geprobeerd te praten over:

1. het voetbal
2. het wielrennen
3. mijn nieuwe auto
4. het weer
5. fietsen met zulk mooi weer
6. mijn verkoudheid

Hij doet soms zijn best om interesse voor te wenden, maar na twee zinnen schudt hij ongelovig zijn hoofd, keert de verbeten trek terug om zijn mond en zegt hij: 'Ze willen niet, hè. Ze willen het echt niet.'
En hij heeft gelijk: de dokters willen niet. Ze zijn niet uit principe tegen euthanasie. Ze hebben het al vaak toegepast, lang voor het wettelijk toegestaan was. Ze hebben mijn bompa's verzoek ernstig overwogen. Maar na overleg met collega's zijn ze tot het besluit gekomen dat hij niet in aanmerking komt. Hem doden kunnen ze niet met hun geweten in overeenstemming brengen.
Hem zichzelf zien doden blijkbaar wel. Het is een merkwaardig ethisch onderscheid. De vuile, trage dood is moreel meer toegestaan dan de snelle, propere.

15

Er is een psychiater aangesteld om herhaaldelijk, over een redelijke termijn gespreid, zijn uitdrukkelijke en zelf geformuleerde wens aan te horen, en met hem te overleggen of er geen redelijke alternatieven zijn.
Er is een moreel consulente, die ongeveer hetzelfde doet.
De behandelende geneesheer komt elke dag kijken of de wens nog steeds uitgesproken wordt. Er is een tweede arts aangesteld, die hetzelfde doet. En kijk, daar duikt een derde arts op, om zeker te zijn.
Hij doet niets anders dan tien keer per dag hetzelfde zeggen: 'Ja, ik wil dood, nee, ik wil geen alternatief, ja, ik vind dit ondraaglijk lijden.'
Zijn die mensen doof?
Bompa is van een generatie waar de man één keer zijn wens uitsprak, en die wens was wet. Zijn hele leven heeft dat gegolden, over minder belangrijke onderwerpen dan dit. Niemand legt hem uit dat herhalen in de procedure zit, dat het in tien verschillende rapporten moet staan, gespreid over een maand.
Hij is bars, hij is boos, hij scheldt zijn dokters uit. Dat werkt tegen hem.
'Uw grootvader is een zeer dominante man.'
'Hij toont weinig respect.'
'Hij *wil* de alternatieven niet overwegen.'
'Het is een depressie. Dat gaat over.'
'Meneer Lorreyne', heeft de psychiater hem toegesproken. 'U hebt iets te willen, maar wij ook. U vraagt ons een gunst, en wij kunnen die vraag al dan niet inwilligen. Als u dat niet kunt begrijpen, dan wens ik u goedendag.'
Het is geen *gunst*, het is zijn *recht*.

16

Saskia en ik hebben nog niet aan onze families verteld dat we uit elkaar zijn. In afwachting daarvan blijven we voor de buitenwereld koppel spelen. Ze komt mee naar een familiefeest van mij.
Bomma verjaart. Het is haar eerste feest met haar kinderen zonder dat haar man de baas over haar speelt, zonder dat hij opstaat en tot haar gêne tegen niemand in het bijzonder een toespraak houdt, of het nu bij een van de kinderen thuis of op restaurant is: 'Ik zeg heeeee God, het is *genoeg* geweest, hè makker! Het mag gedaan zijn.'
(Op elk verjaardagsfeest, het zijne of het hare, smeekte hij om de dood. Zijn blinde ogen opgeslagen naar de God in wie hij enkel dan geloofde, armen als Mozes gespreid voor een bord eendenborstfilet met kroketjes: neem mij op in het rijk der hemelen.)
Bomma heeft een verjaardagskaart gekregen die muziek speelt als je haar openvouwt. *Happy Birthday* van Stevie Wonder. *Hap-py birthday to you, hap-py birthday.* Het hele feest lang. Om gek van te worden.
'Oooo Tom', glundert bomma. 'Zo'n mooie kaart heb ik nog nooit gezien!'
(Ze is negentig. Ze moet ooit al eens een muzikale verjaardagskaart gezien hebben.)
We kijken naar het nieuws. Het gaat over de moord op Ann en Eefje. Bomma kijkt met grote ogen.
'Wat is dát allemaal?!'
We kijken haar vreemd aan.
'Ma, dat weet ge toch? Dat is die Dutroux!' roept moeder, hoewel bomma niet doof is.

Bomma schudt haar hoofd. 'Je weet dat ik niet slim ben.'
Ik doe alsof het normaal is dat iemand niet weet wie Dutroux is. Ik teken de man op een stuk kladpapier, neem twee kranten met artikelen over de zaak, noem de namen van de vermoorde meisjes, speel de Witte Mars na, evoceer het spaghetti-arrest en hobbel door de kamer ter imitatie van Michel Nihoul. Bomma kijkt het verbaasd aan.
'Allee, dat ik dat allemaal gemist heb. Ik zal juist in de gang geweest zijn.'

17

Er staat iets te gebeuren. De Marokkaanse gemeenschap roert zich. Het zal niet lang meer duren of ze komt naar buiten. Op een positieve of negatieve manier, dat zal afhangen van hoe de regerende klasse reageert. En ik krijg de kans dat in primeur te brengen. Ik krijg het voorrecht om gerespecteerde woordvoerders van de Marokkaanse gemeenschap te spreken. Ik word verwacht om een halfuur voor middernacht in vzw Al Jazeera in Borgerhout, en alles zal duidelijk worden.
Dat is wat Ahmed Al Eboudi, een vage kennis die ik ooit eens ontmoet heb op een open dag van een of ander allochtoon centrum, me aan de telefoon meldt. 'Je weet dat ik om mijn vrienden geef. Ahmed zorgt voor mooie stukjes in de krant.'
Een halfuur voor middernacht? Is dat een tijdstip voor een persconferentie? En wat is dat voor gezwollen, pathetisch gezwets over gerespecteerde woordvoerders? Ik ken die mannen een beetje: nog een koekje, nog een theetje, wat hebben ze een respect voor me en uiteindelijk hebben we vier uur gepalaverd en is er niets gezegd. Maar goed: hier zit ik dan, een halfuur voor middernacht, in vzw Al Jazeera. Stel dat ik echt een wereldprimeur krijg.
(Nu lieg ik mezelf voor. Het is een kans om eens in een Marokkaanse vzw te komen, die geheimzinnige etablissementen waarover gefluisterd wordt dat het drugsholen zijn en onderduikadressen voor illegalen, maar die ondanks die avontuurlijke geruchten oersaai en ongezellig lijken. Hoe zal ik mijn allochtone broeders anders leren

kennen dan in hun natuurlijke habitat? Bovendien: ergens streelt het mijn multiculturele ego, altijd blij met een nieuw laagje vernis. Anderen schrijven over onze moslimvrienden, maar ik ken ze echt! Ze bellen me op! Ze respecteren me! Een nacht in de vzw, vier uur zwetsen en mijn geloofwaardigheid als opiniemaker kan er weer tegen. Voor mij geen ivoren toren: ik adem, ik zweet, ik lééf diversiteit.)

Ahmed is te laat.

(Uiteraard.)

Al Jazeera lijkt op een parochiezaal. Kil, te groot, te leeg, flikkerende witte buislampen, metalen toog. Aan de muur hangt een dartsbord, een pro-Palestinaposter en een affiche van *The Talented Mister Ripley* ('sexy en dodelijk'). Er staan twee biljarttafels. Ook al heet het café Al Jazeera, de tv staat op een Arabische muziekzender. Ik weet niet wat ik zie. Schaarsgeklede dames! Wiegende Arabische borsten! Strakke kontjes! Er zijn geen moslims meer.

Op de kaart staan drie drankjes: muntthee, chocolademelk en milkshake. Ik neem muntthee omdat de twee andere me al te belachelijk lijken – ik wil niet afgaan voor al die stoere mediterrane mannen. Dan zie ik dat de helft van hen zelf een chocomelk of aardbeienshake nuttigt. In hun snorren hangen roze melkrestjes.

Waarom hebben oudere Arabische mannen altijd snorren? Weten ze dan niet dat die je nors doen kijken? Dat ze alle mannen op elkaar doen lijken? Ik zit tussen tientallen nurkse mannen, stuk voor stuk het evenbeeld van Saddam Hoessein.

Uiteraard zijn er geen vrouwen. Het geeft het gezelschap iets triests. Tientallen mannen kijken naar wiegende bor-

sten in videoclips, terwijl die borsten gewoon bij hen aan tafel hadden kunnen zitten.
Ik wacht op Ahmed en probeer te doen alsof het normaal is dat een jonge blanke man alleen in een Marokkaans café zit. De snorren met hun milkshakes proberen te doen alsof zij het ook normaal vinden. Iedereen is hier welkom. Van onder hun borstelige wenkbrauwen werpen ze vluchtige blikken op mij. Als ik toevallig net dan opkijk om een vluchtige blik op hen te werpen, doen zij alsof ze naar de televisie kijken, en ik alsof ik nieuwe thee bestel. Al gauw heb ik buikpijn van de thee.
Ze spelen mens-erger-je-niet. Het heeft iets idioots, volwassen mannen die milkshake drinken en mens-erger-je-niet spelen. En opgaan dat ze doen in dat spel! Er wordt gevloekt en gelachen, heftig gediscussieerd en met handgebaren duidelijk gemaakt dat de ander een smerige zet heeft gedaan.
Soms kijkt er een lachend in mijn richting en roept iets in het Arabisch of het Berbers of een andere taal met veel keelklanken. Het klinkt goedmoedig en ik lach hartelijk terug. Kijk eens hoe harmonieus wij samenleven.
Twee uur heb ik op Ahmed gewacht! De belangrijkste reden waarom ik ben blijven zitten, is omdat weer opstappen me wel zeer verdacht gemaakt zou hebben: jonge Vlaamse man komt een uurtje in Marokkaanse vzw zitten, praat met niemand en gaat weer weg. Als dat geen Staatsveiligheid is, wat dan wel? De tweede reden is dat Ahmed me na een uur gebeld heeft om zich te verontschuldigen. Hij zou er dadelijk zijn. Hij was in slaap gevallen.
(Moeten er nog meer clichés worden bevestigd? Nee? Kunnen we dan verder?)

Als Ahmed eindelijk binnenkomt, moet hij eerst iedereen in het café begroeten. Er moet op ruggen worden gemept, er moeten vrienden worden omhelsd, er wordt tegen schouders gebokst, handen worden met veel omhaal geschud. Er wordt getrakteerd en traktaties worden aanvaard. Daarna krijg ik eindelijk ook een hand en wordt het raadsel van mijn verdachte aanwezigheid opgelost: geen Staatsveiligheid, vriend van Ahmed.

Ik ben ondertussen doodmoe en niet echt meer tot lange gesprekken in staat. Ik wil naar bed. Maar voor Ahmed begint de avond pas. Hij komt bij me zitten en bestelt onmiddellijk erwtensoep voor me. Ik heb geen honger en lust geen erwtensoep, maar durf niet te weigeren. De soep smaakt doordringend naar olijfolie.

Ahmed is voorzitter van een van de vele tientallen organisatietjes die de Marokkaanse gemeenschap telt. Ze is genoemd naar het dorp in Marokko waar de leden vandaan komen en haar eerste bestaansreden is het organiseren van financiële hulp voor de achtergebleven familieleden in dat dorp. Hoewel de leden al meer dan dertig jaar in België zijn, is het pas recent dat de vereniging haar blik op België heeft gericht.

Maar dan ook definitief! (Plots verandert Ahmeds toon. Hij wordt bitter.) Al te lang zijn de moslims als tweederangsburgers behandeld! (Volgt een opsomming van hoe hij als tweederangsburger behandeld werd.) En dat moet gedaan zijn! Vandaar dat de vereniging gekozen heeft voor de dubbele aanpak: nederigheid en assertiviteit.

Een vreemde combinatie, maar Ahmed legt het uit. Er heerst een negatief beeld van moslims. Een te assertieve houding zou dat alleen maar versterken – zonder steun van het grote publiek geen vooruitgang, dus vegen ze elk weekend de straten van Borgerhout schoon, om de Vlamingen te laten zien dat ze brave loebassen zijn die zich willen inzetten voor hun stad. Ook al hebben zij die straten niet vuilgemaakt! Zij zullen ze schoonmaken! Wadend in de stront van de honden van de Belgen, want Marokkanen hebben geen honden! Kniediep in de drek! Dat de Belgen zien dat Marokkanen een propere stad willen!

En als de Belgen dat gezien hebben, dan gaan de Marokkanen hun rechten opeisen. Met de stront van de Belgische honden nog aan hun broekspijpen.

'Zoals de Arabisch-Europese Liga dat nu al doet?' zeg ik.

Ahmeds blik verstrakt.

'Je denkt dat de AEL beter werk levert?'

Ik stel alleen maar vragen.

'Jij vindt de AEL sterker, omdat zij geen hondendrollen rapen?'

Vragen stellen is mijn werk, advocaat van de duivel, in alle objectiviteit.

'Ik zal je eens wat vertellen over de AEL. Wij zijn met hen gaan praten. We hebben hen uitgelegd wat wij deden. We hebben hen gezegd dat ze met ons konden samenwerken als ze dat wilden. Dat onze gemeenschap zich niet mocht laten verdelen. Weet je wat ze deden? Ze lachten ons uit! "Rapen jullie maar stront, wij doen het echte werk." Dat zeiden ze! Dat je daar nog geen stukje over gemaakt hebt.'

Er zijn ondertussen een stuk of tien mannen om ons heen komen zitten, die goedkeurend mompelen en naar mij lachen en gebaren dat ze geen Nederlands spreken, maar het toch eens zijn met wat Ahmed vertelt. Ze wor-

den allen aan me voorgesteld en in hun ruimere context geplaatst, wat er meestal op neerkomt dat de snor in kwestie enorm veel respect geniet in de gemeenschap en dat naar zijn woord geluisterd wordt, zowel door jongeren als ouderen. Na de voorstelling begint de gerespecteerde snor aan een uitleg van vijf minuten, die door Ahmed onveranderlijk vertaald wordt als 'Hij is zeer vereerd dat je belangstelling toont voor de noden van onze gemeenschap', dan wel als 'Hij zegt dat de media meer aandacht moeten besteden aan de moeilijke positie van onze mensen, in het bijzonder in Borgerhout en in de door Israël bezette gebieden'.
'Dit zijn zeer boeiende mannen. Misschien leuk om eens een stukje over hen te maken?'
'Je had onthullingen', zeg ik.
'Lekkere soep?'
'Zeer lekker.'
'Aaaaaah! De beste Marokkaanse erwtensoep van Antwerpen!'
Ahmed vertaalt in het Arabisch of het Berbers of welke taal ze ook spreken. Er stijgt een goedkeurend geroezemoes op. Een man begint een lange uitleg tegen me. Ahmed vertaalt: 'Hij zegt dat je blank bent en met ons erwtensoep eet, en dat dat je de broeder maakt van ons allemaal.'
Ik ben opgenomen in het erwtensoepverbond.
'Onthullingen?' herhaal ik.
Het blijkt dat er nog vijf andere snorren moeten komen, die zo mogelijk nog meer gerespecteerd worden dan de voorgaande, en wier aanwezigheid dringend noodzakelijk is om mij de onthullingen te kunnen vertellen, ook al spreken ze dan geen Nederlands. Na nog een halfuur

ben ik omringd door vijftien oudere Marokkanen die allemaal op elkaar lijken en die me intensief aanstaren, me onafgebroken toeglimlachen, dichter bij me komen zitten, knikken, nog breder glimlachen maar me nooit aanspreken.
Tot overmaat van ramp gaat Ahmed naar het toilet, en blijft zowel op weg ernaartoe als op de terugweg met iedereen nog even praten. Tien minuten lang zitten de wijze snorren en ik doofstom naar elkaar te grijnzen, respectvol te knikken en eenvoudige boodschappen in gebarentaal over te brengen, die op disproportioneel luid gelach onthaald worden. We zijn allemaal gerespecteerd. Het is drie uur.
Ahmed komt terug en onmiddellijk barst een van de mannen uit in een Marokkaanse furie, waarbij hij driftig naar mij wijst, naar de andere mannen, naar de wiegende borsten op de televisie en naar de barman, die het interpreteert als een teken om nieuwe glazen chocomelk te brengen voor de hele tafel. Ahmed riposteert verontwaardigd, de man gesticuleert choleriek, uiteindelijk zucht Ahmed en wendt zich tot mij.
'Deze man zegt dat de Belgische pers meer moet schrijven over wat er in Israël gebeurt.'
Zullen we doen, beloof ik. De man staat op en komt me omhelzen. De tafel applaudisseert. Morgen op de regionale Antwerpse pagina's: de wandaden van Israël door de jaren heen.
Ik word balorig. Nu begrijp ik wat Marokkanen bedoelen als ze zeggen dat Belgische journalisten niet genoeg moeite doen om de allochtone stem in de pers een plaats te geven – als je er altijd tot drie uur 's nachts voor moet opblijven...

'Onthullingen?' vraag ik.
'Goed goed', lacht Ahmed, en hij trekt veelbetekenende gezichten naar zijn makkers. 'We zijn ongeduldig, ik begrijp het. Goed, hier heb je je onthulling. We gaan een bos kopen.'
'Een bos.'
'Niet nu. Binnenkort. Om barbecues te houden. Iedereen houdt van barbecues. Onze mensen vooral. Maar we hebben geen huizen met grote tuinen en in de parken mag het niet. Dus we dachten: dat is best een leuk stukje voor de krant. Een reportage van onze mensen die barbecuen. Een gewoon, gezellig beeld van gezinnen, helemaal anders dan wat er gewoonlijk in de kranten verschijnt. Als we het bos gekocht hebben en we organiseren onze eerste barbecue, dan ben jij de eerste, nee, wat zeg ik?, jij bent de énige die we bellen! In primeur!'
Als we het bos gekocht hebben? Bedoelt hij dat hij me hier tot in het midden van de nacht gehouden heeft om te beloven dat ik binnen een jaar of vier of vijf of tien of meer dan waarschijnlijk nooit een reportage mag maken over barbecuende Marokkanen?
'Heb je een idee wanneer...?'
Ahmed spreidt zijn armen. 'Insjallah', lacht hij. 'We zijn bezig met een goede plaats te zoeken. Niet te ver van Antwerpen, niet te klein, niet te duur. En we zijn geld aan het inzamelen.'
'Misschien is het leuk om daar een reportage over te maken', zeg ik. 'Een Marokkaanse vereniging die een bos wil kopen om te barbecuen. Dat zie ik zo dit weekend op de nationale pagina's.'
'Nee!' Ahmeds gezicht verstrakt. 'Ben je gek? Als het in de krant komt, dan trekt elk gemeentebestuur zich terug!

Dan maakt het Vlaams Blok een wet die Marokkanen verbiedt om bossen te kopen.'
'Dus ik moet wachten tot het bos gekocht is?'
'Je krijgt het als enige.'
'En je hebt geen idee wanneer dat zal gebeuren?'
'Een mooie, grote reportage, die een positief beeld schetst van onze gemeenschap.'
'Maar het is waarschijnlijk dat het nog wel een paar jaar op zich laat wachten.'
'Vroeger, als Allah wil. Maar ik begrijp je. Jij bent journalist, voor jou moet het snel snel snel gaan. Wel, dan heb ik nog iets voor je. Volgende week komt de Marokkaanse consul naar Antwerpen. Hij komt kijken naar een basketbalwedstrijd. En wie zit er naast hem op de tribune?' Hij wijst op zichzelf. 'Een grote eer voor onze vereniging en een erkenning van ons werk. Daar zit een mooi stukje in!'

18

Naar mijn Atheneum, aan de Mechelsesteenweg, gingen bijna duizend leerlingen. Het was een van de grootste scholen van Antwerpen, ze bevond zich in het hart van een stad waar grote concentraties migranten woonden. Toch zag je ze nauwelijks. Ik herinner me niet dat er ooit één allochtoon kind in mijn klas zat. Terwijl op die andere niet-katholieke monsterschool van Antwerpen, het Atheneum op de Rooseveltplaats, niets anders dan Marokkanen en Turken en Afrikanen en Russen en God weet welke nationaliteiten schoolgingen. Mijn school trok kinderen aan van ver uit de rand, kinderen zoals ikzelf die elke dag een halfuur fietsten of in de tram zaten of door hun ouders gebracht werden, en toch was er geen enkel Marokkaans of Turks kind dat tien minuutjes fietste naar die witte burcht.

Niettemin was mijn school een voortrekker in de antiracistische beweging. Ik herinner me nog goed de grote hand-in-handbetogingen, die in de vroege jaren 1990, na de eerste overwinningen van het Vlaams Blok, door de stad liepen, en die door het Blok geparodieerd werden als 'hand in hand, terug naar eigen land'. Ze waren bedoeld om de wereld te laten zien dat een grote meerderheid van de Antwerpenaars niet voor het Blok had gestemd, en werden aangevoerd door grote drommen scholieren die nog niet mochten stemmen. Onze school was ruim vertegenwoordigd. We hadden zelfs vrij gekregen. De school vond het belangrijk dat haar leerlingen politiek bewust waren. We tekenden Hitlersnorretjes op verkiezingsfoto's van Filip Dewinter, we lazen de columns van Tom Lanoye in *Humo* en we schreven Vlaams Blok als Vlaams Blok, als ging het om een heavy metal band. Wij waren het meedogenloze verzet.

De ochtend van zo'n betoging gingen we met een groepje van onze school naar het Sint-Lievenscollege, dat niet ver van onze school gelegen was. Maar wat een wereld van verschil! Een katholieke school, een uniformschool, het kon niet anders of dit was een bolwerk van rechts-conservatieve krachten die de opgang van het Vlaams Blok niet ongenegen waren. En kijk: de school verbood haar leerlingen om deel te nemen aan de betoging. Wat hadden we anders verwacht? Ook de nazi's vonden in de Kerk een trouwe bondgenoot. Maar dat was buiten ons gerekend! Wij gingen posten voor de schoolpoort, om de seutebezen in hun belachelijke uniform te dwingen partij te kiezen.

We hebben wat afgelachen. Ocharme de jongetjes in hun uniformpje, trillend van schrik als ze ons zagen, de kloeke jongeren van het officiële onderwijs. We versperden hun de doorgang. 'Vandaag staan alle jongeren paraat tegen de fascisten', zeiden we.

'Maar wij hebben toets', trilde een jongen van dertien.

'Toets? Ha! Als morgen de nazi's door de straten marcheren, als de deportaties beginnen, als tienduizenden onschuldigen over de kling worden gejaagd en men vraagt jou: "Heb je iets gedaan om dat te stoppen?" – zeg jij dan: "Nee, want ik had toets"?'

Een razende directeur kwam ons wegjagen. Die betoging kon net zo goed in het weekend of op woensdagmiddag. Nu liep ze vol jongeren die zich van de boodschap niets aantrokken, maar slechts een excuus zochten om te spijbelen!

Ha, hoe hebben we hem weggejoeld! Katholieke fascist! Altijd excuses om de eigen lafheid te verbergen, zo kennen we de Kerk. De paus steunde Hitler, Sint-Lievens doet het weer!
(Tijdens de ene betoging die plaatsvond in het weekend was er niemand van onze school. Ik ook niet. Betogen in het weekend – wat voor lol was daar nu aan?)

Daar liepen we dan, honderden leerlingen van Antwerpens monsterschool, allemaal blank en tegen racisme, scanderend van 'Vlaams Blok, rot op!' en 'Nie wieder Faschismus!' Gezellig. In de buurt liepen Marokkaanse jongeren van onze leeftijd. Het was de eerste keer dat ik ze van zo dichtbij zag.
Nou dat was schrikken. Energiek dat ze waren! Ze renden door de rangen van de betoging en deden aan schaduwboksen, nepworstelen en schijnkarate. En ze liepen in zulke grote groepen! Ik had een of twee vrienden bij me, met wie ik rustig praatte en af en toe slogans riep. Zij waren met zijn twintigen, dertigen tegelijk, allemaal jongens (waar waren de meisjes?), en het leek alsof ze elk moment echt konden gaan vechten.
Wij waren blanke jongeren uit de middenklasse. Wij hadden ouders die opgegroeid waren in de jaren zestig. Wij hadden niet geleerd om te gaan met die cultuur van mannelijkheid, fysieke kracht en opzichtige seksualiteit. Wij hadden geleerd dat mannelijkheid iets was waar je zeer mondjesmaat mee omsprong, iets dat leidde tot oorlog, moord en verkrachting. Onbewust minachtten we het luidruchtige van de Marokkanen, hun brallerige haantjesgedrag.
Ik had het echt moeilijk, die dag. Ik was zestien en voor-

zitter van het zelf opgerichte Anti-Macho-Comité. Ik was schrijver van de brochure 'De Macho. Herkennen en Ontwijken'. Ik had ze gekopieerd in vijftig exemplaren en op school uitgedeeld. (Oké, ik was raar.) En hier liep ik, op een betoging ter verdediging van macho's!

En dan waren er de verhalen. Moeilijk te plaatsen verhalen. Bijvoorbeeld dat van mijn oom Herman. Hij was onderwijzer in een concentratieschool – de oorlog was lang genoeg geleden om het woord te mogen gebruiken – in Borgerhout. Op een dag vroeg en kreeg hij zijn overplaatsing. Overspannen. Een incident te veel.
Het was nochtans een banaal incident geweest. Oom Herman stond op de speelplaats. Hij hield toezicht tijdens de speeltijd. Hij was nerveus.
'Meester meester meester!'
Alleen daarvan al werd hij gek, van hun gewoonte om elke zin te beginnen met een stortvloed van meester meester meester, veel luider en brutaler en dwingender dan Vlaamse kinderen. Hoe vaak had hij hun al uitgelegd dat een meester een advocaat was?
'Meester, Hassan heeft vier tepels.'
Daar stonden ze, met tien tegelijk. Waarom konden ze nou nooit in kleine groepjes rondlopen, of alleen? Waren ze bang, alleen?
'Dat kan niet, Abdeslan.'
'Jawel jawel meester, jawel meester, meester meester, Hassan heeft vier tepels.'
'Niemand heeft vier tepels.'
Minutenlang geschreeuw. Hermans ooglid begon te trillen. Ze zagen het! Ze merkten dat hij zenuwachtig was! Ze gingen hem pakken. Ze hielden hem voor de gek.

Hoe moest hij zich uit deze situatie redden? Kon hij zich gewoon omdraaien, of was het zijn plicht te bewijzen dat mensen geen vier tepels konden hebben?
'Hahaha', deed hij. 'Heel grappig.'
'Wilt u ze zien, meester meester?'
'Ik hoef Hassans tepels niet te zien, Abdullah. En ga een beetje achteruit. Straks doen jullie me nog vallen.'
'Maar hij heeft er vier, meester. Gelooft u ons niet, meester?'
Hij was nu overvloedig aan het zweten. Het vocht trok kringen onder zijn oksels, ze zagen het, ze wisten het. Er stonden nu zeker vijftien jongens om hem heen, altijd alleen maar jongens, waar waren hun meisjes? Ze troepten om hem samen als wilden ze hem kelen. Ze ondermijnden zijn gezag. Deze rotjochies, die op alle vakken een nul haalden of een drie of een vier en hem zo gedwongen hadden om zijn toetsen makkelijker te maken, omdat het niet aanging om een hele klas te laten overzitten – zij lachten hem uit op zijn eigen speelplaats!
'Het kan me niet schelen!' viel hij uit. 'Al heeft Hassan twintig tepels en een lul op zijn voorhoofd, ik wil het niet weten!'
Stilte.
De jongens hielden hun adem in.
Zijn geduld verloren. Een verboden woord uitgesproken. Hij zag aan hun gezichten dat ze het gehoord hadden. Lul. Hij had lul gezegd. Hij, een leraar. Zijn zelfbeheersing verloren. Bang gemaakt door kinderen die met tien tegelijk om hem samentroepten en bleven aandringen met hun futiliteiten.
'Geen twintig tepels, meester. Vier.'
En Hassan trok zijn T-shirt omhoog. Nu nog zag Herman

ze voor zich: de vier tepels van Hassan. De twee onderste waren niet helemaal doorgekomen, maar toch duidelijk zichtbaar: twee donkere kringen onder Hassans lichtbruine vel. Extra ogen, die hem spottend aankeken: je kunt niet eens kinderen van tien jaar aan.
'Kijk eens aan', zei hij.
Kijk eens aan. Meer wist hij niet te zeggen. Hij gebaarde met zijn hand dat Hassan zijn shirt mocht laten zakken. Diezelfde dag nog vroeg hij zijn overplaatsing aan naar een school in Wilrijk, waar toen nog geen Marokkanen woonden.

Wat zeg je als je zo'n verhaal hoort? Je lacht eens: oom Herman kon zijn baan niet aan. Maar dat samentroepen, dat te dichtbij komen, dat aandringen tot het bijna bedreigend overkwam – ik hield daar ook niet van. Maakt mij dat tot een racist?
De vader van mijn toenmalige vriendin, Roger, was directeur van een grote lagere school in het centrum van de stad. Meer dan driehonderd leerlingen, zesentwintig nationaliteiten, haast geen Belgen. Roger was een grote man met een warrige baard die altijd op sandalen liep, de karikatuur van de progressieve vader. Hij hield ervan om ons, idealistische zielen, in de war te brengen met verhalen uit de praktijk.
Bijvoorbeeld. Er was eens een Marokkaanse leerling die zeer onregelmatig naar school kwam. Het was een jongen van veertien, die in het laatste jaar van de lagere school zat. Op een dag zag Roger hem in een café zitten. De eerste dag dat de jongen zich weer op school vertoonde, riep hij hem bij zich.
'Sorry, directeur, dat ik niet op school ben geweest, maar

mijn broer was ziek en er was niemand om voor hem te zorgen', verontschuldigde de jongen zich meteen.
Roger besloot het spel mee te spelen.
'Dat is vreselijk!' zei hij. 'En nu ben jij toch naar school gekomen, en is je broer alleen thuis? Dat kunnen we niet laten gebeuren. We zullen hem gaan halen.'
De jongen vertrok geen spier en stemde ermee in. Toen ze bij hem thuis aankwamen, was er natuurlijk van de broer geen spoor.
'Mijn moeder zal hem meegenomen hebben naar haar werk', zei de jongen, waarop Roger antwoordde: 'Laten we daar voor alle zekerheid gaan kijken. Stel dat je broer alleen de straat op is gegaan. Dan moeten we de politie waarschuwen.'
Toen zag je de jongen zweten, want van hun moeders zijn ze bang!
'Laten we moeder maar niet storen. Abdel is waarschijnlijk genezen en naar school gegaan.'
'Yusef', zei Roger. 'We zijn nu al een uur aan het rondrijden. Waarom geef je niet gewoon toe dat je al die dagen in het café zat? Ik heb je daar gezien.'
Yusef ontplofte bijna van woede.
'Directeur! Ik nooit café directeur! Ik moslim directeur!'
Roger was net als mijn ouders een man die godsdienst haatte. Glimlachend zei hij tegen ons: 'De islamitische cultuur is van een hemeltergende hypocrisie, vergelijkbaar met de Vlaamse katholieke cultuur in de jaren vijftig.'
Als je durfde te protesteren, antwoordde hij: 'Ik ken de realiteit, jongens. Ik zie ze elke dag. Daar kunnen jullie met je boeken niet tegenop.'
Was dat racisme? Zo'n aardige man!

Ik besloot om bevriend te raken met allochtonen. Hoe kun je solidair zijn met mensen die je niet kent? Ik voelde me onwennig in hun nabijheid, maar dat kwam door een gebrek aan kennis. Alleen liefde en vriendschap leidden tot echt begrip.
Probleem: waar vond je ze? Zelfs mijn vrienden hadden geen vrienden die bevriend waren met allochtonen. Vrienden maakte je op school, in de jeugdbeweging, in een club... Maar noch op mijn school, noch op de universiteit, noch in de milieubeweging waar ik een paar jaar lid van ben geweest ontmoette ik allochtonen. Ze waren nergens. Je zag ze uit de verte. Je kon toch niet zomaar op straat iemand aanspreken: 'Hallo, ik wil bevriend zijn met een allochtoon. Zin om een milkshake te drinken?'
Ik ging naar het fitnesscentrum. Daar kon je er tientallen leren kennen. Ik zag meteen ook Vlaamse volksmensen. Twee vliegen in één klap. Maar na drie keer was ik het beu om in die katrollen te bengelen. Waren er geen minder idiote manieren om mijn horizont te verbreden? Daarbij: in het fitnesscentrum zag je alleen fitnessmensen. Fitnessmensen waren yukkie.
Ik werd supporter van FC Turksport, een amateurclub die openstond voor alle etnieën en nationaliteiten, maar door haar naam alleen Turken aantrok. Na twee wedstrijden gaf ik er de brui aan. Ik had een hekel aan voetbal. Hoe moest dat nu? Mijn leefcultuur week te veel af van de hunne. Ik kwam op geen enkele plaats waar zij ook kwamen.
De journalistiek bracht redding. Ik was telkens vrijwilliger om verslag uit te brengen van persconferenties van het Platform voor Allochtone Jongeren, de Federatie van Marokkaanse Verenigingen, de Federatie van Marok-

kaanse Democratische Organisaties, de Liga voor Democratisering en Emancipatie van Marokkaanse Vrouwen, de Vereniging voor Ontwikkeling en Emancipatie van Moslims, de Federatie van Turkse Vooruitstrevende Verenigingen, de Unie der Turkse Islamitische Culturele Verenigingen, de Liga van Imams, het Platform van Imams, de Liga van Moskeeën, de Unie van Moskeeën, de Democratische Federatie van Vooruitstrevende Gematigde Moslims en het Berber Platform – persconferenties die telkens hooguit tien regels kregen, maar waar ik elke keer uren nadien nog muntthee zat te drinken met woordvoerders en allochtone leiders die elkaar het licht in de ogen niet gunden. De Liga van Verenigde Marokkaanse Democraten vond de Democratische Federatie van Marokkaanse Liga's een lege doos, een handpop van de Belgen die alleen zichzelf representeerde en uit niets dan collaborateurs bestond. 'Als er iemand collaboreert, dan de Unie van Gematigde Moskeeën', sneerde de Federatie van Niet-Gelieerde Islamitische Democraten, waarop die Unie huilde dat het de ándere Unie was, de Unie van Verenigde Progressieve Moslims, die de zaak verraden had. De Raad van Afrikaanse Gemeenschappen verweet het Platform van Afrikaanse Gemeenschappen dat het geen enkele Afrikaanse gemeenschap vertegenwoordigde, en vice versa. Het Berber Platform verweet de Arabische Federaties dat ze de Berbers arabiseerden. 'Het Berber Platform?!' spuwden die op hun beurt. 'Wat is dat, behalve een door de Vlamingen opgerichte nepfederatie om onze krachten te breken? Dood aan die mediageile verrader, broer van zijn zus, die hoer die met iedereen in de integratiesector geslapen heeft om te komen waar ze nu is!'

‘Aaaah, de integratiesector! Dood aan het Centrum voor Infiltratie en Sublimatie, dat instrument van het Systeem om het eengemaakte Front der Islamitische Zelforganisaties tegen elkaar uit te spelen en de gerechtvaardigde eisen te bedelven onder bureaucratie.’
‘Om te zwijgen van de media, die altijd de verkéérde woordvoerders aan het woord laten.’
‘Nog een geluk dat jij, Tom, weet wie er écht voor de Gemeenschap spreekt.’
Uren later, met diarree en maagpijn van de muntthee, zwalkte ik naar de redactie, om mijn tien regeltjes te tikken.

De AEL was anders. De Arabisch-Europese Liga was de eerste van de honderden miniorganisatietjes die de indruk wekte dat ze over een achterban beschikte. Al deed die in het openbaar dan niet veel meer dan het scanderen van de naam van haar leider, Dyab Abou Jahjah.
De eerste keer dat Abou Jahjah op de voorgrond trad, stond ik daar ook. Dat wil zeggen: ik stond geprangd tussen zijn stoottroepen. Op 3 april. Een illegale betoging op de Meir, een herdenking van de slachting in Sabra en Shatila.
(Sabra en Shatila! Als de Vlaamse moslims voor iets talent hebben, dan zonder twijfel voor het kiezen van merkwaardige prioriteiten. Komen ze ooit op straat voor meer werk, beter onderwijs, minder racisme? Betogen ze ooit voor zichzelf? Nooit gezien. Maar als het gaat om solidariteit met de Palestijnen, dán staan ze met honderden hun kop eraf te schreeuwen: ‘Bush! Sharon! Assassin!’ Alsof de eerste socialisten nooit betoogd hadden voor de achturendag of betaalde vakantie, maar wél tegen

de uitbuiting van spoorwegarbeiders in pakweg Angola. Internationalisme, oké, maar alleen internationalisme?)

Het was min of meer toevallig dat ik op die eerste betoging aanwezig was. Ik was klaar met mijn stukken toen het bericht binnenliep dat er een niet-aangekondigde betoging aan de gang was. Ik was in een ijverige bui en stelde voor even te gaan kijken.

Ik wist niet wat ik zag. Zulke boze mensen had ik nog nooit gezien. Kinderen van nog geen zestien hadden wit-zwarte sjaals voor hun mond en neus geknoopt en klommen in de jonge, veel te dunne boompjes. Ze zwaaiden met hun Palestijnse vlaggen alsof het Israëlische leger zelf voor hun neus stond. Terwijl het toch maar de Antwerpse politie was, die aan de bezetting ook niet veel kon doen.

De agenten waren in gevechtskledij verschenen. Ze hadden zware helmen op en droegen grote schilden. Twee cordons hadden de betogende kinderen klem gezet op het laatste stuk van de Meir. Een beetje een ongelukkige plaats, aangezien zich daar alleen winkelpanden met uitnodigende etalages bevinden. Ondanks alle intifada-imitaties sneuvelden er toen echter geen ruiten.

Ik zwaaide naar Jonas, mijn fotograaf. Hij zwaaide terug. In die seconde werd zijn grote lens gestolen. Razend ging hij achter de dief aan, maar die was in de menigte verdwenen. Rik, een Belgafotograaf, vloekte dat zijn portefeuille verdwenen was. 'Zorg dat er morgen in elke krant staat dat het criminele klootzakken zijn', vloekte hij tegen zijn journalist.

(Verwachten ze echt een positief artikel als ze ons eerst bestelen? Hebben ze dan niks geleerd van de socialisten? Discipline! Verantwoordelijkheid! Zelfbeheersing!

Alleen wie zijn achterban in de hand houdt, boekt politiek succes.)
Een man kwam uit de menigte met de lens van Jonas.
'Die is van u? Alstublieft. En sorry.'
Mijn boosheid zakte. Mijn angst niet. Ik zat ingesloten tussen politiecordons die elk moment konden chargeren, en naast me stonden twee pubers vlaggen te verbranden alsof ze er rijk van zouden worden. Ik was de enige blanke tussen honderden Marokkanen die razend waren om een conflict in een land, duizenden kilometers ver, tussen mensen die ze persoonlijk niet kenden, van wie ze de taal niet spraken en die nooit zouden weten dat Mohamed uit Mortsel hun lijden gewroken had door in een winkelstraat te Antwerpen brullend in een jong berkje te klimmen.
Ik manoeuvreerde me zo voorzichtig mogelijk naar de kant, bang dat de woede van de betogers zich van de boompjes op mij zou richten als ik hen te ruw opzij zou duwen. Ik geraakte aan de zijkant van de Meir. Ik hees me op een vensterbank, om wat boven het gewoel te zitten. Kijk. Niet ver van de vlaggenverbrandende en boompjesvernielende jongens was er een put in de massa. Daar lagen een twintigtal mannen op hun knieën. Te bidden. Tussen die razende jongeren, tussen de vlammen en het gekrijs, leidde een imam het gebed. In plaats van die jongeren te laten ophouden met bomen vernielen! In plaats van ervoor te zorgen dat de betoging verliep zoals een betoging moet verlopen! Wat deden ze daar op hun knieën?
Wat waren dit *rare* mensen!

'Tom Naegels?'
O mijn God, ze gaan me mollen. Voor me stond een jongen van mijn leeftijd, gekleed in jeans en trui. Hij zag er vriendelijk uit, maar hij had een Palestijns vlaggetje in zijn hand en ik wantrouwde iedereen die dag. *No way* dat ik van mijn vensterbank afging. Moest hij maar naar me opkijken. Dan zou hij wel drie keer nadenken voor hij hamas-jihad-hezbollah scanderend mijn sokken in brand stak.
'Ali Ouhida. Politiek secretaris van de Arabisch-Europese Liga. Wij organiseren deze betoging, die helaas door politieprovocatie uit de hand loopt.'
Politieprovocatie? De politie stond daar gewoon, met hun domme helmen en hun rare schilden. Ze hield de massa alleen maar tegen.
'U zou moeten horen wat ze tegen ons zeggen. Racistische beledigingen. Geen wonder dat onze jongens boos zijn.'
Als deze kinderen, die hier voor mijn neus tegen de metalen rolluiken van de winkels opsprongen, boven hun eigen lawaai en dat van hun medebetogers uit één woord hadden verstaan van wat de politie zei, dan hebben Marokkanen de beste oren van alle volkeren.
'Ik ken uw werk', ging Ouhida verder. 'Mag ik u iets laten zien?'
'Als je me hier uit krijgt', zei ik.
'Het cordon wordt zo dadelijk opgebroken. Ze laten ons in kleine groepjes gaan.'
Zo gebeurde. Ouhida leidde me langs de opgewonden scanderende jongeren, die per se via de joodse wijk naar huis wilden gaan. Er kwam een waterkanon aanrijden. Ouhida schudde het hoofd. 'Zie je die provocatie?'

'Ik wil u met eigen ogen laten zien hoe de politie ons behandelt. Zodat er toch één journalist is die de waarheid schrijft.'
Hij bracht me naar zijn auto, een klein oud Fiatje met een deuk in de deur. 'Heeft een agent gedaan. Om me te provoceren. Bij wie moet ik dat aangeven?!'
We stapten in. Hij startte en reed langzaam langs de betogers, die in groepjes afdropen. De meesten gingen niet meteen naar huis, maar bleven rondhangen op het kruispunt met de Frankrijklei of op de Rooseveltplaats. Politiebusjes reden rond om hen toeterend tot voortgang aan te sporen.
We reden in de richting van het Astridplein. Het ging traag, aangezien het verkeer opgehouden werd door de jongeren, die met tegenzin naar huis gingen en aan lijdzaam verzet deden. Ze bleven hangen op zebrapaden, ze dwongen de busjes om te stoppen in het midden van de straat, waardoor er weer opstoppingen kwamen.
Ondertussen waren Ali Ouhida en ik in gesprek geraakt. Mijn ergernis was weggeëbd. Nu zag ik een best aardige jongen van mijn leeftijd die gedreven over zijn organisatie praatte – en over zijn leider, Dyab, amper vier jaar ouder dan ik, die de ambitie had om de Vlaamse Malcolm X te worden. Terwijl we praatten, kreeg hij telefoon van Abou Jahjah. De vrienden spraken Engels. 'Mijn Arabisch is niet goed genoeg', grijnsde Ali verontschuldigend. 'Ik wil het wel studeren, maar het is moeilijk.'
Ali was pas getrouwd. Zijn vrouw en hij wilden een gezinnetje stichten. Makkelijk was dat niet, want Ali had geen werk. Zijn vrouw zorgde voor het inkomen. Hij wou weten of ik geen baantje voor hem had. Op de krant

bijvoorbeeld. Hij zou geen slechte journalist zijn. Of bij de televisie? Had ATV geen hulp nodig? Desnoods zou hij kabels slepen. Hij had het geld echt nodig.
'Kijk.'
Ali stopte zijn woordenvloed en wees naar een enorme reisbus met een blauw zwaailicht erop, die het Astridplein kwam opgereden. Hij werd geflankeerd door een vijftiental overvalwagens, die het hele plein afzetten. Errond zwermden tientallen agenten met wapenstok, schild, zware helm, kogelvrij vest en zware laarzen. Ze hadden Duitse herders bij zich.
'Het gaat om die kinderen.'
Ali wees naar een zijstraat van het plein. Daar zat een grote groep jonge kinderen ingesloten door agenten.
'Ze waren gewoon naar huis aan het gaan!'
Hoe hij dat wist, was me een raadsel. We kwamen net aan. Ik had niet gezien wat er aan de hand was. Maar het waren wel erg jonge kinderen. De meeste waren niet ouder dan twaalf. Er waren veel meisjes bij, kokette allochtone meisjes in mooie kleren, met dure handtasjes, mooi opgemaakt. Ze werden allemaal opgepakt door de agenten en in de bus gezet. De kinderen huilden. Velen gingen op de grond zitten en dwongen de politie hen naar de bus te slepen. Daarbij werden ze aangespoord door mensen van de communistische PvdA, die zich onder de kinderen gemengd hadden.
Ali schudde zijn hoofd. Hij belde weer met Dyab. Ze spraken af dat ze de volgende dag in de tegenaanval zouden gaan. Persconferentie samenroepen. Politieprovocatie aanklagen.
Terwijl we wachtten tot de overvalwagens het plein ontruimd hadden, zette Ali een cd'tje op. Chris de Burgh.

'Mijn idool', zei hij. 'Dat van Dyab ook, overigens.'
Waarop hij lyrisch de biografie van de Ierse zanger begon te vertellen. De Burgh, dat wist ik misschien niet, was een echte wereldreiziger. Geboren in Argentinië, had hij als kind gewoond op Malta, in Nigeria, Zaïre en Ierland, vele Vlamingen konden er een voorbeeld aan nemen. (Ondertussen waren groepjes betogers begonnen met bushokjes in elkaar te trappen.) Zijn ouders hadden een twaalfde-eeuws kasteel tot hotel omgebouwd, en daar leerde hij de hele wereld kennen. Dat hij in zijn beginjaren geen succes had, zorgde er alleen maar voor dat hij met zijn voeten op de grond bleef – een les die Dyab en hij zich ook voorhielden. (Politiebusjes werden met stenen bekogeld.) Wist ik dat hij zijn eerste hit in Brazilië scoorde? Typisch voor de kosmopoliet De Burgh. (We waren aan de Ommeganckstraat aangekomen, waar jongeren over auto's liepen, spiegels afbraken en antennes verbogen. Hé, ik herkende mijn collega Dimitri, verscholen achter een van de auto's. Faitsdiversjournalist, het was een heel andere baan...) De Burgh was bovendien de enige niet-Duitse artiest die uitgenodigd was op het concert bij de eenmaking van Oost- en West-Duitsland in 1990. Al zou hij wel vooral blijven voortleven door het onsterfelijke *The Lady in Red*...
Waarop Ali en ik, vals, met tremolo in de stem, in zijn Fiatje onze versie van de klassieker ten beste gaven.

The lady in reeeeed is dancing with me
Cheek to cheek
There's nobody here
It's just you and me

It's where I wanna be
But I hardly knoooooow this beauty by my side (ik: wooooo)
I'll never forget the way you look tonight

En wij maar naar Khaled luisteren...

Breed glimlachend nam ik veel later op de avond afscheid van Ali Ouhida. Ik was met hem mee naar huis geweest, in de Seefhoek, waar ik zijn fantastische vrouw ontmoette, alsook de Vlaamse Malcolm X, Dyab Abou Jahjah. Allemaal jofele jonge mensen. Samen zongen we *The Lady in Red* tot we schor waren. Er waren koffiekoeken en liters thee, en een poes die Leona heette, naar de Antwerpse burgemeester. We spraken af om allemaal samen eens te gaan eten.
Ik wandelde naar huis door de Offerandestraat, waar de betogers, om hun broeders in Palestina te wreken, de ruiten van de winkels hadden ingeslagen en, daartoe geprovoceerd door de politie, de duurste kleren uit de etalage geroofd hadden. Ik nam me voor Ali en Dyab een geschiedenis van het Belgische socialisme cadeau te doen, zodat ze de vergelijking zouden kunnen maken wie de meeste resultaten geboekt had, Malcolm X of Camille Huysmans.

19

Ik heb Nadia bij me uitgenodigd voor een diner. Ik heb het licht gedimd, kaarsjes aangestoken, een jazz-cd opgezet en ik heb gekookt. Paprikahapjes uit de oven. Struisvogel met gestoofde tomaten met tijm en rozemarijnaardappeltjes. Kwaliteitseten. Man van de wereld. Gezellig en smaakvol.

Nadia komt binnen, stelt verbaasd vast dat mijn flatje in schemerlicht baadt en gaat de verlichting hoger zetten. Ze houdt haar handen achter haar rug.

'Ik heb een cadeau voor je', fluistert ze. Dan laat ze triomfantelijk een rommelig pakje zien, dat met tien soorten kleefband bij elkaar wordt gehouden.

'Tadaam!'

Ze houdt zo van verrassingen.

Ik trek de kleefband los, voorzichtig, om de verpakking niet te scheuren. Uit de berg inpakpapier haal ik een plastic sneeuwuil tevoorschijn, die rust op een boomstronk.

Nadia kijkt gespannen lachend toe.

Aan de ene kant van de stronk groeien paddestoelen, aan de andere frisse gele lentebloempjes. Welk seizoen is het nu? denk ik.

Dat is wat ik denk. In plaats van vertederd te zijn omdat Nadia een verrassing voor me gezocht heeft, in plaats van het gebaar te appreciëren, in plaats daarvan kan ik alleen denken aan die onnozele paddestoel en dat bloempje en dat die nooit tegelijkertijd op dezelfde boomstronk kunnen groeien.

'Je vindt het prachtig?' vraagt Nadia onzeker.

'Het is prachtig', zucht ik. Het klinkt gespeeld, maar gelukkig vindt ze de uil zelf zo mooi dat ze mijn aarzeling niet merkt.
(De uil staat nog altijd op mijn boekenkast. Als vrienden me bezoeken, vragen ze: 'Is dat in afwachting van de Gouden?')
'Aan tafel!' roep ik. Vol spanning en trots leid ik haar naar de tafel, waar de struisvogel en de gestoofde tomaatjes zorgvuldig geschikt op mijn mooiste borden liggen te dampen.
'Hmmm, lekker', zegt ze. 'Heb je mayonaise?'
Mayonaise? Op paprikahapjes en struisvogel en rozemarijnaardappeltjes?
'Ja, lekker, mayonaise', smikkelt ze.
Goed: mayonaise. Ze gooit een enorme kwak op mijn stoofpotje en prakt dat door elkaar met de aardappelen. Mijn hart bloedt.
'Het is oké dat ik tv kijk?'
Zonder mijn antwoord af te wachten loopt ze naar mijn stereo en snoert mijn kwaliteitsmuziek de mond. In de plaats zet ze de televisie op. Ze zapt tot ze een wel heel erg foute komedie gevonden heeft, een slecht doorslagje van *Home Alone*: een jongetje is alleen thuis terwijl twee domme dieven proberen in te breken. Hij maakt hun het leven zuur door hen te laten uitglijden op zijn rolschaatsen, tien kilogram zure snoep op hun hoofd te laten neerstorten en hen van het dak op een auto te laten vallen die dan wegrijdt, waardoor ze eraf rollen, net op de grasmachine die start en met hen over het gazon rijdt tot ze eraf springen en op een riek trappen die patsboem in hun gezicht terechtkomt.
Nadia schatert tot de mayonaiseprak uit haar mond valt.

'Kijk, domme dief, hij bots op andere dief!'
Ik ervaar een vertedering die tranen in mijn ogen brengt. Wat moet ik met haar? Hoe kan ik een relatie hebben met iemand die van slapstick houdt?
Misschien moet ik haar gewoon laten zien wat ik mooi vind, denk ik. Misschien brengt dat ons dichter bij elkaar. Na het eten stel ik voor om naar *Shine* te kijken, een prachtige film over een Australisch wonderkind, de pianist David Helfgott, die gek wordt onder de tirannie van zijn vader. Ontroerend zonder tranerig te zijn! Geestig zonder dijengeklets! Subtiel!
'Is de hele film zo?' vraagt ze na tien minuten.
'Wat bedoel je met "zo"?'
'Zoals dit. Praten.'
'Ze gaan niet met hun koppen tegen elkaar lopen, als je dat bedoelt.'
'Mag ik gaan chatten?'
'Blijf nu nog even kijken! Dit is echt een mooie film.'
We zitten in stilte te kijken. Ik naar de film, Nadia naar alles in de kamer. Misschien, denk ik, moet ik een paar aanwijzingen geven die haar helpen de film beter te begrijpen.
'David Helfgott is joods', zeg ik.
'En?'
'Zijn vader heeft zijn familie verloren in de kampen. Daarom wil hij zijn eigen familie zo wanhopig bij zich houden.'
'Kampen?'
'De holocaust.'
'Odocau?'
Is het belangrijk voor een relatie dat je partner weet wat de holocaust is? Natuurlijk niet! In relaties gaat het om

vertrouwen, passie, respect, niet om iets dat zestig jaar geleden gebeurd is in een ver buurland.
Niettemin. Er is niets dat je hoeft te weten, behalve wat de holocaust is. Dat is toch zo? De holocaust is het ergste wat de mensheid ooit overkomen is. De Armeense genocide, de slachtingen in Rwanda, napalmdoden in Vietnam, Sabra en Shatila – allemaal erg, maar ze horen tot een reeks van tienduizenden vreselijke dingen die in de loop van de geschiedenis gebeurd zijn. Sommige ken je, andere niet, afhankelijk van je scholing en interesse. Maar de holocaust! Mensen worden *geboren* en weten wat de holocaust is.
Er staat ontzetting op mijn gezicht geschreven. Minachting ook, vrees ik. Ik zie het aan haar reactie. Haar uitdrukking wordt hard. 'Je denkt dat ik dom ben!' sist ze. 'Omdat ik andere films leuk vind.'
Ik ontken vier keer. Met de films heeft het niets te maken. Ik begin aan een uitleg over de holocaust, probeer haar te doen inzien waarom het zo belangrijk is. De eerste industriële slachting! Bureaucratische moord! Nooit eerder op een dergelijke schaal! Met de bedoeling een heel volk! Dat mak als lammetjes! Knapste koppen van Europa! Altijd vervolgd! Ik haal de dertig boeken over het onderwerp uit mijn kast, laat foto's zien van Hitler en van de bergen uitgemergelde lijken in Auschwitz, lees voor uit het dagboek van Anne Frank.
Het is een symbool van racisme, betoog ik. Misschien dat ik daarmee een brug kan slaan naar haar eigen leven. Iedereen die ooit het slachtoffer werd van racisme móét weten wat de joden is overkomen – vandaag beledigen ze je op straat, morgen staan de treinen klaar.
Nadia lacht bemoedigend.

'Dus dat is wat jou interesseert', zegt ze. 'Het is leuk om een vriend te hebben van wie ik kan bijleren.'
Lacht ze me uit?
'Mag ik nu gaan chatten?'
Mokkend blijf ik voor *Shine* zitten. Ze heeft gelijk, houd ik me voor. De een houdt van Rachmaninov, de ander van slapstick. De een weet wat de holocaust is, de ander kan goed dansen. Het is smaak, en interesse. Als mens zijn wij allen gelijk.

20

Bomma en bompa hadden een typisch vooroorlogse relatie: een man en een vrouw die niets gemeen hadden, enkele maanden toevallig op elkaar verliefd waren, onmiddellijk trouwden en de rest van hun leven doorbrachten met elkaar te pesten.

Ze zijn één zomer gelukkig geweest. De zomer van 1938. Ze gingen zwemmen, wandelen en fietsen. Daarmee verborg bompa dat hij geen gezellige man was, iemand die liever in de natuur was dan danste, die liever boeken las dan vrienden maakte, die liever nadacht dan praatte. Ze trouwden in de herfst.

De eerste jaren van hun huwelijk werkte bompa, las zijn krant en ging naar de vergaderingen in het Volkshuis. Bomma was thuis en zorgde voor Layla, mijn moeder, hun enige kind, die in het laatste jaar van de Tweede Wereldoorlog geboren werd.

Het heeft niet veel gescheeld of moeder was nog voor haar eerste verjaardag gestorven. Toen Antwerpen geterroriseerd werd door de vliegende bommen, was bomma met haar aan het wandelen toen het luchtalarm begon te loeien. In paniek parkeerde ze de kinderwagen naast een winkel en rende zelf naar binnen. 'Ik dacht er niet bij na', zei ze. 'Ik dacht: ik krijg die *voiture* daar nooit binnen!'

Bompa brulde drie dagen lang. Welke ontaarde moeder deed zoiets? Er zaten geen hersens maar stront in haar kop!

Vanaf toen kleineerde hij haar elke dag, vaak met rijmpjes die hij zelf ludiek vond. Toen ze de aardappelen liet aanbranden, prikte hij boven het fornuis een papier met een spreuk erop: 'Dit weet zelfs het stomste dier, patatten koken niet langer dan een kwartier'. Het was haar verboden het te verwijderen. Toen ze vergat om tomaten te kopen, tekende hij op een groot wit papier een tomaat, kleurde ze in, knipte ze uit en kleefde ze tegen de deur. 'Wat wordt daar rot en plat? Het is de tomaat die Ma vergat!' Toen ze met haar fiets door het rood reed, verkocht hij haar fiets. Als ze op de radio een populair deuntje meeneuriede, zette hij loeihard een plaat met opera op. Hij las zijn krant en vroeg: 'Wat vind jij daar nu van?' Goed wetend dat ze zich niet interesseerde voor politiek. Als ze geen antwoord gaf, snoof hij in onze richting: zie waar ik elke dag mee moet omgaan.

Ze heeft van hem willen scheiden. 'Goed,' zei hij, 'maar ik hou Layla.' Bomma deed niet eens de moeite om te informeren of dat kon. Ze borg de plannen op. Toen moeder haar later vertelde dat hij gebluft had, zei ze gelaten: 'Je weet dat ik geen slimme ben.'

Daarmee vocht ze terug: ze speelde de rol die hij haar had toegedacht. Tien keer per dag herhaalde ze het: 'Je weet het, ik ben geen slimme, ik heb niet het verstand van onze pa.' Ze wreef het hem keer op keer in: ik zal een domme vrouw zijn, en ik zal je er elke dag aan herinneren dat jij je leven lang aan mij geketend zit.

Zodra bekend was dat bompa problemen had met zijn gehoor en zijn gezicht, zei ze tegen iedereen, luid genoeg opdat hij het kon verstaan: 'Het is toch spijtig dat hij niets hoort, en niets ziet. Hij, zo'n intelligente man, die in alles geïnteresseerd is! Hij ziet graag het voetbal, hij volgt de politiek... Dat kan nu allemaal niet meer! Dat is erg, hoor. Heel erg.'

Of: 'Ik heb één geluk, en dat is dat ik goed zie en goed

hoor. Ik ben geen intelligente vrouw. Ik heb niet het verstand van onze pa. Maar mijn ogen en mijn oren, die zijn in orde. Daar ben ik gelukkig om.'

De laatste jaren van zijn leven werd bompa actiever dan ooit. Zeker nadat de problemen met zijn ogen en oren waren begonnen, schakelde hij in een hogere versnelling. Arme bomma. Die had zich er net op ingesteld om haar laatste jaren rustig te slijten.

Zo wilde hij naar een rockconcert. (Nu ja, iets met een kinderkoor en dansende fonteinen in een park.) Maar hij kon niet alleen. Bomma moest mee.

'Er was veel jeugd.'

Daar had ze van genoten. Van al die jonge mensen die plezier maakten.

'En hij is gevallen. Hij.'

En zij had hem mogen oprapen en thuisbrengen, in het donker, in een modderig park. Was hij helemaal zot geworden?

Bompa deed alsof hij de tirade niet kon horen. Zijn doofheid was erger naargelang van de omstandigheden.

Hij ging naar Metropolis naar de film *(Toy Story)*. Daar vond hij niet veel aan. Maar zo'n grote zaal!

Op reis wou hij ook. Naar de Sinjoortjes in Blankenberge. Het was een marteling voor bomma. Alleen al koffers pakken bezorgde haar stress. Toch gingen ze. Had ze niet de kracht om koffers te pakken, ze had nog minder de kracht om tegen hem in te gaan.

'En weet je wat hij dan wil doen? Rally's! Hij! Hij is blind! Hij is doof! Hij kan niet stappen! Dus wie mag die rally doen? Ik ben ook bijna negentig. En ik moet op zo'n hoge duin kruipen, omdat er een antwoord bovenop ligt! Ik gleed weg in dat zand, ik, met mijn schoenen. Ik zeg: "Bob, dat gaat niet." Hij doet alsof hij mij niet hoort!'

De leiding van het vakantiekamp was hen moeten komen zoeken, omdat ze bij zonsondergang nog steeds ergens in de duinen rondploeterden.

Maar hij had gezwommen. Hij, die in zijn jeugd de ene medaille na de andere verzamelde. Sterzwemmer Bob Lorreyne, die makkelijk de Schelde overzwom en terug. Nu, op zijn zesentachtigste, had hij drie baantjes getrokken in het zwembad van het hotel. 'Zo'n magere oude vent in een zwembroek', sneerde bomma.

De vakantie was in mineur geëindigd. Drie dagen voor ze naar huis zouden gaan, kreeg moeder telefoon van bompa: 'Ons ma is niet goed. Kom haar halen.'

Bomma rukte hem de hoorn uit de hand: 'Ik heb niks, kind.'

Bompa: 'Ze houdt zich flink. Ze wil u geen last bezorgen.'

Bomma: 'Gaat ge mijn eigen kind tegen mij opzetten, ambetante vent?!'

Moeder reed naar zee. Daar zat bomma, lijkbleek in een strandstoel, kermend van de pijn. Bloedende maagzweer, bijna maagperforatie, ze kon nog net op tijd naar het ziekenhuis worden gebracht.

Toen bomma in het ziekenhuis lag, stortte ook bompa in. Ook een maagzweer. Ze lagen in hetzelfde ziekenhuis, enkele kamers van elkaar, ziek van elkaars kwaal, slachtoffer en dader tegelijk.

Het weerhield hem er niet van om het volgende jaar weer naar zee te willen. Maar deze keer hield hij rekening met haar. Ze mocht thuisblijven. Hij telefoneerde, waar zij bij zat, naar een pas weduwe geworden vriendin. Of die met hem op reis wou?

De schande!
Bomma: 'En hij doet dat waar ik bij zit! Alles om mij te kleineren!'
Bompa: 'Als ik haar meeneem is het niet goed, en als ze mag thuisblijven is het ook niet goed. Ze is een ontevreden vrouw, uw bomma.'
Helemaal op het einde heeft hij het proberen goed te maken, dat leven van bevelen en minachting. Te laat, te weinig, te zeer op zijn manier, maar niettemin.
'Ma', beval hij. 'Het wordt warm dit weekend. Gij gaat een koude schotel maken. En zondag wandelen we naar het park en eten we daar. Dan hebt gij ook rust.'
'Och god! Hij zal bepalen wanneer ik mag rusten. Dat hij doodvalt, dan zal ik rust hebben.'
Toen hij thuiskwam van een wandeling, zei hij: 'Ik heb een nieuwe oven voor u bij.' Vijf minuten later kwamen twee mannen een oven leveren. 'We *hadden* nog een oven! Een hele goeie! Hij deed nooit iets in de keuken. En ineens komt hij thuis met een oven.'
Nu bompa zijn laatste weken doorbrengt met een luier aan en een buisje in zijn penis, is bomma daar niet in het minst van onder de indruk. Ze is enkel gegeneerd omdat moeder zijn pyjama's en onderbroeken wast. Ze wil dat zelf doen. Het is haar man, haar vergissing, en ze zal die doorstaan tot het einde.

21

Het is door bompa dat ik Nadia heb leren kennen. Dat gebeurde drie maanden geleden.

Ik was het beu om hem thuis te zien zitten, tierend en scheldend tegen al wat mis ging in de wereld. Als hij werkelijk de wereld wou verbeteren, als hij echt zo geboeid was door het migratievraagstuk, waarom werd hij dan geen vrijwilliger in een inburgeringscursus? Ik koesterde vaag de hoop dat hij, toch een verstandige man met grote idealen, door nieuwkomers te leren kennen meer begrip voor hen zou opbrengen.
Ik ging mee. De eerste ontmoeting vond plaats in Borgerhout, in de lokalen van het Antwerpse onthaalkantoor. We zouden een klas Russischtaligen ontmoeten, die er net een half jaar les over België op hadden zitten. De bedoeling was dat ze ons vragen zouden stellen over onze cultuur.
Bompa was de enige oudere Vlaming. De enige volksmens ook. Alle andere autochtonen waren jong en zagen eruit alsof ze in een mooi, groot, zelf gerenoveerd huis woonden, met blauwe deur en een bewust verwilderd gelaten achtertuin. Ze droegen krijtstreepbroeken en gekke brilletjes en hun kapsels waren nonchalant verward. Ze knikten bemoedigend naar de Russen, raakten al voor de sessie met hen in gesprek, zochten de organisatoren op, waren geïnteresseerd in de moeilijkheden die opdoken bij het organiseren van zo'n inburgeringscursus.
Nee, bompa was niet de enige oudere. Er was ook nog een vrouw van rond de zestig. Ze droeg een grote gou-

den bril, had haar geblondeerde haar opgestoken en keek streng in het rond. Ze had culturele brochures bij zich. Daar liep ze mee te wapperen.
Ik bracht bompa tot bij zijn stoel. De jonge deelnemers met hun verwilderde tuinen knikten mij toe: leuk, je hebt je opa meegenomen. Fan-tas-tisch dat hij op zijn leeftijd nog zo positief is, zo opbouwend, zo betrokken. Ze hadden geen idee hoe betrokken hij kon zijn.
Bij aanvang zei bompa niet veel. Het leek alsof zijn doofheid hem parten speelde. Hij hield zijn ogen gesloten, wat hij altijd deed als hij geconcentreerd luisterde. Af en toe schudde hij zijn hoofd. Dat kon twee dingen betekenen: of hij hoorde niet alles wat er gezegd werd, of hij ergerde zich.
Het gesprek verliep met de hulp van een tolk. De Russen vroegen waarom Belgen een afspraak maakten als ze hun vrienden wilden bezoeken. Vrienden, dat zijn toch mensen bij wie je op om het even welk moment kunt binnenvallen? Wij probeerden uit te leggen dat dat niet betekende dat wij minder gastvrij waren, maar raakten verstrikt in ons betoog.
De oudere dame zorgde voor een eerste onbedoeld grappig moment. Ze zei: 'Weet je wat ik raar vind? Dat jullie ons nodig hebben om Belgen te leren kennen. Er is zoveel dat je hier kunt doen! Er is zoveel cultuur in Antwerpen. Ga naar een tentoonstelling. Ga naar een toneelstuk. Ik heb al mijn kaartjes al gekocht, voor alle voorstellingen die ik wil zien. Overmorgen is het de Nacht van de Poëzie.'
De Nacht van de Poëzie! Deze mensen spraken nauwelijks Nederlands, en zij ging hun Peter Verhelst opdringen. Als ze het al begrepen, dan vroegen ze onmiddellijk

hun repatriëring aan. Maar de tolk vertaalde gedwee, en sommige Russen schreven op: *nagt pozi*.

'Wat vinden jullie van de oorlog in Tsjetsjenië?' vroeg een Tsjetsjeense vrouw.

Heel erg! Wij Belgen vonden die oorlog heel erg. Het was vreselijk wat het Tsjetsjeense volk te verduren had.

'En de terroristische acties van de Tsjetsjenen dan?' riep een Rus.

Afschuwelijk! Terrorisme was nooit goed te praten. Dat vonden wij, Belgen, allemaal.

'Wie heeft er gelijk in het conflict volgens de Belgen?'

Iedereen heeft zijn eigen waarheid, en uiteindelijk is de weg van het overleg het beste voor iedereen. Als de wapens zwijgen en het hart spreekt, en als we naar onze kinderen luisteren want de jeugd is de toekomst. Maar vooral: het kan de Belg geen lor schelen. Hij ziet geen verschil tussen Tsjetsjenen en Russen, Polen, Roemenen, Kazakken, Georgiërs, Ingoesjen, Serviërs, Kosovaren of Armenen. Jullie zijn allen broeders van het Oostblok! Vergeet jullie oude geschillen! Gooi af dat sektarische nationalisme! Welkom!

Ik ging op in het gesprek en ik verloor bompa uit het oog. Ik had eraan moeten denken: niet kunnen zien en slecht horen frustreert hem, frustratie maakt hem boos, en als hij boos is, dan ontploft hij.

'Waaraan denken jullie, als jullie aan Russen denken?' wilde een van de nieuwkomers weten. Wij gingen al klaar zitten voor een opsomming van alles wat ons mooi en leuk leek aan de Slavische cultuur, van Dostojewski over melancholische mannenkoren tot de pracht van het Kremlin, maar we werden onderbroken door bompa. Hij stak zijn hand op, wat meer leek op 'Iedereen stil!'

dan op 'Mag ik het woord alsjeblieft?'
'Ik ken niks van Russen...' zei hij.
De tolk vertaalde. De jonge Vlamingen knikten bompa glimlachend toe. Mijn handen zweetten.
'Maar ik weet één ding', ging hij verder. 'Ze slapen altijd op de vloer. Hun kleren liggen overal rondgestrooid. In hun appartementen is het vuil en er liggen wapens op de grond! Ik ben in een appartement geweest en die mannen stonden altijd klaar om hun jas aan te schieten en het af te trappen. De week erop zitten er dan nieuwe Russen en de week daarop wéér nieuwe. Denk je dat wij dat leuk vinden?'
Iedereen keek gegeneerd naar zijn schoenen. Ik probeerde de situatie te redden.
'Je hebt die niet zelf gezien, bompa. Het was op tv. Je bedoelt die documentaire over criminele illegalen die we gisteren gezien hebben. Dat heeft niets te maken met het feit dat ze Rus zijn.'
Bompa deed alsof hij me niet hoorde.
'Ze hebben ons misschien bevrijd,' zei hij, 'maar wat ze nadien gedaan hebben achter de Muur, dat is niet goed te praten. Ik zeg: heeeej Stalin, uw ideeën zijn schoon maar wat ge ermee doet, dat kan ik niet goedkeuren.'
Ik gebaarde tegen de anderen dat ze hier dringend moesten onderbreken. Maar bompa's tussenkomst had de sfeer veranderd. 'Waar ik aan denk,' zei de oudere vrouw, 'dat zijn forsgebouwde mannen met vierkante koppen, die in grote BMW's cabrio rijden. Ze dragen van die zwarte leren jassen, en inderdaad, zoals meneer zegt, wapens.'
'En ze drinken wodka!' juichte een jonge vrouw.
Jaaaa, wodka! Het hek was nu helemaal van de dam. De jonge krijtstreepgebroekte Belgen dachten aan zwarte

wenkbrauwen die in een dikke streep doorliepen, aan hardvochtige vaders zonder werk die wodka distilleerden – alweer wodka! – uit rotte aardappelschillen, aan mensen die er dolgraag uit wilden zien als gewone westerlingen maar daar altijd net niet in slaagden. Te sterk geblondeerde vrouwen met donkere haarwortels en plastic schoenen, net dat tikje te goedkoop, die kleine stijlfoutjes, die mode van drie seizoenen geleden – dat was het Oostblok voor ons, Belgen. We zeiden het maar gewoon zoals het was, we waren hier om de waarheid te zeggen.

Grote consternatie onder de Russen. 'Ik nodig u uit om naar Sint-Petersburg te komen!' riep een onder hen. 'Dan zult u zien dat Russen geen dronkelappen zijn. Dat we even modern zijn als jullie! Dat onze cultuur rijk is!'

'Waarom bent u dan weggegaan?' vroeg bompa.

'Ik werk voor Agfa België', zei de Rus. 'Het bedrijf heeft mij gevraagd om hier te komen wonen.'

'Heeft uw eigen land u niet méér nodig?'

Een gesluierde vrouw in de hoek vond het mooi geweest. 'Dat zijn de Russen waar u het over heeft! Dronkelappen, criminelen, agressoren! Wij zijn Tsjetsjenen! Wij hebben oorlog met de Russen!'

Waarop de Russen en de Tsjetsjenen onderling ruzie begonnen te maken. Het duurde een vol kwartier voor de tolk de gemoederen wat bedaard had. Daarna beëindigde hij, zeer verstandig, de bijeenkomst.

Het kostte me moeite om de organisatoren van de inburgeringscursus te overreden om bompa nog toe te laten. Wat voor beeld wilden ze de nieuwkomers geven van de Belgen? wierp ik hen voor de voeten. Dat we allemaal jong en hip en rijk en mooi en gestudeerd waren? Dat we dol waren op buitenlanders? Was het niet goed om er ook een oudere, volkse Vlaming bij te hebben? Een beetje scherp van tong en kort van stof misschien, maar ook in het echte leven zouden ze wel eens moeilijke Belgen tegenkomen.

Daar hadden ze niet van terug.

Bompa had niet eens door dat hij iedereen tegen zich in het harnas had gejaagd. Hij had zich best geamuseerd.

De nieuwkomers in die tweede sessie waren anders. Frans- en Engelstalige Afrikanen, Spaanstalige Latijns-Amerikanen, een paar mensen uit het vroegere Oostblok, ze zaten allemaal door elkaar. Er waren drie tolken, maar het was de bedoeling dat we zo veel mogelijk Nederlands zouden spreken.

In plaats van een groepsgesprek deden we nu activiteiten om elkaar spelenderwijs te leren kennen. Pictionary, bijvoorbeeld. Je kreeg een Nederlands woord, dat je zo snel mogelijk op een blad van de flip-over vooraan met tekeningen moest uitbeelden. De ploeg die het woord het eerste raadde, kreeg een punt. Ik kreeg het woord 'dierentuin' en tekende een olifant en een giraf achter tralies. Het werd meteen geraden. Een Afrikaans meisje uit een andere ploeg kreeg het woord 'snoepje' en tekende een zwart blokje, dat ze minutieus begon in te kleuren, tot het werkelijk git-, gitzwart was. Ze was teleurgesteld toen niemand het raadde.

Door bompa's blindheid kon hij tekenen noch raden. Hij kneep zijn ogen dicht en probeerde te verstaan wat wij door elkaar joelden.

Tweede activiteit: vul een papiertje in met simpele vragen, zoals

1. Mijn naam begint met een?
2. Wat is je favoriete eten?
3. Wat is je favoriete kleur?
4. Heb je broers of zussen?
5. Wat doe je het liefst in België?

De papiertjes werden door elkaar geschud en opnieuw uitgedeeld. De bedoeling was dat je de eigenaar van een papiertje ging zoeken aan de hand van zijn antwoorden. Je stelde de vragen, en als hij vijf keer het juiste antwoord gaf, dan was hij het.

Hilariteit troef, vooral met Abu uit Liberia die zo dol was op aardappelen dat hij ze bij elke maaltijd at, ook bij het ontbijt, en die een wel erg merkwaardige manier had om België te leren kennen: hij nam een pendelbus tussen Antwerpen en Hasselt, of Antwerpen en Aalst, of Antwerpen en ergens anders, en bekeek alle dorpen die hij onderweg tegenkwam heel nauwkeurig. Hij kende meer dorpen dan ik, en wist precies waar ze lagen.

Derde activiteit: Banaan en Meloen, een soort stoelendans. De helft van de deelnemers werd ingedeeld bij de groep Banaan, de andere helft bij de Meloenen. Eén iemand stond in het midden. Hij of zij riep, naar keuze, 'banaan!' of 'meloen!' Daarop moesten alle bananen of meloenen als de weerga opspringen en op een andere stoel gaan zitten. Degene die het laatst ging zitten, diende van plaats te verwisselen met de persoon in de kring, en moest een opdracht uitvoeren.

Bompa stond niet op. Had hij dan niet gehoord dat er 'banaan!' geroepen was? Goed dan, doof of niet, hij

moest in het midden van de kring. Zijn opdracht was: draag een gedicht voor.
Hij zweeg lang. Ik vroeg me af of ik hem de opdracht opnieuw zou uitleggen. Of was hij gewoon aan het nadenken over een gedicht?
Uiteindelijk sprak hij.
'Wat ik wil weten,' zei hij, 'is waarom ge naar hier gekomen zijt.'
De tolken rolden met hun ogen. Ik stond half op maar bompa hield me tegen. Hij liep op mij toe.
'Ziet ge Tom hier? Tom is mijn kleinzoon. Hij heeft een goeie job. Hij kan het zich veroorloven om hier onnozel te staan doen met u, en "banaan!" te roepen. Hebt gij enig idee hoe hard ik heb moeten werken opdat mijn kleinzoon dat zou kunnen doen?'
Hij bleef rustig praten. Dat was misleidend.

'HEBBEN JULLIE GROOTOUDERS EVEN HARD VOOR JULLIE GEVOCHTEN?'

(Bompa alsjeblief. Ik wil hier nog vaker komen.)

'Is er iemand hier die in zijn eigen land heeft gevochten om het goed te hebben? Beseft gij aan wie ge het te danken hebt, dat het hier zo'n plezant land is om te wonen? Zo'n plezant land is het hier, dat de hele wereld hier wil zijn! Beseft gij wie dat land zo plezant gemaakt heeft? IK. Wij hebben ook armoede meegemaakt. Wij hebben ook meegemaakt dat we aan het begin van de dag niet wisten of we 's avonds nog werk zouden hebben en dat we aan het begin van de week niet wisten wat we aan het einde zouden eten. Maar wij zijn gebleven. En wij heb-

ben gevochten om ons leven beter te maken. Voor onze kinderen. En voor onze kleinkinderen. Maar niet, het spijt me, niet voor u.'
'Zie uzelf eens bezig. "Banaan!" "Meloen!" "Aardappel!" En maar lachen. Oooo, wat is het goed om op kosten van een ander en op het zweet van een ander de plezante te komen uithangen. Wat is het leuk om in andermans huis te eten, te drinken, te spelen, te lachen. De heer des huizes zal wel werken. Wel, mannen, die heer des huizes ben ik en ik zeg: bedankt dat ge mijn kleinzoon geamuseerd hebt, ga nu terug naar uw eigen huis. Als het daar nog niet zo mooi is als hier, *maak* het daar dan zo mooi als hier!'

Bompa liep naar buiten en verwachtte dat ik hem zou volgen. Ik kon moeilijk anders: alleen raakte hij nooit thuis.
In de auto zei ik heel rustig: 'Als ik je thuis heb afgezet, dan rijd ik terug om me voor jou te verontschuldigen. En ik ga sméken dat ik mag blijven komen.'
Hij deed alsof hij me niet hoorde.

22

Nadia zat tijdens die laatste sessie in mijn groep, de Bananen. Voor bompa zijn tirade begon, had ik al even met haar gesproken. We zaten naast elkaar en telkens als er 'banaan!' geroepen werd, wisselden wij twee gewoon van stoel. Makkelijk zat, zo was je zeker dat je nooit als laatste ging zitten.
Ze sprak niet genoeg Nederlands om bompa's uitval begrepen te hebben. Toen ik hem thuis had afgezet, teruggekomen was en me verontschuldigd had, raakte ik weer met haar in gesprek. Bleek dat ze al een jaar in Antwerpen woonde en nog nooit in het Museum voor Schone Kunsten was geweest. Ik beloofde haar een rondleiding. Dat was de bedoeling van de cursus. Dat we samen eropuit trokken, dat we los van de sessies met ons allen activiteiten zouden doen. Met ons allen, daar had ik niet zoveel zin in. Toch niet nadat ik Nadia had ontmoet. Mijn wens om het legioen nieuwkomers het naar de zin te maken in hun nieuwe land, kreeg plots een zeer specifieke invulling.

Het eerste dat Nadia me liet ontdekken: ik ben een typische man. Ik geniet ervan als een veel jonger meisje met een bewonderende blik naar me luistert, en op de juiste momenten uitroept: 'Amai, jij weet veel!'
En reken maar dat ik veel weet. Heeft ooit iemand beweerd dat kunstgeschiedenis nutteloze kennis is? Het is de basis van elke geslaagde verleiding. Ik rende door het museum en improviseerde over stromingen, schilders en thema's. Wat maakte het uit dat de helft niet waar was

en de andere helft omstreden? Wist zij veel! Ik vertelde over de tragische teloorgang van de middeleeuwse goudverf, de voorliefde van Antoon van Dijck voor rode gordijnen (zelfs midden in een bos) en de opkomst van ik-schilder-u-voor-een-raam-met-een-wei-op-de-achtergrond-schilderijen. Wat een indruk maakte ik!
Er is een tijd geweest dat ik vol minachting neerkeek op oudere mannen die op jonge vrouwen vielen, en op meisjes die zich lieten inpakken door om het even welke ervaren charmeur. Het uitspelen van je leeftijdsoverwicht, wat voor kunst was daar aan? Met persoonlijkheid had dat bitter weinig te maken. Dat vond ik toen ik achttien was, en al mijn vriendinnen een man van vijfentwintig zochten. Nu had ik er heerlijk veel minder moeite mee. Waarom onze vaders hiermee gewacht hebben tot hun vijfenveertigste, het is een raadsel.

De dag na mijn rondleiding werd ik verwacht bij Nadia thuis. Ze woonde in een klein flatje in de Lange Beeldekensstraat, in de Seefhoek, een wijk waar Vlamingen niet komen als ze er niet hoeven te zijn. Ze kookte voor me: in de pan gebakken curryworsten (die ze meegebracht had van de slager waar ze werkte) met rijst in een saus van gefrituurde aubergine, geprakt met citroensap en pindakaas. Soedanees, zo beweerde ze. Het zag eruit als hondenkots, maar was lekker.
Tijdens het koken leerde ik haar Nederlands.
Ik: 'Ik *schep* nu de curryworst *op*.'
Zij: 'Dus jij bent de *opschepper*.'
(Jaja. Haha.) We klonken met ijskoude rode wijn, die ze speciaal voor mij was gaan kopen en nog snel even in de diepvriezer had gelegd.

Na het eten keken we televisie. Probleem: Nadia had geen kabel, de antenne deed het niet en ze had maar één videocassette. Daarop stond de viering van de onafhankelijkheid van Pakistan, waarin op artistieke wijze de oorlogen tegen de Britten en tegen India geëvoceerd werden. We zagen een Indische generaal uitroepen: 'Zelfs met een tak in de hand kunnen de Pakistanen ons verslaan!' Waarna zijn collega gestileerd in hoonlachen uitbarstte – dat hem dra verging toen de vastberaden Pakistanen hen inderdaad versloegen!
We zagen Indische soldaten onheilspellend naar een hoop doeken toe dansen, die een stad voorstelde waar een hevige, legendarische slag was geleverd. Pakistaanse soldaten dansten hen van de andere kant tegemoet. Nadia legde uit dat er in de echte oorlog natuurlijk niet gedanst werd: dat was het evocatieaspect. Het Indische en het Pakistaanse leger zetten een ingewikkelde choreografie in die een vreselijk bombardement moest verbeelden. Pas gebombardeerde burgerslachtoffers walsten huilend naar de veiligheid, of heupwiegden kreunend ter aarde. Nadia zong mee met de oorlogsliedjes.
Tijdens de toespraak van de president, die een halfuur duurde, zijn we beginnen te kussen. Sindsdien zijn we het bewijs dat de liefde culturen overstijgt. Het symbool van de multiculturele, verdraagzame, open maatschappij. Een voorbeeld voor de wereld.

(O ja. Ik was toen nog met Saskia. Nog drie maanden. Toen besefte ik dat het vertrouwde nooit op kon tegen het nieuwe.)

23

Er is de eerste kus, er is de eerste keer seks, en er is het moment waarop je beseft dat je echt verliefd bent. Bij mij kwam dat tijdens de derde bijeenkomst van de inburgeringscursus.
Er werd van ons, Belgen, gevraagd dat we elk met een nieuwkomer de straat zouden opgaan, om toevallige voorbijgangers vragen te stellen. Over feestdagen. Het onderwerp deed er uiteraard niet toe, het was de bedoeling dat de nieuwkomers Nederlands zouden praten, en eventueel iets zouden bijleren over Belgische feesten.

1. Hoe viert u Kerstmis/de ramadan/Chinees nieuwjaar? Met vrienden/familie/alleen...
2. Wat is het leukste aan Kerstmis/de ramadan/Chinees nieuwjaar?
3. Welke cadeautjes koopt u? (Als de vraag in een winkel wordt gesteld:) Welke cadeaus verkoopt u?
4. Wat is uw favoriete plaats in Antwerpen en waarom?
5. Stel dat u een dag de premier was van dit land, wat zou u dan veranderen?

Wat die laatste twee vragen ermee te maken hadden, was mij ook niet duidelijk.
Uitstekend idee. Ga in het donker, met een bijna zwarte Aziatische, willekeurig Vlamingen aanspreken op de Turnhoutsebaan, waar mensen al angstig wegrenden als je gewoon de weg vroeg. Een prijs voor het genie dat die opdracht bedacht had. Ik haat het sowieso al om onbe-

kende mensen aan te spreken, laat staan de agressieve marginalen die van deze straat het bolwerk van het Vlaams Blok maakten.
(Volksmensen, Tom! Je hebt sympathie en respect voor hen.)
Geen sprake van dat ik een sliert Afrikanen, Arabieren en Tsjetsjenen achter me ging meesleuren. Laat iemand anders maar de klappen krijgen. Ik nam Nadia bij de arm en ging alleen met haar op pad. Mijn plan: een halfuur naar het café gaan en dan terugkeren met zelf ingevulde, nagemaakte vragenlijsten.
Dat was buiten Nadia gerekend. Zij had zin in de opdracht. De eerste de beste voorbijganger, een Marokkaanse twintiger, klampte ze al aan.
'Hoe viert oe Kersmies, de damdam en Chinees noejaar?' vroeg ze.
'Wat?' fronste de man geërgerd.
'Oe virt oe-'
'Ze wil weten hoe u de ramadan viert', zei ik.
Onmiddellijk kreeg de man een achterdochtige trek om zijn mond. Waren we het Heilige van het Heilige aan het bespotten? Besmeurden we de islam? Ha-tsjakka, een vreselijke dood wachtte ons!
'Waarom wil ze dat weten?'
Ik legde de opdracht uit.
'En zij wil weten hoe ik de ramadan vier?'
'Ja. Hoe gaat dat feest in zijn werk? Eerst eten jullie niet, maar na zonsondergang laten jullie je gaan, nee?'
Ik heb in mijn leven nog nooit zo'n minachtende blik toegeworpen gekregen.
'De ramadan,' zei hij, 'is geen feest. De Heilige Maand Ramadan is niet iets als Kerstmis, met cadeautjes en mu-

ziek. De Ramadan is een heilige plicht, een versterving, een offer aan Allah, groot is Hij!'
Ik vertaalde voor Nadia. Ze knikte en schreef: 'Kado en muzik.'
'Wot ies leukst aan damdam?' ging Nadia verder.
De man keek geschokt.
'Er is niets leuks aan de ramadan!' zei hij. 'De ramadan is niet bedoeld om leuk te zijn.'
'Kom kom', zei ik. 'Na afloop is het toch feest? Brallen, vreten, bioscoopzalen op hun kop zetten?'
'Mijn plicht aan Allah is geen feest!' riep de man. 'Het is boetedoening. Het is een offer. Wij ontzeggen ons lichaam zijn voedsel, opdat Allah ziet dat onze ziel aan Hem toebehoort.'
'Jaja', lachte ik. 'Pasen is ook het lijden van Christus, maar vooral chocolade-eieren zoeken.'
De man werd hoogrood. Hij draaide zich om en beende verder zonder me nog een blik waardig te keuren.
Nadia vroeg wat ze moest opschrijven. 'Het feest achteraf', zei ik. 'Eten, heel de nacht opblijven en films verstoren door te roepen en te gsm'en en over de stoelen te kruipen.'
We bezochten een telefoonwinkel en een pittabar. Daarna bereikten we café Roma. Nadia maakte aanstalten om naar binnen te gaan. Ik probeerde haar tegen te houden. Café Roma was verboden toegang voor iedereen die niet op het Vlaams Blok stemde. Alle mannen hadden er snorren, de vrouwen droegen joggingpakken, de kinderen waren dik en dronken bier vanaf hun vierde. Dit was geen café om met een buitenlandse binnen te gaan.
Dat wilde ik Nadia uitleggen, maar nog voor ik kon be-

ginnen, had ze de deur al opengeduwd en gebaarde naar mij: jij met je vooroordelen...
Nadia voelt gewoon niet aan wanneer ze niet welkom is. Ze leek geen last te hebben van de golven van vijandschap die op haar afkwamen. Was ik de enige die de hatelijke blik van de dienster opmerkte?
'Wat zal het zijn?' snauwde ze tegen mij.
Toen had ik geen zin meer om iets te bestellen.
'We gaan dadelijk weer weg. We willen alleen wat vragen stellen.'
Ze snoof en maakte zich uit de voeten. Ik wilde ook weg. Ik was bang dat deze mensen Nadia zouden gaan uitschelden. Als het daarbij bleef. Kijk hoe bedreigend ze keken, hoor hoe plat ze Antwerps spraken. Dit waren leden van een vijandige volksstam!
'Kort', fluisterde ik in Nadia's oor. 'Eén vraag, dan gaan we.'
Ze begreep niet waarom ik zo snel weg wilde. We waren hier pas! Ze liep vrolijk op twee mannen toe die zo te zien al drie dagen in dit café zaten. Ze ging naast hen zitten en lachte hen toe met haar liefste glimlach.
Was ze gek geworden? Ze zouden haar mollen!
'Mag ik vraag?' zei Nadia.
De ene man had een warrige zwarte baard en kleine oogjes van de drank. De andere was klein, kaal en had een dun snorretje. In zijn nek groeide nog wat haar.
'Aan mij stel je geen vragen!' bralde de man met de baard. Hij trok mij naast zich op de bank en sloeg zijn enorme arm om mijn schouder.
'Waarom mag ze aan jou geen vragen stellen?'
'Daarom niet!'
Hij lachte vet.

'Wiens initiatief is dit?' vroeg de andere.
'Van de stad Antwerpen', zei ik.
(Fout. Ik wist het zodra ik het zei.)
'Och hoort hier! Van de stad! En waarom doet de stad niets voor ons?'
'Omdat jullie niet nieuw zijn in dit land', bromde ik.
'Hoe virt oe Kersmies?'
'Hier', zei de baard, die nu plots wel wilde meedoen.
'In café?'
'Waar anders?'
Nadia dacht na. Ze kon tientallen plaatsen bedenken die leuker waren om Kerstmis te vieren.
'Thuis', zei ze.
'Dit is mijn thuis!'
'Met wie virt oe Kersmies?'
'Met niemand.'
'Alleen?'
'Ja, alleen, ja!'
'U geen familie?'
'Nee!'
'U geen frouw?'
'NEE!'
'U geen vrienden?'
'NEE GODVERDOMME!'
De baard raakte buiten zinnen. Ik probeerde Nadia duidelijk te maken dat ze geen vragen meer moest stellen, om ongelukken te vermijden.
'Wil u frouw?' vroeg ze.
'Als ge wilt afkomen, 't mag altijd!'
Volgde een luide rochellach, die gedeeld werd door het halve café, dat meeluisterde. Ik haalde opgelucht adem. Nadia vatte moed door haar plotselinge succes.

'Wat zou oe doen als u primjé was?' vroeg ze.
Eén vraag had ik toch gezegd? Eén vraag, dan wegwezen. Wij hoorden hier niet. Wij waren ongewenst, gehaat, uitgespuwd, deel van een wereld die deze mensen niet aanvaardden. Ik verborg mijn gezicht in mijn handen. Uitgerekend die vraag, in dit gezelschap... Nu zouden we het horen: makakken buiten, de postjespakkers op het schavot, de doofpotten open en de partij van het volk aan de macht.
'Dat alle mensen wat beter overeenkomen.'
Het was de kale man met de dunne snor die het antwoord gaf. Hij bedoelde het duidelijk als een geste van goede wil. Ik beloonde hem met een stralende glimlach. Fijn, dan zouden we nu maar opkrassen, de heren hadden het duidelijk druk...
Ik gebaarde tegen Nadia dat ze moest opschrijven op ons antwoordenblad: als meneer eerste minister was, dan zouden de mensen beter overeenkomen. Blank en zwart, rijk en arm, de zon schijnt voor iedereen. Een boodschap van warmte en solidariteit waar we allemaal iets van kunnen leren. Recht uit het hart van het volk. Eenvoudig, en o zo waar.
'Dat is ni job van minister', zei Nadia.
Kon ze dan nooit haar mond houden?
De kale man keek verbouwereerd. De baard kwam zijn vriend te hulp: 'Ha nee? En van wie dan wel? Van de burgemeester misschien?'
'Dat moet oe zelf doen', zei Nadia. 'Wat zou oe doen als oe eerste mister was?'
'Awel en wij zeggen dat we elkaar beter moeten verstaan!' brulde de baard. 'Is dat zo moeilijk? Dat de stad Antwerpen dáár eens voor zorgt in plaats van geld te

geven aan zwarte popkes om onnozele vragen te komen stellen in mijn café!'
De kale was ondertussen aan een onsamenhangend verhaal begonnen tegen mij, over hoe moeilijk het was om in een beschutte werkplaats te werken en dat zijn ene arm lam was en zij waren toch ook mensen? Hè, waren zij ook geen mensen? (Ik beaamde: zij waren ook mensen.) Dat moest ik toch begrijpen, dat zij het ook moeilijk hadden maar als ze iets durfden te zeggen, dan waren ze racist. Dat kon toch niet?
Ik luisterde maar half; de dronken baard ging nu helemaal door het dak. Nadia legde hem de vraag keer op keer opnieuw voor: gegeven de bevoegdheden van een premier in dit land, wat zou zijn eerste beleidsmaatregel zijn?
'Gratis bier!' riep hij uiteindelijk.
'Da is job primjé!' juichte Nadia.
Tevreden nam ze haar antwoordblad en schreef op: 'gratis bir'. De baardaap lachte en begon tegen haar hetzelfde gesprek, over dat hij toch ook een mens was, ook al had hij dan geen vrouw en vierde hij Kerstmis op café.
Op dat moment werd ik verliefd op haar. Op slag. Reddeloos. Mijn Nadia, die een Blokcafé binnendrong en overwon.

24

Bomma haalt eindeloos herinneringen op aan de zomer waarin ze bompa ontmoette, de enige zomer waarin ze gelukkig was. Ze vertelt over dancing Magique in Borgerhout, 'een deftige dancing. Je kwam er niet binnen met een pet op'. Bob was niet zo'n danser, en bomma zei tegen haar vriendin Melia: 'Nu heb ik er een opgedaan met houten benen!' Maar zwemmen dat hij kon! Zwemmen! Veel beter dan zij. Als zij het Albertkanaal over geraakte, dan was ze al blij. Hij zwom met zijn vrienden de Schelde over en terug, om een borst op te zetten. De vrouwen bleven op de oever achter. Melia zei: 'Salut, ik ga zitten!' En dat deed ze op de zak van haar vrijer. Een tijd later kwam die jongen uit het water en zei: 'Amai, nu heb ik honger! Waar is mijne zak?' Zijn pistolets waren plat! Ja, dan konden ze nog eens lachen...

Het stormt vreselijk. Bomma zegt: 'Ik kan niet zeggen dat we een goede zomer hebben.'
'Het is september, bomma.'
'Dat is ook waar.'
Na een poosje zegt ze: 'En we verjaren weeral bijna!'
'Je bent net verjaard, bomma.'
'Dat is ook waar.'
Alles is waar.

's Avonds kijken moeder, bomma en ik naar *National Geographic Channel*. Het gaat over een groep walrussen die naar Walrus Island trekt, waar een ijsbeer zich heeft verborgen. De ijsbeer sluipt langzaam naar de walrussen

toe, onheilspellende muziek zwelt aan en bomma zegt: 'Och zie, hij is een wandelingeske aan het maken.'
De muziek wordt onheilspellender, de beelden wisselen elkaar steeds sneller af. Sluipende ijsbeer – nietsvermoedende walrus – klauwende ijsbeer – slapende walrus. Het is duidelijk dat de ijsbeer elk moment kan toeslaan en bomma zegt: 'Zijn ze u vergeten, jongen? Ziet daar, zij zijn daar aan 't slapen en gij zijt een wandelingeske aan 't maken.'
Als de walrussen in beeld komen, zegt ze: 'Dat zijn lelijke beesten. Ik kan niet zeggen dat ik het schone beesten vind.'
Tot op het moment dat die ijsbeer de kudde walrussen inloopt en er één verscheurt, heeft ze niet door wat er aan het gebeuren is. Ze heeft zelfs niet door dat het om twee verschillende dieren gaat. Terwijl, laten we wel wezen, een ijsbeer niet op een walrus lijkt.

25

Moeder is zenuwachtig. Ze heeft papieren bij zich waarmee bompa zijn aanvraag kan doen. Het moet op papier staan, zegt de wet. Ze is bang, boos, verward, nerveus, ze voelt zich schuldig en is daarom kwaad op zichzelf. De twee andere mannen in de ziekenhuiskamer kijken ons verwijtend aan. Hier is de familie die haar eigen stamvader ter dood brengt, een zwakke man die willoos tekent, zijn eigen dochter vertrouwt en zie! Zie wat ze hem aandoet! Een op de erfenis beluste boze dochter die haar bedlegerige vader zijn eigen doodvonnis laat tekenen.
De mannen glimlachen.
Ze weten van niks.
Wij zijn de liefhebbende familie die opa niet vergeet. Kijk naar hen, zij liggen hier eenzaam.
Een van hen laat luide, rollende, lang aanhoudende winden. Hij kijkt alsof zijn kont niks met de rest van hem te maken heeft.

Moeder is onhoudbaar kordaat. Alsof ze zelf een operatie leidt. Het maakt me suf. 'Allez, bewéég nu eens!' snauwt ze tegen mij. 'Sta – daar – niet – zo!'
Hoe moet ik dan staan?
Hoe staan andere mensen die hun bompa helpen met sterven?

Ze stopt me de papieren in de handen. Ik moet tekenen als getuige, nee dáár.
Móét het zo sloom, moet iedereen het *zien* misschien wat we doen?

Ze tekent zelf op de verkeerde plaats.
'Volgens mij moet bompa hier tekenen.'
'Jamaar, je zegt net zelf dat *ik* hier moet tekenen!'
(Ik heb niks gezegd. En zeker niet dat zij daar moest tekenen.)
'Ze zullen het wel verstaan', zegt ze, met een blik naar de verpleegsters die op de gang rondlopen en niet binnen mogen komen.
We zien er verdacht uit, we handelen verdacht, we staan verdacht – de boze familie die opa, nog amper bij zijn verstand, een vervalst testament laat tekenen. Ik laat alles na aan mijn kleinzoon Tom, omdat ik zijn walkman mocht lenen.

Vrrrrrrrrrrrrrrt
De surreële toets: door ons paniekerige gestuntel heen, de onverstoorbare scheten van de vriendelijk toekijkende man.

Bompa glundert. De hoop doet hem er jonger uitzien, minder zwak. Hij glimlacht zelfs. Zijn dochter komt hem redden. Zij heeft het uitgezocht, zij kent de kanalen, zij weet aan welke touwtjes ze moet trekken, de weerstand van de dokters zal smelten als sneeuw voor de zon, nu zal het niet lang meer duren. Enkele dagen nog, en zijn wens wordt bewaarheid.
Het einde van de week, zo schat hij zelf.
(Nog een maand, dat zegt de wet. Als ze dit duidelijk niet door hem zelf opgestelde ding aanvaarden.)
Maar dan zal hij wel eerst zijn eigen aanvraag moeten ondertekenen. Acht keer, alle vier de formulieren aan voor- en achterkant. En die zijn te klein gedrukt voor

zijn slechte ogen, de ruimte voor de handtekening is onduidelijk, hij kan niet voldoende rechtop zitten om te tekenen en we hebben niets om het papier op te leggen. De schetenlater, die onze moordpoging al tien minuten geïntrigeerd gadeslaat, zegt dat hij 'een boek' heeft.
Nu ben je medeplichtig, makker!
Het blijkt een foldertje. Nauwelijks steviger dan het te ondertekenen papier.

LOSER!

Ik vind een schotel waar de maaltijden op gebracht worden. Na verwijdering van het lege bord, het halfvolle glas, het bestek, het onaangeroerde yoghurtpotje en de wikkel van een Zippreep, blijkt dat iemand er saus op gemorst heeft. Die heeft een kleverige vlek gemaakt. Maar goed, het zal dienst moeten doen.

'Bij mijn duim, pa!' commandeert moeder.
'Nee pa, HIER!'
Ze blaft hem af, hij glimlacht.

Eén handtekening belandt tussen de gedrukte tekst.
Eén overlapt met die van moeder.
Eén komt wonderwel goed terecht.
De volgende valt van het blad af.
Op alle papieren kleeft een bruine sausvlek. Maar de opdracht is volbracht. Bompa krijgt zijn dood.

26

Het is de bedoeling dat ik ga kijken naar een debat met Dyab Abou Jahjah, de wonderboy van de Arabische gemeenschap, de nieuwe Malcolm X, de ayatollah in maatpak, Abu Jihad. (Nu ja, debat: hij praat met een communist en een linkse internetjournalist die hem op elk punt gelijk zullen geven.) Sinds onze eerste ontmoeting, na de desastreuze betoging op de Meir, is hij als een komeet het politieke firmament in geschoten. Met provocerende uitspraken domineert hij al maandenlang de media. Hij is het gezicht van de nieuwe, mondige allochtone generatie, die het niet meer pikt. En nu gaat hij in de politiek. Hij heeft een partij opgericht, in alliantie met de communisten, die het Vlaams Blok zal wegblazen. De krant heeft me gestuurd in de hoop dat de revolutie gepreekt zal worden. Wordt er iets minder gepreekt, dan hoef ik er geen stuk over te maken.

Ik ben te laat. Op weg naar de zaal word ik ook nog eens opgehouden door een groepje jonge Marokkanen, die mijn vriendschap zoeken.

‘Hé hé hé hé hey’, zeggen ze.

Ik ben een vlotte kerel. ‘Hé hey’, zeg ik.

‘Meneer meneer meneer.’

‘Mevrouw mevrouw’, grap ik. Ik weet hoe ik die jongens moet aanpakken. Ze lachen hard.

Of ik van de politie ben? Nee, dat ben ik niet. Aha, want zij zijn van de ordedienst van Abou Jahjah. Ik glimlach: de jochies zijn amper zestien, als ze al zo oud zijn. ‘Heel knap’, zeg ik. Ik loop verder. Ze volgen me.

‘Hey, uw moeder is een hoer.’

'Nee hoor, ze is schooldirectrice', zeg ik.
'Jawel jawel, uw moeder is een hoer.' Hij roept zijn vrienden erbij. 'Hey hey, zijn moeder is een hoer, hè?' Iedereen blijft breed lachen, dit is een amicaal gesprek onder gelijkgestemde Antwerpenaars. Omdat ik niet boos word, krijg ik een hand en een kameraadschappelijke klap op de schouder. 'Gij zijt ne goeie!' Ik heb de test doorstaan: beledigd worden en blijven lachen, dat is samenleven met respect voor elkaar.
Bij de ingang van de zaal word ik begroet door Ali Ouhida. Hij zegt dat het debat al een halfuur bezig is en dat de zaal stampvol zit, maar dat ik naar binnen mag.
Het kleine zaaltje is inderdaad tot de nok gevuld. Het publiek zit zelfs op de trappen, meestal jonge mensen, zowel allochtonen als blanke Vlamingen. Van die laatste opvallend veel mooie jonge vrouwen met wit-zwartgeblokte Palestijnse sjaals.
Het debat is al voorbij. We zijn aan de vragenronde. Vooraan in de zaal heeft een man een microfoon in zijn hand. Hij is aan het vertellen over de Vietnamoorlog en Amerikaans imperialisme en de Golfoorlog en olie en George W. Bush en de Antwerpse politiecommissaris Luc Lamine die om duistere reden met die internationale bende in verband staat en de Eerste en Tweede Wereldoorlog en niet te vergeten Stalin en Trotsky, de positie van de vrouw in de moslimlanden en de manier waarop de Antwerpse media het Vlaams Blok een forum geven...
Als hij tien minuten lang al deze kwalen van de moderne tijd opgesomd heeft, vraagt de moderator hem vriendelijk om af te ronden.
'Zijn we hier op tv misschien?' snauwt de man. 'Moet alles in tien seconden worden uitgelegd? Dit zijn serieuze kwesties!'

'Laat hem uitspreken!' roept een vrouw in de zaal.
'Kunt u dan misschien een vraag stellen?' probeert de moderator.
'Dit *is* een vraag!' blaft de vraagsteller. En verder gaat hij, over Israël en Libanon en het verraad van Lumumba en de vliegtuigen die het fascistische Chili gekocht had met steun van de Belgische regering en dat zijn lezersbrieven nooit gepubliceerd worden in *De Morgen*, de krant die beweert dat ze progressief is – instemmend hoongelach bij het publiek – en dat hij een betoging heeft georganiseerd die...
Ik kijk naar Abou Jahjah en vraag me af of dit is hoe hij het zich voorgesteld had, de strijd voor de emancipatie van het Arabische volk: eindeloos debatten voeren in kleine kamertjes voor altijd dezelfde mensen?
Ik hou het voor bekeken. De revolutie wordt vanavond niet gepreekt, dat zie je zo. Ik verlaat de snikhete zaal en begeef me naar Ali aan de ingang.
Hij is in gesprek met drie oudere Arabische mannen in djellaba. Ik blijf op een afstandje wachten.
Een bodyguard – nu ja, een van de forse jongens die Dyab Abou Jahjah overal vergezellen en die voorgesteld worden als zijn lijfwachten, al hebben ze geen opleiding en zijn ze niet meer dan wat ze zijn: werkloze Marokkaanse jongens die veel tijd met fitness hebben doorgebracht – kijkt me wantrouwig aan. Ik glimlach om hem gerust te stellen.
'Wat?' vraagt hij.
'Niets', zeg ik.
'Ik vraag: wat?'
'Dat hoor ik.'
Ik glimlach opnieuw.

Hij komt dreigend dichterbij, tot hij vlak voor mij staat. Hij is twee koppen groter dan ik en dubbel zo breed. Hij loopt zogezegd per ongeluk tegen me aan. Dan lacht hij plots breed en slaat me op mijn schouder.
'Alles goed?'
Ja, alles goed.
Mep! 'Alles goed?'
Nog eens mep! 'Alles goed?'
'Hou op', zegt Ouhida.
De lijfwacht kijkt verstoord, maar loopt weer naar zijn plaats. Ali komt zich verontschuldigen. 'Hij is een goeie gast. We houden alleen niet zo van journalisten.'
Tegen de goeie gast zegt hij: 'Deze hier is een uitzondering.'
Ik krijg een smalende grijns.
De drie oudere mannen met wie Ali heeft staan praten, horen ook dat ik journalist ben. Ze komen om me heen staan en beginnen een verwarde theorie uit de doeken te doen die erop neerkomt dat de rellen van april, waarvoor de AEL verantwoordelijk werd gehouden, eigenlijk veroorzaakt werden door de politie, die infiltranten heeft in de Arabische gemeenschap die betaald worden om herrie te schoppen.
'Anders heeft de politie niet genoeg werk, en dan krijgen ze minder geld van de regering! Het draait allemaal om geld.'
Ik beloof dat ik het zal onderzoeken. Tevreden druipen ze af.
Na de meeting loopt het gangetje voor de zaal vol met toeschouwers. Ik schat dat het er tweehonderd zijn. Ze kwetteren opgewonden door elkaar. Vier Marokkaanse pubermeisjes giechelen in plat Antwerps over de lijfwachten van Abou Jahjah.

'Ik geef u de kracht van Abou Jahjah', roept een van hen, en legt plechtig haar handen op het hoofd van haar vriendin.
('Hij luistert naar Chris de Burgh!' wil ik roepen. 'Zo cool is hij nu ook weer niet!')
'Ben jij Tom Naegels?' vraagt een bebaarde man.
Ik antwoord bevestigend.
'Wat een talent, hè', zegt hij.
'Ach, het is vooral hard werken', zeg ik.
De man fronst vragend. O, hij bedoelt Abou Jahjah.
'Zoals die man kan praten. En hij heeft gelijk!'
Ik vraag of hij lid is van de AEL.
'Nee-hee. Ik ben een groene tot en met. Onze partij zou naar die man moeten luisteren!'
Het is even wachten, maar daar begint het dan toch: het scanderen van 'A-bou Jahjah! A-bou Jahjah!' Een groepje jongens bezet het trottoir en een deel van de straat en zet zijn enthousiaste chant in. Voor hen is politiek iets als voetbal. Automobilisten die de hoek omrijden denken dat ze in een rel terechtgekomen zijn: je ziet hun verschrikte gezichten, ze versnellen onmiddellijk. Het groepje loopt, nog steeds scanderend, naar de Groenplaats.
Gezellig, zo'n meeting van de AEL. Beetje als een jeugdbeweging. En zoveel mooie jonge vrouwen. Echt jammer dat ik niet geëngageerder ben.

27

Ik ben bij Nadia als ik de sms krijg. Hij komt van een collega en spoort me aan om de regionale tv-zender ATV op te zetten. Nadia is aan het kijken naar *Coming to America*, met Eddy Murphy als Afrikaanse prins die een lief gaat zoeken in New York. Het is moeilijk om haar ervan te overtuigen die film even af te zetten voor het nieuws. Ik moet wachten tot de reclame.

Eerst heb ik niet door wat er gebeurt. Het beeld maakt voortdurend slagzij. Het enige wat ik kan onderscheiden zijn tientallen mensen die voorbijlopen. Daarna zie ik dat er geduwd en getrokken wordt. Waarschijnlijk is de cameraman zelf betrokken bij dat duwen en trekken, want het beeld gaat nu helemaal kantelen. Ik zie een vriendin van me die voor de regionale omroep werkt, die met haar microfoon uit het gewoel probeert te raken.

Pas als journaliste en cameraman zich bevrijd hebben en van een grotere afstand kunnen filmen, zie ik wat er gebeurt. Er zijn rellen aan de gang op de Turnhoutsebaan. Wat broeide is uitgekomen. Groepjes Arabische jongeren rennen heen en weer, springen op wagens, trappen ruiten in en vechten met de politie.

Ziehier de reden waarom ik geen goede journalist ben: ik kan mijn emoties niet bedwingen. Mijn bird's eye view, mijn bedachtzame, genuanceerde opinies, mijn objectiviteit en *cool* blijven alleen overeind als het om onbelangrijke feitjes gaat. Of als iets heel ver weg, of heel lang geleden gebeurd is.

Ik zit voor de televisie te trillen van woede. Ik denk de ergste dingen. Heel racistische dingen. Maar is het racis-

me? Of gewoon een instinctieve afkeer van geweld, een diepe haat die opborrelt als ik mannen zie die losgeslagen en brullend van auto tot auto springen – ik kan het niet helpen, ik denk smerige makakken, boeren uit Marokko, walgelijke primitieve achterlijke bananenschijters. Dat is wat ik denk, maar is dat racisme? Het is emotie van het moment die zoekt naar het ergste scheldwoord dat ze kan bedenken. Of is racisme altijd emotie van het moment?
Ik ga naar de keuken om te huilen.

Als ik terugkeer, staat *Coming to America* weer op. Hoe kun je naar Eddy Murphy kijken als enkele straten verder de oorlog uitgebroken is?
'Waarom huil je?' vraagt Nadia.
'Heb je de beelden niet gezien?'
'Van daarnet?'
'Dat is op de Turnhoutsebaan. Niet ver hiervandaan.'
'Het zijn Marokkanen.'
'Het is in mijn stad.'
'Niet waar jij woont.'
'Mag het nieuws weer op? Je hebt die film al drie keer gezien.'
Met tegenzin zapt ze weg.
We zien de burgemeester en de commissaris van de politie. Een commentaarstem legt uit wat er gebeurd is. Eerder op de avond heeft een oudere Vlaamse man met een geweer gevuurd op zijn Marokkaanse buren, een vader en zijn zevenentwintigjarige zoon. De vader kon ontkomen, de zoon werd getroffen. Hij overleed voor de deur van zijn ouderlijke woning. De dader werd opgepakt door de politie. Een grote massa allochtonen spoedde zich naar de woning. Ze begonnen een rel te schoppen.

Emotie één: woede, gericht tegen de dader. De vuige racist! (Dacht de man die vijf minuten eerder tierde over smerige makakken.)
Emotie twee: woede, tegen racisten in het algemeen, die al jaren de harten en de geesten van mijn stad verzieken. Het moest er eens van komen, dat er één zijn geweer nam en iemand afknalde. Er is geen Vlaming of hij heeft racistische reflexen. Ik ook!
Emotie drie: woede, gericht tegen de relschoppers. Oké, er is een jongen vermoord, maar die kunnen ze toch niet allemaal gekend hebben? Niemand heeft zoveel vrienden. En dan nog: als er een vriend van mij vermoord werd, dan zou ik machteloos op de grond zinken en huilen. Ik zou maanden tot niets in staat zijn. Wat *is* er met die mensen, dat hun verdriet zo snel boosheid wordt? Felle emoties, daar verkramp ik van; ik sluit me op, ik wil stil liggen in het donker, ik wil *alleen* zijn als ik verdrietig ben. En wat hebben ze met grote groepen? Als *ik* een groep zie, zeker een boze, dan weet ik niet hoe snel ik die moet ontvluchten – snel snel, straatje in, naar huis toe, vooral niet opgeslorpt raken in dat gewoel van een uitzinnige, redeloze menigte. Wat *is* het met die mensen, dat ze zo graag menigtes vormen, zo graag in groep boos zijn?
Er is niets dat ik begrijp van die beelden. Behalve dat onredelijke mensen dingen stukslaan. Dat jongetjes, veel jonger dan ik, de politie jennen en met gsm's andere jongetjes opbellen om de politie nog meer te jennen – dat is toch geen verdriet?
De heftigheid van mijn emoties maakt me bang. Ik *ben* geen racist. Ik zou liever sterven dan een racist te zijn. En toch, bij het zien van die beelden... Slopende woede.

Boos op niemand. Boos op alles en iedereen. Op mannen. Op machoculturen. Op volkeren uit het Zuiden. Op jongens met te veel testosteron. Op moslims. Op Arabieren, het moeilijkste volk van deze tijd.

Beelden van de burgemeester. Ze zegt met stellige zekerheid dat het niet om een racistische aanslag gaat. Hoe weet zij dat zo zeker? Het is pas gebeurd!
Beelden van Dyab Abou Jahjah. Hij zegt met stellige zekerheid dat het om een racistische moord gaat. Hoe weet hij dat zo zeker? Het is pas gebeurd!
Volgens Abou Jahjah heeft de moordenaar, voor hij schoot, 'smerige Taliban!' geroepen. Kijk eens aan. Heeft hij dat gecheckt? Was hij erbij? Heeft hij in een uurtje het gerechtelijk onderzoek gedaan? Of bauwt hij geëmotioneerde pubers na?
Woede!
Ik ga zitten en hou mijn hoofd in mijn handen. Al die stukgeslagen ruiten. Stel je maar voor dat je winkelier bent. Stel het je maar voor. Waarom gebeuren zulke dingen nooit met Russen, Chinezen, Turken, Koreanen, Pakistanen, Afrikanen, Ecuadorianen...? Waarom doet Nadia dat niet? Wat *is* er met Arabische jongens dat hen zoveel bozer maakt dan die anderen?
Nadia is naast me komen zitten en streelt mijn hoofd.
'Waarom zo triest? Je weet toch dat Arabieren uitschot zijn?'
'Hoe kun jij dat nu zeggen? Je bent zelf zwart.'
'Arabieren zijn blank.'
'Arabieren zijn niet blank! Europeanen zijn blank!'
'Arabieren zijn even blank als Europeanen!'
'Dat is niet waar! Arabieren zijn bruin!'

'Niemand houdt van Arabieren. Ook wij niet.'
Ze geeft me wat ik nodig heb: een excuus om me te verliezen in sociologenpraat. Ik hervind de bird's eye view. Het is hun schuld niet. Het is het systeem. Achterstelling, racisme, zelfhaat. Minutenlang vertel ik mijn cursus Racisme, Etniciteit en Intercultureel Samenleven na.
Ik voel me beter.
Nadia zet *Coming to America* weer op.

28

De volgende dag zijn de emoties geluwd en ben ik opnieuw een verdraagzame jongen. Ik denk zelfs, met rebelse trots, dat het misschien geen kwaad kan, een beetje oproer. Een paar winkelruiten, een telefoonhokje, wat auto's... misschien is het nodig om aandacht te eisen voor de problemen van onze allochtone broeders. Zolang ze beleefd blijven, gebeurt er toch niets.

En daarbij: rellen? Opstootjes, dat waren het. Incidenten. Feiten. In Zuid-Afrika, daar heb je rellen. Wat een hysterie. Hoeveel ruiten zijn er nou gesneuveld? Tien? Twintig? En wat zijn een paar kapotte ruiten vergeleken bij die jongeman die gisteren het leven liet? Denk je dat hij alle aandacht krijgt in de kranten vandaag? Twee, drie paragraafjes over de moord, en vier bladzijden over de rellen. Ziehier de prioriteiten van de Vlaamse pers.

(Waarom ben je niet naar buiten gegaan om zelf te kijken wat er aan de hand was? Met je perskaart hadden ze je zo doorgelaten.)

(Ben je gek? Ik, in een oorlog?)

(Een échte journalist was gaan kijken.)

(Ik ben een bird's eye view-journalist.)

Met dit heerlijke gevoel van warme rebellie loop ik de redactie binnen.

'Het is nogal wat met die zwarte mannen, hè Tom', word ik begroet door een stem die ik vaag herken. Ze hoort toe aan een collega die normaal op het Brusselse hoofdkantoor werkt. Er is versterking gekomen van de nationale redactie. Ze zijn met zijn drieën.

'Je gaat vandaag toch niet de grote linkse filosoof uithangen, hè Naegels?'

Ik heb niet eens iets gezegd!
'Je ziet waar je met al je theorieën gekomen bent. Geef toe: al die moestafa's lopen achter die bandiet met zijn geschoren smoelwerk aan. Geef die opgefokte mannekes de eerste de beste ayatollah uit Sjokowakije, en daar staan ze met hun allahoe akbar.'
'Grooohohohohoho!'
De drie collega's uit Brussel lachen de grohoho-journalistenlach. 'Grohoho!' lach ik mee.
Hij is me goedmoedig aan het provoceren. Hij maakt een lolletje. Collega's onder elkaar. In werkelijkheid is dit een progressieve man, gedreven door grote liberale en humanistische waarden. Dat blijkt uit zijn commentaarstukken, die met regelmaat racisme veroordelen.
Ergens is er in die vreemde subcultuur van mediamensen de gewoonte ontstaan om de taal van de straat te imiteren. Beschaafde, gestudeerde mannen doen zich voor als seksisten, homofoben, fascisten, racisten en liefhebbers van harde porno. Ook ik spreek over 'bruin mannen' voor Marokkanen en 'zwartologen' voor integratiewerkers, als ik het al niet heb over 'makakkologen', in mijn lucidere momenten.
'Heeft er iemand een nummer van de bonobo's van het stadsbestuur?'
Het is grohoho-humor, journalistenhumor.
'Maar godverdrek!' vloekt onze collega, nadat blijkt dat er op het stadhuis niet onmiddellijk wordt opgenomen. 'Liggen waarschijnlijk nog in hun bed! Zijn nog aan het koffiekletsen! Logisch dat het hier naar de kloten gaat, als je ziet wat voor onbenullen hier aan het hoofd staan. Neem nu op, bonobo's!'
Op dat moment wordt er opgenomen. Zijn stem veran-

dert onmiddellijk van timbre en beleefd doch dringend eist hij dat hij de burgemeester kan spreken.
'In vergadering? Mevrouw, wij zijn de grootste krant van Vlaanderen. Het zou jammer zijn als de burgemeester niet aan het woord kon komen. Zegt u tegen haar dat ze na haar vergadering onmiddellijk naar mij terugbelt?'
'Vergadering', smaalt hij als hij de hoorn neergelegd heeft. 'Aan de koffieklets, daar zit ze!'

Ik krijg mijn opdracht van de dag. Ik moet op zoek naar Mohamed met de Megafoon. Zo heet hij natuurlijk niet echt, maar het alliteereert leuk. Mohamed met de Megafoon was de man die, volgens de collega die gisteren ter plaatse was, de gemoederen wist te bedaren door in het heetst van de strijd de megafoon te nemen, op de vernielzuchtige jongeren toe te stappen en hen toe te spreken. Hij is de held van de dag. In die hoedanigheid moet ik hem portretteren. 'Tom Naegels portretteert Megafoon Mohamed en laat hem vertellen hoe hij, met gevaar voor eigen leven, de losgeslagen jongeren bedaarde. De man vertelt hoe hij op hun eergevoel werkte en dreigde hun moeders erbij te halen. Tom Naegels laat hem zeggen dat, als mannen met autoriteit uit de Marokkaanse gemeenschap hun verantwoordelijkheid durven op te nemen, de jongeren in toom kunnen worden gehouden.'
Ik bel naar Mohammed Chakkar, voorzitter van de Federatie van Marokkaanse Verenigingen.
'Dag Mohammed, ik ben op zoek naar de held van de dag, de man die met zijn megafoon de jongeren in bedwang hield.'
Mohammed: 'O ja, is hij de held van de avond? Ja 'allo!

Wij waren met zijn zessen, wij hebben met zijn zessen onderhandeld, en hij was er ook bij maar of hij nu zoveel gedaan heeft...'
O.
Ik val even stil.
Ik begrijp wat er gebeurd is. Iemand heeft dit verhaal bedacht tijdens een redactievergadering, en nu hoopt men dat het ook echt gebeurd is. Het is mijn taak om daarvoor te zorgen.
Ik bedank Mohammed en bel naar mijn chef in Brussel. Ik leg hem uit dat het verhaal volgens mij anders in elkaar zit. Er zijn *zes* helden van de dag, niet één.
Mijn chef lacht. 'Ik begrijp dat die Moestafa Tsjakka ook graag in de krant wil en dat hij een beetje jaloers is dat we iemand anders held maken.'
'Ja maar... Wat als er echt zes...'
'Dat is nu eenmaal kranten maken, Tom. Wie de megafoon bemachtigt, is de held. Heel jammer voor de andere vijf, die ongetwijfeld ook hard gewerkt hebben, maar zes helden, dat gaat niet. Bovendien: we hebben die man met de megafoon op foto, de anderen niet.'
Mijn warme gevoel van rebellie is verdwenen. Ik ben zelfs geen bird's eye view-journalist meer. Dit is gewoon mijn werk. Ik doe wat men mij vraagt.

Ik wacht twee uur voor ik weer begin rond te bellen. Ik draai op mijn stoel, bekijk mijn e-mail, surf wat rond, ga naar het toilet, zoek naar manieren om onder mijn opdracht uit te komen maar vind er geen. Ik haat Mohamed met de Megafoon.
Ik wil net, ten einde raad, opnieuw beginnen als fotograaf Jonas de redactie binnenkomt. Hij is foto's gaan

nemen van een 'serene herdenkingsdienst' ter nagedachtenis van de vermoorde Marokkaanse jongen. Of dat was het plan. Toen hij arriveerde op de serene dienst werd hij in elkaar geslagen door vijf jochies. Toen hij wilde wegrennen, achtervolgden ze hem. Twee hebben hem vastgegrepen, de andere drie hebben zijn camera stukgeslagen.

Een camera van 10.000 euro! Hij heeft een lening moeten aangaan om die te kunnen kopen! Zijn baan hangt af van die camera! Zonder dat ding is hij werkloos! Hij heeft geen geld om een nieuwe te kopen! Hij is zelfstandige, de krant betaalt dat nooit terug!

De camera van een vriend van mij is vernield door kleine jochies die het leuk vinden om boos te zijn, die graag in groep boos zijn, die graag alles in groep doen omdat ze als individu niets voorstellen. Wat tril ik van woede.

Jonas nog meer. Zijn lippen beven, zijn handen schokken, zijn ogen spuiten haat. Met toegesnoerde keel krijgt hij niets anders over zijn lippen dan 'smerige makakken, vuile smerige kutmakakken'. Het is de emotie van het moment. Jonas is een goedlachse, hartelijke jongen, gunt iedereen een plaats onder de zon, maar hoe kun je geen racist zijn als je net aangevallen bent door kereltjes die half zo oud zijn en op school hadden moeten zitten?

Waarom zitten ze niet op school?

Een vrouwelijke collega begint te huilen omdat Jonas 'makakken' heeft gezegd. Ze loopt naar de gang. Als ik haar achterna ga, stuurt ze me weg.

'Het zijn hier allemaal racisten!' huilt ze. 'Jonas, die idioten van Brussel die denken dat ze grappig zijn met hun moestafa's hier en hun bruine mannen daar.'

(Maar dat is toch geen racisme! Het is ofwel emotie van

het moment, ofwel de ironische taboedoorbrekende gewoonte van hoogopgeleiden om laagopgeleiden te imiteren. Je kent ons toch? Zien wij eruit als racisten?)

Mohamed met de Megafoon. Het is mijn taak om hem te vinden om hem te laten zeggen wat wij graag hebben dat hij zegt. Na twee uur begin ik weer. Ik bel naar een woordvoerder van de Unie van Moskeeën. Ik heb geluk. Hij heeft net in vergadering gezeten met Mohamed. 'Bel binnen een uurtje terug. Dan ben ik uit vergadering en dan geef ik je zijn nummer.'
Na een uur zegt hij: 'Said Mdaouchi heeft het nummer, ik niet.'
Ik bel naar Mdaouchi, de voorzitter van de Unie van Moskeeën. 'Ik zit nu in vergadering maar bel me binnen vijf minuten.'
Vijf minuten later staat de gsm af. Pas een uur later kan ik hem weer bereiken. Ik krijg een nummer. Dat blijkt fout. Ik bel terug naar Mdaouchi: 'Ik zit nu in de auto maar bel me binnen een halfuur.'
Halfuur later: gsm staat af.
Ik ben niet alleen boos omdat ik een artikel moet schrijven dat niet waar is, ik ben ook gegeneerd omdat ik zoveel mensen moet storen met mijn domme opdracht. Al deze prominente Antwerpse moslims zijn de begrafenis van de vermoorde jongen aan het regelen. Zij houden contact met de gebroken familie, ze proberen hun boze jongeren in bedwang te houden, ze onderhandelen met politici om de situatie onder controle te krijgen. Hun werk heeft zin. En ik moet hen storen omdat ik een held moet maken van een man die geen held is maar die we toevallig op foto hebben.
Uiteindelijk, laat op de dag, ontdek ik dat Mohamed met

de Megafoon een jonge medewerker is van de Marokkaanse ambassade, maar ik krijg hem niet aan de lijn. Hij wil niet of hij mag niet – de vrouw bij de ambassade begint haast hardop te lachen als ik zeg dat hij de held van de voorbije avond was. 'Ik denk dat hij daar maar heel eventjes geweest is, hoor.' Ten einde raad maak ik een stuk over hoe zes oudere Marokkanen met gezag de jongeren kalmeren. Ik citeer Mohammed Chakkar en laat hem al de dingen zeggen die mijn chef in Brussel graag heeft dat oudere Marokkanen zeggen. Ik leg het hem later wel uit.
(Ik heb hem niets hoeven uit te leggen. Het stuk is nooit verschenen.)

29

Moeder heeft beslist dat er over de rellen niets tegen bompa verteld mag worden. Alle informatie gaat via haar. Alles wat hem boos kan maken (en alles maakt hem boos), en alles wat hem niet interesseert (en niets interesseert hem) wordt door haar afgeblokt. Het liefst heeft ze het als ze zelf de onderwerpen kan aangeven, waarna de bezoeker in kwestie het verhaal mag afmaken.
'Onze Tom is naar Brugge geweest', galmt ze dan, bijvoorbeeld. Ze wacht op zijn reactie. Als hij knikt, dan is het onderwerp goedgekeurd en dan mag ik vertellen over mijn uitstap naar Brugge. Haalt hij zijn schouders op, dan wordt er niet verder op ingegaan.
Als ik de kamer binnenkom, zit bompa rechtop en houdt zich vast aan het handvat boven zijn hoofd. Zijn pyjama hangt los over zijn knokige schouders. Hij buigt zich voorover naar moeder, zijn persoonlijke raadgever, opdat hij geen woord mist van wat zij zegt.
Moeder ziet mij eerder dan hij. Ze bereidt hem voor op mijn komst, opdat hij niet te erg schrikt. Ze stopt met praten en kijkt in mijn richting. Ze raakt zijn hand aan. Ze zegt luid: 'Zie eens wie hier is!'
Ik leg mijn hand op zijn schouder. Iets te vroeg. Hij schrikt toch, kijkt wild om zich heen, weet niet wat er gebeurt, krijgt me niet in zijn blikveld. Even is hij in paniek, en staat hij op het punt in huilen uit te barsten (dat gebeurt vaak en vroeger nooit). Dan merkt hij toch mijn contouren op, of mijn haarkleur, of mijn geur... wat hij ook gebruikt om mij te herkennen.
'Tom, jongen!'

Hij opent zijn armen om me te omhelzen, verliest daardoor zijn greep op het handvat en valt hulpeloos in zijn kussens. 'Tom, jongen', vloekt hij met gesloten ogen.
Ik buig me over zijn bed en omhels de kleine broodmagere man, die vloekt onder mijn omhelzing.
Het is alweer een week geleden dat ik bompa bezocht heb. Het verwijt hangt als een gas in de kamer. Mijn bompa ligt op sterven en ik kom één keer per week! De rest van de familie komt bijna dagelijks...
'Ge ziet, pa', zegt moeder. 'Hij is u niet vergeten.'
Ze draait messen graag drie keer in de wond. Ik zoek koortsachtig naar een enigszins aanvaardbaar excuus, maar moeder is me voor. 'Ge weet, hij heeft veel werk, hè pa.'
Werk doet het altijd bij bompa. Werk is het belangrijkste.
'Hij heeft een verkoudheid, onze Tom.'
Even wachten, bompa knikt, ik mag.
Het is maar een verkoudheid. Wat kan ik daar over vertellen?
'Gisteren had ik koorts', zeg ik met tegenzin.
Bompa reageert niet.
'Luider!' beveelt moeder.
'Dat ik gisteren koorts had!'
Nu heeft bompa het wel gehoord. Ik had koorts. Nou en? Hij is aan het sterven! Hij haalt zijn schouders op. Onderwerp afgevoerd.
Nu weet ik weer waarom ik weinig kom. Ik kan niet tegen de stiltes. Mijn bompa ligt op sterven, we zouden diepe gesprekken moeten voeren over de Essentie, maar het enige wat we doen is zwijgen, en af en toe pogen meer dan drie zinnen te zeggen over een banaliteit.

Zo zitten we een halfuur bij elkaar. Moeder haalt onderwerpen aan, kijkt of bompa ze goedkeurt, ik zeg er drie zinnen over die bompa al dan niet verstaat, dan haalt hij zijn schouders op en valt het gesprek stil.
Ik ga weg. Ik heb getoond dat ik van mijn bompa hou.

30

Dyab Abou Jahjah zit in de gevangenis. Waarvan hij beschuldigd wordt, is onduidelijk. Mijn krant schrijft dat er wapens gevonden zijn in zijn flat. Nog diezelfde dag blijkt daar niets van te kloppen. Toch loopt onze gerechtsjournalist nog drie dagen glunderend rond: geen enkele andere krant had het!

In het parlement zegt de premier dat de AEL maar één doel heeft: *no-go*-zones creëren waar de politie niet durft te komen zodat de criminaliteit er welig kan tieren. Waar hij dat vandaan heeft, is onduidelijk. Een Antwerpse schepen, tevens parlementslid, eist dat de wet wordt veranderd om de AEL erbuiten te stellen. Een week later wordt Abou Jahjah vrijgelaten. Van criminaliteit is geen sprake. Toch wordt de premier enkele maanden later met overweldigende meerderheid herkozen. Een rechtzetting komt er nooit.

Het nieuws toont beelden van Abou Jahjah die de relschoppers ophitst. Twee dagen later toont het nieuws beelden van Abou Jahjah die de relschoppers kalmeert. Welke conclusie we daaruit moeten trekken, is onduidelijk.

De rellen gaan verder. Drie dagen lang. Kranten vullen zich met lezersbrieven. Vlamingen begrijpen niet waarom Marokkanen zoveel heisa maken over een moord. Het is vreselijk, natuurlijk, tragisch, maar hey, gebeurt elke dag! Als er een Belg vermoord wordt, slaan wij dan alles stuk? Marokkanen begrijpen niet dat Vlamingen glas belangrijker vinden dan een mensenleven. Een familie doorstaat een tragedie, en jullie zeiken over een paar auto's en wat ruiten. Voor de Marokkanen staat het vast dat het om een racistische moord ging. Voor de Belgen staat het even vast dat dat niet zo was. De moordenaar was waanzinnig! O, en een gek kan niet racistisch zijn?

Ik sta al zo'n kwartier te drentelen voor café Roma. Ik heb de opdracht gekregen om reacties te sprokkelen bij de buurtbewoners. Overdag luwen de rellen, om na zonsondergang weer met volle kracht los te barsten. Het is twee uur 's middags. De Turnhoutsebaan ligt er rustig bij. Op enkele gesloten rolluiken na is niet te merken dat dit een strijdtoneel is geweest.

Ik kijk door het raam. Baard en Kale, die me zouden kunnen herkennen van de vorige keer, zijn er niet. Bovendien is Nadia niet bij me. Ik zie alleen snorren en trainingspakken. Ik ben bang van snorren en trainingspakken.

Maar ik heb mijn schild: ik ben journalist. Ik mag anders zijn dan de klanten, ik hoef hun vriend niet te worden, ik heb een goeie reden om hen aan te spreken. En: ik werk voor een krant die dicht staat bij het volk. Ook al zie ik er niet zo uit, door mijn werk ben ik een van hen. Diep in mijn gedachten heb ik een snor.

Niettemin: ik blijf nog vijf extra minuten aarzelen, tot ik vrees dat ze me zullen zien en de politie bellen of me in ieder geval taxeren als een gek, waardoor ik mijn kansen op een interview helemaal vergooi.

Niemand kijkt op als ik binnenstap. Er zit een man of tien, in stil gebed rond hun pintje. Alleen pintjes. Geen andere bieren, geen andere dranken.

Ik zie meteen met wie ik moet praten: vier mannen met nekhaar en bruine tanden die luid in gesprek zijn. Ze lij-

ken me ongeveer even oud als ik, al is dat moeilijk te zeggen.
'En toen gaf ik hem een kopstoot en dat brilleke vloog tien meter verder!' roept de luidruchtigste. Ik tast angstig naar mijn bril.
'En dat meisje, dat krijste gelijk dat ze gekeeld werd!'
Ik ga aan het tafeltje naast hen zitten, wil koffie bestellen, bedenk me en bestel een pintje. Wat een naïviteit. Alsof ik met dat ene pintje, dat detail van volksheid, mijn hele uiterlijk kan tenietdoen, dat brilletje doen verdwijnen, die nette trui, die plooibroek.
Uiteindelijk raap ik mijn moed bij elkaar en ga naast de man die brilletjes wegmept en meisjes keelt zitten.
'Excuseer.'
Fout! Wie zegt er nu 'excuseer'? Waarom niet meteen 'met mijn welgemeende verontschuldigingen'? Wat is er mis met 'sorry'? En spreek Antwerps, verdomme! Hoe wil je hun vertrouwen winnen met dat halfbeschaafde nepdialect?
'Sorry, mag ik even storen?'
'*Even*, hè makker.' Hij imiteert mijn bekakte accent op vileine toon. (Het is *efkes*, dat weet ik toch.) 'Hou me niet te lang wakker, ik moet nog slapen met ons Conny.'
Vette knipoog. Conny is de vrouw achter de bar. Ze protesteert voor de vorm. 'Dat zou je wel willen, geobsedeerde!'
'Ge moogt gerust zijn!' kraait hij.
De oudste van de vier komt me te hulp. Hij legt zijn zware arm om mijn schouders en zegt: 'Zeg het maar, jongen, je moet op hem niet letten, hij doet maar wat onnozel. Hoe heet ge?'
'Tom', mompel ik.

(Niemand hier heet Tom. Op zijn minst Tommy.)
'Nog een pint voor onze maat Tom! En voor ons ook allemaal! Op zijn kosten!'
Weer een bulderlach.
Ik noem de naam van de krant waarvoor ik werk.
'A-haaaaaaaaa! De Gazet!'
Ze staren me aan. Ze slaan op tafel. Hoe is dat nu mogelijk? Ik werk voor de krant die ze al heel hun leven lezen! Ze hebben het al dikwijls tegen elkaar gezegd: eigenlijk zouden zij eens in de krant moeten komen. Wat zij allemaal al meegemaakt hebben! Wat moeten ze doen om ook eens een keer...? Met mij praten? Gewoon nu met mij praten? Maar dat is ongelooflijk!
De magie werkt elke keer. Wanneer je in een gesprek met volkse volksmens bent, zeg altijd dat je journalist bent van mijn krant. Alles wordt je vergeven.

Nu ben ik deel van de groep. Ik word uitgebreid voorgesteld. De man die brilletjes wegmept, heet Randy, bijgenaamd Bambi, bijgenaamd Andras Pandy. Naast hem zitten Franky, bijgenaamd Stafke Porno; Eddy, bijgenaamd Bolleke; en Danny (geen bijnaam). Eddy is de vader van Danny en de oom van Franky. Ze zijn vaste klanten van café Roma. 'Wij zijn de favoriete Romaboys', bulderen ze.
'Wij zijn van café Roma, en vrijdags allemaal in coma!'
Ze rijmen graag.
Uitbaatster Conny heeft ook een bijnaam: kwartel. 'Allez, een serieuze kwartel, meer een fazant', brult Eddy en Randy gooit daarbovenop: 'Conny, laat uw tetten eens meten? Onze maat Tom hier wil uw tetten meten.'
Ik lach schaapachtig: nee hoor, ik wil haar borsten hele-

maal niet meten. Haha, die Randy toch.
De pintjes worden gebracht. Ik betaal om mijn net verworven vriendschap niet op de proef te stellen.
Als ze horen waar mijn reportage over gaat, doen ze wat ik ook altijd doe: ze brengen de Borgerhout-mythe in stelling. Om indruk te maken? Omdat ze ervan genieten om zichzelf voor te stellen als harde overlevingskunstenaars in het getto? Of is het voor hen echt realiteit?
'Dat is hier Mekkatown hè', zegt Randy, de beste woordspeler van de groep. 'In Amerika hebt ge Chinatown en hier is het Mekkatown. Of Irangate, een gat vol Iranezen.'
'Toch zeker de linkerkant van de Turnhoutsebaan. Aan de rechterkant is het nog een beetje koffie met melk, maar aan de linkerkant is het honderd procent pure Arabica.'
'De Bronx, dat is onze hof.'
'Zie – met die Marokkanen', onderbreekt Franky. 'Wij kennen heel veel Marokkanen. Daar zit crapuul tussen maar ook goei mannen. Heel veel van mijn maten zijn Marokkanen.'
'Ik spreek zelfs Marokkaans', beweert Danny, en hij demonstreert het.
Twee minuten lang voeren ze een gesprek dat in het Arabisch geweest kan zijn, of anders in een goed gespeeld neptaaltje om mij in de maling te nemen. (In de maling? Waarom niet meteen 'in het ootje'? Spreek Antwerps! Bij uw lul gepakt, gezjost, gesjareld, gefokt, bij uw sjokkedeizen, gekoeioneerd, afgezeken, in de zeik gezet – leer die taal!)
'Vroeger waren ik, mijn broer en twee zussen de enige Belgen op school in de Vincottestraat. De enigen die

Vlaams spraken op die school waren wij, en de leerkrachten. De hele dag hoorden wij niks anders dan Marokkaans. Op de duur sprak iedereen het: de leerkrachten ook.'

'Ik woon hier al vijfendertig jaar', vertelt Eddy. 'Ik heb de tijd meegemaakt vóór de Marokkanen. Toen was zelfs de sneeuw nog wit. Mijn buurman is een Marokkaan. Da's een mens van vijfenvijftig jaar, nog een hele traditionele – ge kent ze wel, hij gaat met vier op reis en hij komt met acht terug. Als ik mijn auto in 't straat zet, dan houden zijn kinderen die in het oog. Als ge ze kent, dan doe ze u niet veel. Maar er is veel *reucht* tussen. Klein mannen van twaalf, dertien jaar die ambras zoeken. Hebt ge er ambras mee, dan roepen ze hun broertjes van zestien, zeventien jaar, en die roepen hun broers van vijfentwintig jaar, en dan hebt ge ambras met de hele santeboetiek. Zo is het ook nu gegaan, met die rellen.'

'Zie – die rellen', zegt Franky. 'Dat zit zo: ze hebben een beetje gelijk, en een beetje niet. Ge moet niemand afknallen, en ge moet geen ruiten insmijten. Alle twee verkeerd, en alle twee juist. Snapt ge dat?'

'Ze hadden die moordenaar uit zijn kot moeten lokken en die in elkaar slagen. Dat was juist geweest. Niet die mannen met een winkel.'

'En wij staan allemaal achter Abou Jahjah... met een mes.'

'Mijn buurman, die is te braaf voor de wereld. Hij zei het ook: "Over die rellen, daar kan ik niet veel over zeggen." Dat zei hij. Te goed voor deze wereld.'

'Maar voor een stuk moet ge ze toch gelijk geven. Marokkanen, die zijn solidair. Als er een Marokkaan last heeft, dan staat daar direct twintig man rond om die te helpen. Als ge ambras hebt met zo één Marokkaan: dat is geen ramadan hè, dat is een heel Suikerfeest. Een Belg, als die ziet dat iemand problemen heeft, dan loopt die rap weg. Een Belg keert voor eigen deur, áls hij nog keert, maar die komt niet op voor zijn volk.'

Daarop volgen oorlogsverhalen over treffens met Marokkaanse bendes. Ze praten om beurten, en wie praat komt naast mij zitten en slaat zijn arm om me heen. Wie het woord wil overnemen, komt aan de andere kant zitten en slaat zijn arm om mijn andere schouder. Ze kijken wat ik opschrijf, nemen soms mijn pen af, schrijven het zelf. Over die keer dat er bij Danny was ingebroken, en dat iedereen uit de buurt wist welke Marokkaan het had gedaan, en andere Marokkanen waren het tegen Danny gaan zeggen, en die was op de gast afgestapt en had gezegd: 'Kerel, ofwel geeft ge alles terug en dan spreken we er niet meer over, ofwel krijgt ge een rammeling die ge van uw leven niet meer vergeet, als ge nog leeft om het te kunnen onthouden.' Waarop hij alles had teruggekregen.

'Het is bewezen dat wij, Belgen, het intelligentste volk ter wereld zijn, wist ge dat? Nee? Schrijf dat dan maar op! Dat is geweest op tv. Waar dat een Belg ook komt, hij zal zich aanpassen. Hij zal zich altijd verstaanbaar maken. Een Hollander, die kent maar twee talen.'

'En be-talen, dat kent hij zeker niet.'

'Zeg', zegt Eddy, en hij slaat weer zijn arm om me heen. 'We zijn nu aan het zwanzen, maar er zit veel waarheid in.'

Waarom beantwoordden deze mannen niet aan het cliché? Dit zijn toch Vlamingen uit de laagste sociale klasse? Waar blijft de ongecontroleerde stroom van woede, het gebral over smerige makakken die ons alles afpakken? Wat moet ik hier nu mee?

Al kun je ook niet zeggen dat ze geen racisten zijn. Ondanks hun belijdenis van vriendschap met de buren, ondanks het feit dat ze Arabisch spreken of doen alsof, ondanks hun beweringen dat er veel goeie tussen zitten knettert hun vierstemmige tirade van 'makak' en 'koeskoestrut' en hoe ze gevochten hebben met die en die bende. Of is dat gewoon het leven van de volkse man in deze buurt?

Cafébazin Conny mengt zich in het gesprek: 'Maar ze moeten niet beginnen met mijn kinderen Arabisch te leren op school! Want dat willen ze! Als ze mijn Kevin Arabisch willen laten spreken, dan zullen ze met mij te maken krijgen! Onze Kevin is een Belg en dat moet zo blijven! Ik leer hem vechten. Een paar dagen geleden had onze Kevin bijna een makak zijn arm gebroken. Ik zeg: ge moet dat niet *bijna* doen, ge moet dat *echt* doen!'

'Meneer, het gaat niet om die rellen, het leven is hier al jaren on-leef-baar', roept een andere klant. 'Wij worden hier bespuwd, uitgelachen, beroofd en afgeslagen. Het is hier de hel, simpelweg de hel. Kijk, meneer, ik ben door en door katholiek. Ik ben lector in de kerk, maar ik heb tegen de pastoor gezegd: het woord "verdraagzaamheid" spreek ik niet meer uit. En de pastoor geeft mij gelijk! Als je ziet hoe ze voetballen: die bal *moet* door de ruiten, de dingen *moeten* kapot. Weet je waar ik bang voor ben? Dat ze onze monumenten zullen verwoesten! En dat gáán ze doen! Alles wat onze voorouders opgebouwd hebben zullen ze vernielen. Nee, meneer, alle beschavingen zijn bezig met ze buiten te keren. En ze heb-

ben gelijk. Schrijf het maar op: zet ze op een boot op de Schelde en boem!'
(Ja. Kijk. Dát is racisme. Onredelijk, wild, naar alles trappend, zonder excuus. Eindelijk.)
Er komt nog iemand bij ons tafeltje staan. Het is een man die ik eerder niet opgemerkt had, maar die qua stijl even erg uit de toon valt als ik. Hij doet denken aan een oudere Amerikaanse senator. Zijn golvende, bijna witte haar is keurig geknipt, hij draagt een lichtgrijs maatpak en zijn gelaat lijkt wel van plastic. Hij straalt succes, krachtdadigheid en onverwoestbaarheid uit. Hij stelt zich voor als vertegenwoordiger van Roomkoetje zuivelproducten. En districtsraadslid van het Vlaams Blok.
Hij legt zijn hand, die groot is als een kolenschop, op mijn schouder. Rond zijn rechterwijsvinger zit een verband. Gevolg van een gevecht met een Marokkaan die bij hem wilde inbreken, vertelt hij. 'Ik heb hem goed liggen gehad. En hij mij. Ik heb het moeten laten opereren. Och, eerst wilde ik niet. Zo'n vingertje.'
Hij lacht zacht. Alles wat hij doet en zegt klinkt zacht, minzaam, warm, geruststellend, maar niettemin mannelijk en sterk. Ik voel me op mijn gemak bij hem.
'Mijn vriend hier' – hij wijst naar de man die 'boem!' riep – 'heeft gelijk. Het gaat niet om de rellen. Mijn vrouw wordt ziek van de problemen met... *allochtonen* moet ge nu zeggen, zeker? Vroeger was ze zo open en tolerant. Ze was de braafste van de klas. Altijd goeie manieren, altijd een goeiendag. Geef haar nu een mitrailleur en ze knalt ze af.'
Hij spreekt langzaam, zodat ik alles goed zou kunnen noteren.

Hij zegt: 'Ze zetten zwerfvuil gewoon voor uw deur. Islamieten hebben geen wooncultuur.'
Hij zegt: 'Ik heb een schoonbroer bij de BOB, en die zegt: "Al wat islam is, liegt alsof het gedrukt staat." En het is waar: ik heb twee Marokkaanse klanten gehad, en ze hebben me allebei bedrogen. Nu weet ik het: ik lever niet aan islamieten. Het staat in de koran: ze mogen christenhonden bedriegen.'
Hij zegt: 'Met de Turken heb je geen problemen, maar hoe komt dat? Omdat de Turken die hier zijn, christenen zijn. Die zijn in hun land weggepest door de islamieten.'
Hij zegt: 'We zijn in een flatgebouw gaan wonen, omdat ze daar tenminste uw ruiten niet kunnen inslaan. Bij ons woonden er ook, in het gebouw. Weet ge wat die man tegen mij zei? "Als jullie aan de macht komen, dan beginnen wij de revolutie! De islam laat niet toe dat het Vlaams Blok aan de macht komt." Ik zei tegen hem: "Dan zullen wij wel eens zien wie de sterkste is, de islam of het Vlaams Blok." En ze hebben het gezien. We hebben ze uit het gebouw gekregen. Nu wonen er geen Marokkanen meer.'
'Bij ons in de straat wonen er ook', zegt Stafke Porno. 'Dat zijn vrienden van mij.'
Roomkoetje glimlacht minzaam. 'Vrienden... Als het erop aankomt, zul je wel zien wie je vrienden zijn...'
'Ik ben trainer geweest van een Marokkaanse voetbalploeg', zegt Danny. 'Daar waren er veel goeie bij.'
'Kom kom, zeker', stuurt Roomkoetje. 'Maar het kan toch erg zijn hè?'
Iedereen beaamt: het kan erg zijn.
Met zijn keurige pak en warme stem heeft Roomkoetje

een natuurlijke autoriteit onder de cafégangers. Ze hebben ontzag voor zijn beschaafde uitstraling, op een manier zoals ze dat voor de mijne niet hebben. Hij vertelt zacht en met humor dat hij graag een eigen partij zou beginnen, radicaler dan het Blok, want dat de leiding hem veel te soft is. Hij zegt dat Marokkanen niet kunnen en niet willen werken, hij zegt dat zijn dochter al vier keer *bevoeld* is (instemming van de andere klanten: ze kennen allemaal vrouwen die bevoeld zijn), dat islamieten niet met hun handen van de vrouwen kunnen blijven, hij zegt dat Vlamingen Vlamingen moeten blijven zoals God hen geschapen heeft en dat Kongo en Zuid-Afrika beter af waren onder de blanken.

Hij vertelt traag, zodat mijn pen kan volgen. Elke zin die hij uitspreekt, overdenkt hij, zich zeer bewust van het feit dat ik hem zal citeren. Soms kijkt hij wat ik opschrijf en kiest een ander woord. Hij wil dat het in de krant komt, want 'de waarheid wordt nooit geschreven. De censuur waakt overal. De stem van het volk wordt nooit gehoord'. Ik beloof hem: zijn stem komt ongefilterd in de krant.

Ik krijg hoofdpijn van hem. Ik wil weg. Dat is onprofessioneel van me. Ik ben op zoek naar de stem van het volk, hier krijg ik ze. Maar deze man maakt me bang. De rauwe volksheid van de Favoriete Roma-boys, die kon ik plaatsen. Het wilde gescheld van de boem!-man ook. Maar deze beminnelijke, intelligente, beschaafde man met zijn geruststellende glimlach en warme stem die steeds hardere dingen zegt, maar op zo'n lieve, keuvelende toon, hij beklemt me.

Ik neem nogal haastig afscheid. De Favoriete Roma-boys slaan me nog eens op mijn schouder, bedanken voor

het pintje en vragen of ik eens terugkom. Roomkoetje geeft me een stevige handdruk en een plastic glimlach. Als ik de deur al uit ben en probeer het beklemde gevoel af te schudden, komt hij me nog achterna. 'Ik was nog iets vergeten te zeggen. Als wij in Marokko zouden doen wat die Marokkanen hier doen, ge weet toch wat er dan met ons gebeurt? Dan schieten ze ons af.'
En weer die minzame glimlach.

31

De avond is gevallen en de eerste groepjes relschoppers verschijnen op de Turnhoutsebaan voor weer een nieuwe nacht van rondrennen, politie ontwijken en autospiegels stuktrappen. Niet ver daarvandaan woon ik een wijkvergadering bij. Terwijl het geweld voortduurt, komen Vlamingen en Marokkanen samen om informeel overleg te plegen. Alleen als we elkaar kennen en begrijpen, kunnen de spijtige gebeurtenissen, schromelijk overdreven door de media, vermeden worden.
Er hangt een ongemakkelijke sfeer in het te fel verlichte lokaaltje van het wijkcentrum. Marokkanen en Belgen hebben al meerdere keren met elkaar overlegd, maar toch is de omgang niet hartelijk. Er staan Arabische koekjes op tafel, van die mierzoete kleverige hapjes, en er is muntthee. Geen wijn of bier. Geen Belgische hapjes. De Vlamingen zijn jong en overwegend vrouwelijk, de Marokkanen oud en uitsluitend mannelijk.
Aangezien de Marokkaanse mannen geen Nederlands kennen, is er een tolk aanwezig. Dat vertraagt de vergadering gevoelig. De tolk, tevens voorzitter van de vergadering, begint met een lange verwelkoming, eerst in het Arabisch, daarna in het Nederlands. Daarop vraagt een Marokkaanse man het woord. Hij praat minutenlang, gesticuleert, vraagt feedback van de andere mannen, die hem met veel misbaar gelijk geven, en als hij eindelijk zwijgt, zegt de tolk: 'Deze man, een figuur met autoriteit in de gemeenschap, vindt dat we meer met elkaar zouden moeten praten.'
Blijkbaar heeft hij daarmee een gevoelige snaar geraakt.

Andere Marokkaanse mannen haken erop in en er ontspint zich een levendig gesprek, dat zo snel gaat en zo emotioneel is dat het voor de tolk onmogelijk is om het te onderbreken. Ruim tien minuten kijken de Vlamingen naar hun tenen, terwijl het Arabische debat steeds heviger wordt. Uiteindelijk beginnen de Vlamingen onderling in het Nederlands te praten. Over hun kinderen, het weer, een film die ze net gezien hebben.
Eindelijk stopt het Arabische debat.
'Deze mannen hebben allen hun bereidheid uitgesproken om vaker met elkaar te praten,' zegt de tolk, 'want enkel als we elkaar beter kennen en begrijpen, kunnen deze spijtige gebeurtenissen vermeden worden.'
'Kunnen we dan misschien beginnen met te praten?' zegt een jonge Vlaamse geïrriteerd. 'Ik merk er niet veel van dat er met mij gepraat wordt. Het zou helpen als de heren Nederlands spraken.'
De tolk vertaalt, commotie bij de Marokkanen. 'Laten we proberen geen verwijten over en weer te sturen', glimlacht de tolk.
Naast mij zit een jongen die ik zestien schat. Hij heet Moestafa, zo heeft hij me eerder gezegd. Hij draagt een djellaba. Voor de vergadering heb ik enkele woorden met hem gewisseld. Daardoor weet ik dat hij Nederlands kent. Toch zegt hij wat hij te zeggen heeft in het Arabisch. Als de tolk hem vraagt of hij alsjeblieft Nederlands wil spreken, snuift hij minachtend. Na vertaling blijkt dat hij zei: 'Onze ouders kennen de islam niet meer. Daarom kennen onze jongeren de islam niet meer. Daarom lopen ze tot twee uur 's nachts over het plein en vernielen ze auto's en winkels. Als de ouders de koran beter zouden lezen, zou dat niet gebeuren.

Een jonge plant kun je in alle richtingen doen groeien, maar een boom niet meer. Dat zegt de Profeet, heilig is Zijn naam.'
(Werd dit echt net gezegd door een jongen van zestien?)
Even pauze, om alle Marokkanen de gelegenheid te geven om 'heilig is Zijn naam' te prevelen. Eén begint aan een heus gebed, of dat denken we toch. De tolk durft hem niet te onderbreken.
Marokkaanse man: 'Wij krijgen steeds de schuld van wat misgaat. De Marokkaan krijgt altijd de schuld. Maar wij kunnen er ook niets aan doen!'
Vlaamse vrouw: 'Ah, het zijn Vlamingen die al drie dagen onze ruiten inslaan?!'
Marokkaanse man: 'Het is de politie. Die beschermt ons niet. Die is racistisch. De jongeren worden opstandig.'
Vlaamse vrouw: 'Maar jullie kunnen toch iets doen om de jongeren binnen te houden. Het zijn toch jullie kinderen?'
Moestafa: 'De islam zal de jongeren binnenhouden.'
Oudere Vlaamse man: 'Is de islam niet vooral het probleem? In jullie cultuur worden jongens als goden opgevoed. Kijk naar Saddam Hoessein. Zo'n dictator vindt ge alleen in Arabische landen. Is dat dan iets met die cultuur? vraag ik mij af.'
Marokkaanse man: 'De Amerikanen hebben Saddam gesteund. Als er veel dictators rondlopen in de Arabische wereld, dan is dat omdat de VS dat zo wil.'
Andere Marokkaanse man: 'Is de Belgische politiek trouwens zo democratisch?'
Nog andere Marokkaanse man: 'Iedereen is tegen Saddam maar Sharon mag doen wat hij wil.'
Magere Vlaamse man met gek brilletje: 'Misschien zou

dit gesprek beter lopen als er ook vrouwen aanwezig zouden zijn.'

Dat wil de tolk niet vertalen. De Vlamingen protesteren hevig totdat hij dat wel doet. Grote consternatie onder de Marokkanen. Minachtende blikken. Moestafa spuwt smalend op de grond. Ik kijk ontzet naar de fluim. IJzig zegt hij: 'Als we allemaal volgens de islam zouden leven, dan waren er geen problemen.'

'Als we allemaal volgens de islam zouden leven, dan sneden we onze vrouwen hun kut eruit en naaiden ze toe!' brult de oudere Vlaamse man.

De andere Vlamingen gebaren tegen de tolk dat hij dát vooral niet moet vertalen.

Een Marokkaanse man probeert de gemoederen te bedaren: 'Het is het onderwijs. Goed onderwijs is belangrijk voor onze kinderen. In Borgerhout zijn er te weinig scholen.'

Vlaamse vrouw: 'Ze moeten *willen* leren, hè. Ik geef al jaren bijles aan kinderen, ook aan die van jullie nationaliteit, of ras, of etnie, hoe moet ik het noemen? Die denken allemaal dat ze na twee lessen Einstein zullen zijn. En als het dan toch trager gaat dan ze verwacht hadden, dan haken ze af. Studeren is een daad van de student zélf. Een diploma krijg je niet zomaar in de schoot geworpen. Ook wij, Belgen, moeten daarvoor werken.'

'Weet je wat jullie scholen met ons doen? Weet je wat ze tegen onze broeders zeggen in jullie scholen?'

'Kijk, dat is het probleem. Jullie denken altijd dat jullie het slachtoffer zijn van een complot. Ik zeg: wérk, en je zult er komen.'

'Vrienden, laten we geen verwijten heen en weer sturen!'

Na een halfuur bedaart de ruzie. Iedereen neemt een

gebakje. Iemand zegt dat de media alles opgeblazen hebben, wat vertaald wordt en door iedereen beaamd. Het gesprek eindigt met eindeloze verklaringen over hoe belangrijk het is dat we blijven praten, want dat we samen wonen in Borgerhout en dat we een gemeenschappelijk doel hebben: Borgerhout aangenaam en leefbaar te maken voor iedereen.

'We hebben de basis gelegd voor een hernieuwde dialoog', besluit de tolk hoopvol. 'De prioriteiten zijn bepaald. De volgende vergadering gaan we concretiseren.'

32

Als ik de familie van de vermoorde Mohamed Achrak één ding zou willen vragen, dan is het of het echt hun eigen wens was dat Mohamed werd begraven tijdens een plechtigheid die half politieke meeting half popconcert was? Of het hun eigen verlangen was, dat de Marokkaanse consul er zou spreken? Of ze er zelf voor hadden gekozen om tien keer op te roepen tot meer verdraagzaamheid, en om geen rellen meer te ontketenen? Het zou een intieme en waardige begrafenis worden. Dus dachten ze aan de enorme, kille sportzaal in het industriepark van Antwerpen-Noord, tussen de slachthuizen, in een buurt waar weinig Belgen wonen en diegenen die er wonen, hebben geen dure wagens. Een buurt met brede lanen waar de politie makkelijk kan chargeren wanneer nodig. Een buurt die tristesse en wanhoop uitstraalt. Uiterst geschikt voor een begrafenis. De eigenaars van de sportzaal gaven hun toestemming toen hen werd verzekerd dat niemand met schoenen, die de vloerbekleding zouden kunnen beschadigen, de zaal zou betreden. Moslims bidden op hun sokken.

Voor ons, journalisten, is in een smalle ruimte voorzien, links van het hoofdpodium, vlak naast de deur naar de kantine. Daar staat een muurtje waarachter normaal supporters de wedstrijden kunnen bekijken. De afspraak is dat de journalisten de dienst niet verstoren, en niet op het muurtje klimmen.

Er is geen plaats meer voor mij. Zoals altijd hebben de televisiezenders alles ingepikt. Alle cameralui staan op het muurtje. Jonas, opnieuw mijn fotograaf, klimt ook

op het muurtje. Ik heb hem wel gezegd dat dat niet mag, maar willen we mooie foto's of niet? De reporter van het TV1- of VTM-journaal probeert Jonas van het muurtje af te trekken. Dat is zijn plaats! Mijn fotograaf wankelt en valt bijna tussen de biddenden. Hij geeft een trap naar achter, raakt de reporter in zijn gezicht.
'Godver, rotte klootzak!'
Een andere fotograaf maakt van de verwarring gebruik om ook op het muurtje te springen. Een van de organisatoren van de begrafenis probeert de nu hardop vloekende en bijna vechtende journalisten te bedaren.
'Heren, dit is een begrafenis.'
'Zorg dan voor een betere service voor de pers!' snauwt een collega. 'Hoe kunnen wij ons werk doen?'
'Meneer, u *moet* uw werk helemaal niet doen. U mag blij zijn dat u erin mag. Dit is een begrafenis, geen persconferentie.'
'Jij moet duidelijk niet om zes uur uitzenden', blaft de reporter.
Tijdens de tussenkomst van de ordedienst zijn enkele fotografen van het muurtje af gekomen. De reporter klautert naar de vrijgekomen plaats.
Het is gezellig om tussen zoveel collega's te lopen, in het hart van het nieuws. Jonas wenkt me. Of ik het nummer heb van de chef in Brussel. Ik zoek het op in mijn gsm en geef hem mijn toestel. Terwijl hij naar het belsignaal luistert, wijst hij naar de zaal met de drieduizend bidders, glimlacht en knijpt zijn neus dicht. Ik concentreer me op de geur. Mijn god, inderdaad. Zesduizend sokken. Twee andere collega's knijpen ook hun neus dicht. Blikken van verstandhouding. Besmuikte lachjes. En zoveel witte sokken! Waarom dragen Marokkaanse

mannen witte sokken? Weten ze dan niet dat dat niet kan? Achter het muurtje bevindt zich de kantine, die voorbehouden is aan de niet-moslims die mee komen rouwen. Veel zijn het er niet. Het Antwerpse stadsbestuur, enkele verdwaalde nationale politici (maar niet de kopstukken), klasgenoten van de broers van Mohamed, en communisten.

Waarom trekken alleen communisten zich het lot van allochtonen aan?

De dienst is bijna helemaal in het Arabisch, of het Berbers, of soms in het Frans. Hoe kunnen wij ons werk doen, als we niet verstaan wat er gezegd wordt?

De journalisten troepen dan maar samen in de kantine. Al valt daar evenmin wat te rapen. De politici hebben afgesproken om, uit respect voor het slachtoffer, geen verklaringen af te leggen. Anders zou het lijken alsof ze politiek garen willen spinnen bij de tragedie. De andere Belgen weigeren ook te praten, meestal uit protest tegen de manier waarop de media de rellen in beeld hebben gebracht.

Zul je nu wat krijgen! Poe-poe, politiek correcte veel te hoogopgeleide linkso's uit rijke families met hun Arafatsjaaltjes en Che-Guevara-T-shirtjes. Hoeveel Palestijnen kennen zij nou echt? Hoeveel volksmensen? Oneindig vervreemd van de kleine man, en toch beweren dat zij als enigen de kleine man vertegenwoordigen. *Wij* zijn de krant van de kleine man! Irritante linkse betweters met hun zogenaamd rebelse antiglobalistische media-internetsites. Hoe kunnen wij ons werk doen als iedereen ons tegenwerkt? We mogen niet op het muurtje staan, we mogen niet flashen, niemand wil met ons praten, mooi hoor, fraai verslag zal dat worden, en dan

schrikken die Marokkanen ervan dat de media tegen hen zijn...
De Marokkaanse consul praat over de goede samenwerking tussen België en Marokko, de spijtige opkomst van extreem-rechts, de uitdagingen die daardoor voor de gemeenschap ontstaan, die zich meer moet inzetten om te integreren, zonder dat dat betekent dat de Vlaamse samenleving zich niet moet openstellen voor het andere. 'De islam is niet de vijand,' zegt hij, 'onverdraagzaamheid is de vijand.' Daarom dat de Marokkaanse regering en de Belgische bla bla bla.
Leuk om dat op de begrafenis van je vermoorde zoon te horen.
Ik bedenk een spel. De glazen deur van de kantine bevindt zich naast de grote ingang van de sporthal. Ze ligt blijkbaar in de richting van Mekka, want alle mannen die binnenkomen, spreiden hun gebedsmatje en smijten zich op hun knieën voor die glazen deur. Het lijkt alsof dat voor ons is, begrijp je? Voor ons, de journalisten, die aan de andere kant van die glazen deur staan. We knikken minzaam: het is goed, jongen, sta maar op, je bent vergeven.
Dat is lachen.
En er blijven maar moslims binnenstromen om de zweetgeur te versterken. Ik krijg er een te pakken voor een reactie, een imposante zwarte in paarse gewaden, met een enorme tulband op. Hij stapt uit een gitzwarte Mercedes en heeft drie bedienden bij zich. Een sjeik, op zijn minst. Of een oplichter. In ieder geval een blaaskaak. 'My friend!' lacht hij, als ik even op zijn schouder tik. Zijn enorme arm slaat hij om mijn schouders. 'These are all friends. All muslims, friends. This is a very, very sad day!'

Zijn lach schalt over het slachthuisterrein. Nee, hij kent Mohamed Achrak niet. Nee, hij is geen sjeik. Nee, geen Marokkaan. Maar hij is moslim, man! Moslim! En als dusdanig geraakt in zijn ziel! Hahaa, geraakt, ja, geraakt!
Ik wandel weg. Zo'n pipo kun je ook niet in de krant zetten.
Even bellen naar de redactie voor meer instructies.
Ik tast in mijn binnenzak.
Mijn gsm is weg!
Mijn bloed kookt. Hoe durven ze! Op de begrafenis van een van hun eigen mannen! Van een islamleraar! Onder het oog van hun god! Smerige, smerige m***!

Pas dan realiseer ik me: ik heb mijn gsm aan Jonas uitgeleend.

Wat een schaamte.

33

Onze vervalste euthanasieaanvraag is afgewezen. De dokters staan pal achter hun besluit: door hun hand zal bompa niet sterven.
Niet dat het nog wat uitmaakt. Door vrijwillige uithongering afgetakeld, zal hij ons binnen enkele dagen sowieso verlaten. Je hoeft geen dokter te zijn om dat te zien.
Hij ligt in bed met mijn walkman op zijn hoofd. Ik kijk lang naar dat breekbare, benige, broodmagere vogelhoofd met die verbeten trekken, met een enorme koptelefoon op de behaarde oren. De trekken van zijn gezicht zijn zo veranderd dat hij voor een ander zou kunnen doorgaan. Hij luistert naar mij, naar mijn stem, die hem mijn boek *Walvis* voorleest, op cassettes van de blindenbibliotheek.
(En jij gaat ervan uit dat het liefste dat mensen willen horen, voor ze de pijp uitgaan, jouw boeken zijn?)
Het is tijd voor de Laatste Sacramenten. Hij weet dat het niet lang meer zal duren voor hij sterft. Dat heeft hem vrolijker gemaakt. Als hij me ziet, zet hij de walkman af, trekt zich opgewekt wat rechter en glundert: 'Het kan niet lang meer duren.'
Hij gaat eerst over tot de Sacramenten.
'We hebben toch vijftig jaar in dat huis gewoond. Dat is dan toch teken dat het goed was.'
'Ons ma en ik hebben het toch vijfenzestig jaar volgehouden. Dat wilt toch iets zeggen.'
'Ik heb u toch zien opgroeien.'
'Ge hebt toch een job, en een goei vrouwtje.'

(Ik zeg niet dat ik die vrouw verlaten heb en nu met een Aziatische ben.)

Nu is het mijn beurt.

> Liefste bompa,
> Je was de beste bompa die ik me kon dromen,
> Uw liefhebbende kleinzoon,
> Tom

Komaan bompa: huilen!!!!

Hij heeft het niet gehoord. Te stil gesproken, ik weet toch dat hij doof is?
In slaap gevallen? Zijn ogen zijn toe, hij reageert niet meer.
Ik herhaal het niet. Zo klef!

34

Hij ligt op de palliatieve afdeling. Hier liggen mensen die er zo erg aan toe zijn dat men ze niet meer wil verplaatsen.
Nu sterft hij echt.
Je ziet het. Niet eten is geen kwestie meer van niet willen. Hij heeft de kracht niet. Hij is niet lang genoeg meer wakker.

Sterven is iets huiselijks, dat heeft men in het ziekenhuis goed begrepen. Roze vloerbedekking, plastic bloemen, lelijke schilderijen.

Dit is de laatste keer dat ik hem in leven zal zien. Ik wil hem nog spreken. Nu ja, ik wil dat hij op zijn minst weet dat ik bij hem geweest ben. Ik wil dat hij wakker is, dat hij me herkent.
Hij slaapt.
Ik heb nog nooit iemand gezien die er zo uitgeput uitziet *terwijl* hij slaapt. Al zijn kenmerkende gelaatstrekken zijn verdwenen. Er is alleen nog die mond, die uitgeput, onderworpen, geërgerd, razend, hulpeloos, verslagen, moegestreden openstaat.
Hij heeft zijn valse tanden niet in. Hij heeft nog twee tanden van zichzelf.
Zijn oren zijn gigantisch. Zijn hoofd lijkt gekrompen, het vel hangt er maar wat omheen, maar die oren! Ze zijn half zo groot als zijn hoofd zelf, en er groeit evenveel haar op.
Als ik zijn handen vastneem, doet hij zijn ogen heel even

halfopen, maar dat kost hem zoveel moeite dat hij ze na enkele seconden alweer sluit. Ik weet niet of hij me herkend heeft. De ogen keken verschrikt, verstoord.

Damn.

Ik zit naast zijn bed en kijk naar hem. Hij slaapt zo *hard*. Schokkend ademend klampt hij zich vast aan zijn deken.

Ik wik Belangrijke Woorden.
Ik schud een beetje aan zijn schouder. De arm is zo dun, ik heb het vel tussen mijn vingers, ik durf niet te knijpen uit angst het bot te breken.

Ik heb Saskia meegenomen, als bewijs dat alles goed met me gaat. Hij zal nooit weten dat we uit elkaar gegaan zijn. Tot in de eeuwigheid gelooft bompa dat ik gelukkig ben, dat mijn leven in de plooi ligt. Van straat. Taak volbracht.
Maar hij wil niet wakker worden om dat te horen.
Koppige vent.

Een verpleegster komt zeggen dat ze hem zo dadelijk gaan 'omkeren', en dat ik dan kans heb dat hij even wakker zal zijn. Hij slaapt al de hele dag, en gisteren ook al. Ze geven hem geen morfine, noch enig ander slaapmiddel. Hij is gewoon op.
In afwachting van dat omkeren zit ik in de roze gang met Sas oude *Dag Allemaals* te lezen. We horen andere mensen rochelen. We kijken naar elkaar en glimlachen. Ik bedank haar omdat ze is meegekomen, omdat ze nog

één keer mee wil spelen in deze idiote vertoning. Ze zegt dat het geen probleem is.
Weg, verleiding van het vertrouwde!

De verpleegsters komen naar buiten met bompa's luier in hun handen. Wat kan daar nog in zitten als iemand al bijna drie weken niet eet?
Maar goed. Mijn moment.
Hij is wakker. Hij herkent me zelfs, vormt 'Tom' met zijn mond, maar ik moet snel zijn: binnen enkele minuten valt hij weer in slaap. Tijd voor de Belangrijke Woorden!
'De mama en de bomma zijn ook geweest', zeg ik.
Niet de belangrijkste woorden, oké, maar hij moet toch weten dat hij niet alleen was, nee?
Hij schokschoudert geïrriteerd.
'Saskia is hier ook.'
Ze komt onwennig dichterbij, zegt 'hallo', maar hij reageert niet.

Hij gaat weer in slaap vallen!
Tijd voor de Belangrijke Woorden!
De Woorden Om Mee Te Nemen Naar Het Hiernamaals!

'Zeg, bompa,' zeg ik, 'als ik je niet meer zou zien: hou je goed, hè.'

35

Als – ik – je – niet – meer – zou – zien?
Hou je goed?????

Hou je goed? De man gaat dood! Hoe kun je je goed houden als je doodgaat? En *waar en wanneer* dacht je hem nog te zien? Aan de *visvijver*? Bij het *biljart*? Wat waren dat voor belachelijke laatste woorden?! Ongetwijfeld de debielste sterfbedtoespraak aller tijden, en jij hebt die gehouden, voor je eigen bompa, die nu naar het socialistische walhalla mag met 'als ik je niet meer zie, hou je goed, hè.' Hou je haaks, gozer, veel sterkte met dat sterven van je, tsjaaaaa, 't is een linke boel, maar we moeten er allemaal door, dus hou je maar flink, laat ze ginderachter niet zeggen dat de Lorreynens mietjes zijn.

(Je hebt hem ook gezegd dat hij de beste bompa ter wereld was.)
En daar ben je *trots* op? Op dergelijke kitsch? O komaan, bompa was slimmer dan dat. De man wist echt wel dat dat de klassieke dingen zijn die je zegt als kleinzoon tegen een stervende bompa. De beste bompa? Je had er maar twee! En tegen die eerste heb je dat *ook* gezegd, toen die stierf. Enfin, je had het willen zeggen als je de ballen had gehad maar daar zat je nog meer klem, daar zat je maar wat met de man zijn hand te friemelen en te glimlachen en hem cola te voederen in een babybekertje en op het einde zei je: 'Je morst, bompa. Zal ik het teutje erop zetten?'
Oké – oké oké: *dat* waren misschien de Belachelijkste

Laatste Woorden ooit. Ik neem dat eerdere terug. De toptwee van Belachelijkste Laatste Woorden ooit:

1. Zal ik het teutje erop zetten? (Tom Naegels)
2. Als ik je niet meer zou zien: hou je goed, hè. (Tom Naegels)

En dat noemt zich schrijver.

36

Toen Camille Huysmans stierf, was hij zesennegentig. Zijn droom was het om honderd te worden. Eerst was het zijn droom geweest om de eerste honderdjarige volksvertegenwoordiger te zijn. Toen hij op zijn negentigste toch uit het parlement gezet was, wilde hij alleen nog de eeuw rond maken. De nacht voor hij stierf, zette zijn vijfenveertigjarige vrouw zich aan zijn ziekenhuisbed. Ze nam zijn benige hand met het droge, gele vel in haar handen en zei: 'Zondag wordt ge honderd jaar. Ge zijt dat vergeten met ziek te worden. Antwerpen hangt vol bloemen.'
Waarom kon ik voor hem niets dergelijks bedenken? Een even mooie uitspraak, die hem zou verzoenen met zijn dood?
(Hij hoefde niet verzoend te worden met de dood.)
De vrienden en familie van Huysmans hebben die laatste jaren, toen hij bitter en onmogelijk geworden was, alles gedaan om het hem naar zijn zin te maken. Toen hij een lovend artikel schreef over de pas overleden koningin Elisabeth, en eiste dat dat met foto op de voorpagina zou verschijnen van zijn blad *De Socialistische Stem*, kon dat niet voor de republikeinse redactie. Toch drukte men speciaal enkele exemplaren van het blad met Huysmans' artikel op de voorpagina. Het waren de enige exemplaren die hij te zien kreeg.
De enige manier waarop Huysmans nog met zijn vrouw communiceerde, was door naar een gat in zijn sok te wijzen, als die gestopt moest worden. Als ze de post twintig minuten te laat bracht, zat hij de hele dag te mokken.

Soms weigerde hij te eten wat zij voor hem had gekookt, hoewel hij nooit een vinger uitstak in de keuken. Toch heeft ze hem op zijn sterfbed dat prachtige verhaal verteld, om hem gelukkig te laten inslapen. En ondanks het feit dat hij zijn partij had verraden en haar dat bij de laatste verkiezing vijftienduizend stemmen had gekost, waren alle socialistische kopstukken op zijn staatsbegrafenis. Burgemeester Craeybeckx, meermaals door Huysmans uitgescholden voor dronkelap, hield een ontroerende rede.

Hadden wij evenveel geduld met bompa? Waren wij even vergevensgezind?

Maar bompa was Huysmans niet! Het was niet omdat *hij* zichzelf even groot achtte, dat *wij* dat ook moesten doen. Huysmans was premier, burgemeester, secretaris van de Internationale. Kom ons niet vertellen dat bompa's werk en later zijn pensioen hem zo stresseerde dat hij niet aardig kon zijn voor zijn vrouw.

Ik zeg tegen moeder: 'Je hebt alles gedaan wat je kon, en dat wist hij.'

37

'Hij is toch oud mogen worden', zegt bomma. Meer woorden maakt ze niet aan hem vuil.
Haar veel te laat herwonnen vrijheid viert ze door de normale maaltijden te vervangen door snoep. 'Ik ben een pateekesmens', zegt ze, terwijl ze met haar vingers door een boterham met kwark, aardbeienjam en bruine suiker ploegt. De korsten heeft ze er afgescheurd. De brokken kwark vallen naast haar mond naar beneden. 'Ik ben een smosser', grinnikt ze tevreden.
Naar de kapper gaat ze ook minder. En ze neemt haar pillen voor haar maag niet meer.
'Ze is haar gendarm kwijt', zegt moeder. 'Maar ze had een gendarm nodig. Ons ma alleen, die laat zich gaan.'
Als ze maar niet vergeet het gas uit te draaien.
Of de stoof af te zetten.
Dat zou nog iets voor ons ma zijn.

Geërfd:
- Twee paar lederen handschoenen, waarvan ik er meteen één verlies
- Vier broeken, nog niet gedragen
- Pyjama's
- Sokken
- Hoed, pronkstuk op mijn boekenkast (nu achter de kast gevallen)
- Een plastic vis die *Don't worry, be happy* zingt.

38

Ik bezoek bomma met Nadia. Voor het eerst. Een grote stap. Niet dat het iets uitmaakt. Bomma noemt Nadia systematisch Saskia. Dat Nadia donker is, schijnt ze niet te merken.

We kijken naar het nieuws.

'Aaaaaaa!' roept bomma, vervuld van weerzin. 'Al die miserie! Mannen, die zien graag miserie. Miserie, en voetbal. Waar ziet gij naar, Saskia? Toch ook niet naar die miserie?'

Nadia begrijpt bomma's Antwerps niet.

'Muziek, dat zie ik graag', gaat bomma verder. 'Er is zo'n programma met twee piano's, en een dame. Dát zie ik graag.'

'*De Notenclub*', zeg ik.

'Ja, dat met die dame en de twee piano's. Dát zie ik graag. Dat is opgewekt.'

Nadia probeert om iets te vertellen, in zeer behoorlijk Nederlands, maar na drie woorden roept bomma: 'Aaaaaaa! Al die miserie! Mannen, die zien graag miserie. Miserie, en voetbal. Waar ziet gij naar, Saskia? Toch ook niet naar die miserie?'

Ik vertaal in het Engels. Nadia noemt de naam van het programma waar ze het vaakst naar kijkt: *The Days of Our Lives*. Bomma antwoordt niet. Na enkele seconden stilte roept ze: 'Aaaaaaa! Al die miserie! Mannen, die zien graag miserie. Miserie, en voetbal. Waar ziet gij naar, Saskia? Toch ook niet naar die miserie?'

Gesprekken met bomma zijn veranderd, sinds bompa's dood. Vroeger vielen er snel vervelende stiltes, omdat elk onderwerp dat ik aandroeg nauwelijks een reactie losmaakte, en ik snel uitgepraat was over die van bomma. Nu herhaalt ze zichzelf gewoon. Soms tientallen keren op een avond. Precies dezelfde woorden, precies dezelfde intonatie. Reageren hoeft niet.

Ik had Nadia beter moeten inlichten. Ze beschouwt bomma's stiltes als beledigend, het feit dat ze Saskia genoemd wordt nog meer.

Bomma heeft nog een manier gevonden om het gesprek gaande te houden. Ze leest de ondertitels voor. Op een normale gesprekstoon, alsof zij tegen mij aan het vertellen is wat de mensen op tv zeggen.

'Tom, *vandaag herdenken wij een zwarte dag*. Ja, dat is wat. *Dag op dag een jaar geleden werd onze democratie in haar hart getroffen*. Och, in het hart, hoort hem. Onze pa, die had het aan zijn hart. *Onze gedachten zijn bij de families van de overledenen.* Wat een miserie... Altijd miserie op dat nieuws. *Wij bidden voor hen.* Da's goed, jong, bidt gij maar. Wat hebben wij daaraan?'

Nadia doet mee. Ik krijg George W. Bush tweestemmig gedubt, met Antwerps en Pakistaans accent. Ik zap weg.

Bij het afscheid omhelst bomma me en bedankt me haast in tranen voor mijn bezoek. Nadia krijgt een kus en: 'Blijf bij hem, Saskia. Ge zijt een schoon koppel, gij twee. Onze pa had u nog graag zien trouwen.'

Ze neemt Nadia bij de arm en leidt haar naar haar kast.

'Dit is een braaf kind', zegt ze.

Nadia fronst.

Bomma wijst op een porseleinen beeldje van een herdersjongen met hond.

'Dat kind hier. Dat hoort ge nu van heel de dag niet!'

Nadia vlucht.

39

Nadia en ik gaan uit elkaar. Het bezoek aan bomma is er te veel aan geweest. 'Bomma is dement', zeg ik, maar dat woord kent ze niet en het maakt niet uit. Mijn familie, ik, mijn vrienden, we leven in een andere wereld.
'Is dat dan niet boeiend?' probeer ik nog. 'Onbekende paden? Nieuwe invalshoeken?'
(Waarom probeer ik altijd te redden wat ik zelf stuk liet gaan?)
'Voor jou is het leuk als er eens iets anders is', zegt ze. 'Voor mij: alles anders. Elke dag. Als mijn man dan ook nog anders is: te moeilijk.'
Ze zegt: 'Jij wil intelligente vrouw.'
'Jij bent een intelligente vrouw.'
'Het is oké. Ik heb andere kwaliteiten.'
(Ze ziet goed en ze hoort goed.)
'Jij wil een vrouw die de juiste kaarsen heeft.'
Ze bedoelt het als grap. Ze lacht en laat me los. 'We zien elkaar nog.'

Perfect. Ik laat een fantastische vrouw gaan, omdat ze de verkeerde kaarsen koopt. Tot zover Tom de ladies' man.

40

Bomma noemt bompa 'mijn man', alsof ik een vreemde ben. Als ik haar bezoek, dan zegt ze: 'Och, dag jongen. Moet ge mijn man spreken? Die zit in de kelder met zijn visgerief.'
'Nee, bomma, ik kom voor jou.'
'Dat is vriendelijk. Ik zal onze pa zeggen dat ge langs geweest zijt.'

Zijn stoel staat voor de televisie. Hij ging altijd zo dicht bij de tv zitten dat zijn neus bijna tegen het scherm drukte. Alleen zo kon hij nog iets zien van wat er zich afspeelde.
'Sinds wanneer zit jij zo dicht bij de tv?' vraag ik.
'Dat is niet van mij', zegt ze. Ze gaat in haar eigen stoel zitten.
'Van wie dan wel?'
Ze kijkt me verward aan. Dan begint ze te lachen. 'Och ja, dat is waar ook!' lacht ze. Ze staat op om de stoel weer onder de tafel te schuiven. 'Het is iets waar ge gewoon aan moet worden.'

'Weet ge hoeveel uw moeder mij wou doen betalen voor de was?' vraagt ze. 'Driehonderd frank. Driehonderd! Ik zeg: "Dat heb ik nog nooit moeten betalen om de was te doen. Kunt ge niet wachten tot ik dood ben, voor ge met mijn geld op de loop gaat?" '
'Moeder heeft zes stukken van vijftig eurocent genomen', zeg ik. 'Dat is drie euro. Dat is honderd twintig frank.'
'Niet waar!' roept ze. 'Ik heb haar ze zien nemen: zes stukken van vijftig frank!'

'Vijftig *cent*, bomma. Drie euro, honderd twintig frank.'
Het venijn trekt uit haar gezicht.
'Och ja, Tom, wat zeg ik allemaal? Ge weet, ik ben geen slimme vrouw. Maar ik heb één geluk: ik zie goed, en ik hoor goed. Spijtig dat onze pa dat niet kan zeggen. Zo'n intelligente man! In alles geïnteresseerd!'

In de badkamer hoor ik haar praten tegen haar dode man.
'Pas op dat ge niet valt', zegt ze. 'Als ge nog eens valt, is het met u gedaan.'
Het water klotst. Bomma lacht.
'Moet ge nu zien. Melia is op de boterhammen van haar vrijer gaan zitten.'
'Nee, blijf nu liggen. Gij altijd met uw vélo. Ge gaat nog eens veranderen in een vélo.'
Het is wachten op de dag dat ze mij niet meer zal kennen. De dag dat ze permanent zal verblijven in die ene zomer met hem, de vier enige maanden van haar leven waarin ze verliefd was. De zomer waarin haar leven zich aankondigde als een staat van voortdurend geluk, de wreedste grap die een zomer ooit met haar uithaalde.
'Laat mij nu maar', zegt bomma. 'Gij hebt genoeg gedaan. Ik zie nog goed. Ik hoor nog. Ik kan nog uit de voeten. Wees nu toch eens voor een keer in uw leven rustig. Leg u, kalmeer, geniet. Aanvaard. Ik ben er... Is dat niet genoeg?'

Meulenhoff | Manteau
Mechelsesteenweg 203, B-2018 Antwerpen
Nieuwe Spiegelstraat 36, NL-1017 DG Amsterdam
www.manteau.be | www.meulenhoff.nl

Boekverzorging: Dooreman & Houbrechts
Zetwerk: Griffo, Gent

Eerste druk maart 2005
Achtste druk februari 2006

De auteur ontving een werkbeurs
van het Vlaams Fonds voor de Letteren

D/2006/0034/213
ISBN 90 8542 008 3
NUR 301